Serial Port Complete

Programming and Circuits for RS-232 and RS-485 Links and Networks

Jan Axelson

Lakeview Research
Madison, WI 53704

Lakeview Research
5310 Chinook Ln.
Madison, WI 53704
USA
Phone: 608-241-5824
Fax: 608-241-5848
Email: jan@lvr.com
WWW: http://www.lvr.com

14 13 12 11 10 9 8 7 6 5 4

ISBN 0-9650819-2-3

Manufactured in the United States of America

Table of Contents

Introduction

This book is a guide to designing, programming, installing, and troubleshooting computer links, including networks of multiple computers. Most of the links described use one of two serial interfaces popularly known as RS-232 and RS-485. The computers may be personal computers, embedded controllers, or any devices that share a common interface. Common uses for these links include data acquisition and control systems.

What's Inside

Putting together a serial link of this type requires expertise both in circuit design, to choose the components that make up the link, and in programming, to write the code that controls the link. This book covers each of these.

PCs

For links that use PCs (personal computers), I describe the architecture shared by the ports in all PCs, and show how to use a port's features, with program code in Visual Basic.

A template project gives a quick start for applications you write. The template includes routines for finding ports in a system, enabling users to select and configure a port, and other general-purpose functions commonly used in applications that access serial ports.

Embedded Controllers

The examples for embedded controllers use one of two popular microcontroller chips: Parallax's Basic Stamp and the 80(C)52-Basic from Intel, Micromint, and other sources. Both are based on popular microcontroller hardware: the PIC and 8051 families. Both can be programmed in dialects of Basic.

Applications

The example applications include circuit designs and code for serial links between two or more PCs and microcontrollers, using RS-232, RS-485, and simple direct links. I also show how to use an RS-232 serial port as the power source for low-power external circuits.

Cables and Interfacing

In a serial link, the proper cable and terminating components can prevent errors due to electrical noise or malfunctioning hardware. This book shows how to choose an appropriate cable and how to select or design the circuits that interface to the cable.

Who should read this book?

Readers from many backgrounds will find this book useful:

Programmers will find code examples that show how to use serial ports on PCs and microcontrollers. Programming a network shared by multiple computers is more involved than programming a link with just two computers. This book explains the options and shows how to avoid the pitfalls.

For **hardware designers,** there are details about serial-port circuits and how to interface to them, including the design of converters to translate between RS-232, RS-485, and 5V TTL logic. Examples show how to implement an RS-485 port on PCs and microcontrollers and how to design links with features like bullet-proof failsafe circuits, high noise immunity, and low power consumption.

For system **troubleshooters,** there are hardware and software debugging techniques, plus code for finding and testing ports and links.

Hobbyists and experimenters will find many ideas, along with explanations and tips for modifying the examples for a unique application.

Teachers and students have found serial ports to be a handy tool for experiments with electronics and computer control and monitoring. Many of the examples in this book are suitable as a starting point for school projects.

And last but not least, **users,** or anyone who uses a computer with serial ports, will find useful information, including advice on configuring and adding ports.

How did you learn all this?

Readers who have found my books useful sometimes ask how I came to know the information they contain. The short answer is that each of my books, including this one, is the result of a continuous cycle of research and experiments.

Many companies do an excellent job of providing information to help customers use their products. Manufacturers of the chips used in RS-232 and RS-485 interfaces have published dozens of application notes. The data sheets for the chips themselves also hold many answers. All of this information is now easily available on the Internet. There are also many good books that cover related topics. See the appendix of this book and Lakeview Research's web site for pointers to many good sources of information.

But in the end there's no substitute for real-life experiments: putting together the hardware, writing the program code, and watching what happens when the code executes. Then when the result isn't as expected—as it often isn't—it means trying something else or searching the documentation for clues. This book is result of many, many hours of such research and experiments.

About the Program Code

The book's program disk includes all of the code presented in the book (and more). All of the code uses some variant of the Basic programming language.

I chose Basic for three reasons. First, much of this book is about trying things out and learning how they work, and Basic's interactive nature makes it a good choice for this. Second, Basic is popular, so many readers will already be familiar with it. And third, Basic is what I know best. Throughout, I've tried to document the code completely enough so that you can translate into another programming language if you wish.

For each example, I assume you have a basic understanding of the language used, whether it's Visual Basic or a microcontroller Basic, and how to create and debug programs. The book focuses on the details that relate specifically to serial communications.

I developed the PC examples with Visual Basic 5. Because they're intended as design tools, and not as finished applications, the disk includes the complete source code but not compiled, executable programs. To compile the programs, you must have a copy of Visual Basic. I tested the code on a system running Windows 95. Visual Basic code is generally compatible with Windows NT as well, but I didn't test under NT.

I also used Visual Basic to illustrate other short calculations. These use Visual-Basic syntax, even when not presented explicitly as a code module. For example, an asterisk (*) signifies multiplication.

For those programming for Windows 3.x, the example code won't load directly into the older, 16-bit versions of Visual Basic, but you can copy and use many of the routines with few or no changes. In some cases, the program disk includes DOS QuickBasic code for use in systems using older or embedded PCs running DOS.

In a similar way, the microcontroller code examples are written for two popular chips, but the ideas behind the code are adaptable to other controllers and languages.

The Visual Basic code uses the line-continuation character (_) to enable a single line of code to extend over multiple lines. The routines within each listing are arranged alphabetically. The microcontroller code has no line-continuation character, and some program lines do carry over onto a second line in the listings in the text. The listings on disk are formatted correctly and should load and run without problems.

About the Example Circuits

I've included many schematic diagrams of circuits that you can use or adapt in serial-port projects. In presenting the circuits, I assume you know the basics about digital logic and electronic circuits. The circuit diagrams are complete, with these exceptions:

Power-supply and ground pins are omitted when they are in standard locations on the package (bottom left for ground, top right for power, assuming pin 1 is top left).
Power-supply bypass capacitors are omitted.
Some chips may have additional, unused gates or other elements that aren't shown.

In the schematics and text, active-low signals use a leading hyphen (-RESET) or an overbar ($\overline{\text{RESET}}$).

For more information on the components, see the manufacturers' data sheets.

Corrections and Updates

In putting together this book, I've done my best to ensure that the information is complete and correct. Every schematic diagram with detail at the pinout level has been built and tested by me, most of it multiple times. In a similar way, I've run and tested every line of code. But I know from experience that on the way from test to publication, errors and omissions do occur.

Any corrections or updates to this book will be available at Lakeview Research's World Wide Web site on the Internet at *http://www.lvr.com.* This is also the place to come for links to other serial-port information on the Web, including software tools, component data sheets, and web sites of vendors of related products.

Thanks!

Finally, I want to say thanks to everyone who helped make this book possible. As with my previous *Parallel Port Complete,* I credit the readers of my articles in *The Microcomputer Journal,* who first prompted me to write about these topics. Some of the material in this book was first published in a different form in the magazine. Others deserving thanks are the folks at companies large and small who have generously provided information and answered questions about these topics over the years.

1

Options and Choices

This book explores one corner of the computer universe: computers that are linked together to monitor and control the world outside themselves. Each computer can exchange information with the others, and each can also calculate, decide, and take action on its own. This type of link requires three things: computers to do the work, programming that tells the computers what to do, and a link to connect them. This chapter introduces options for each of these.

The Computers

Some projects need only a simple link between two computers, while others require three or more computers that connect along a common path. In this book, I use the term *link* broadly, to refer to a connection between two or more computers, while a *network* is a link of at least three computers. Each computer in a link is a *node*, or junction. Usually, each node can both send and receive, though in a simple link some nodes may communicate one-way only.

In the types of link described in this book, the computers may read sensors, switches, or other inputs. They may control motors, relays, displays, or other outputs. Because the computers can communicate with each other, the result is an integrated, intelligent system that enables one computer to react to or control events at another.

The computers may be of any type, and they may be all the same, or a combination. This book focuses on two categories: personal computers and embedded controllers.

A personal computer (PC) may be a desktop machine or a laptop, notebook, or subnotebook. The examples in this book use the family of computers that has evolved from the IBM PC, including the models XT, AT, '386, '486, Pentium, and their many clones and compatibles. But you can use any personal computer that has an appropriate serial interface.

An embedded controller is a computer that's dedicated to performing a single task or a set of related tasks. Embedded controllers tend to be smaller and less complex than PCs. Many are built into, or embedded in, the devices they control. An embedded controller may have no keyboard or display and may be invisible to its users. For example, PC peripherals such as printers and modems contain embedded controllers that enable the peripherals to handle much of the work of printing or communicating over the phone lines on their own.

Many embedded controllers have nothing at all to do with PCs. Cars, video-cassette recorders, and microwave ovens are a few everyday items that contain embedded controllers. Embedded controllers are also popular for one-of-a-kind or small-scale, custom projects that involve simple control or monitoring tasks.

The CPU, or computer chip, in an embedded controller may be the same microprocessor found in PCs, or it may be a microcontroller, which is a computer chip designed specifically for use in control tasks.

Microcontroller chips come in many varieties: 8-bit chips have an 8-bit data path and are popular for use in monitoring and control links, but 4-, 16-, and 32-bit chips are also available. Different chips have different features and abilities, including serial ports of various types, varying amounts of memory for storing programs and data, and low-power modes for battery-powered circuits. A monitoring and control link can use any microcontroller that can connect to the desired interface.

The examples in this book use two microcontrollers: Parallax's Basic Stamp and Intel/Micromint's 8052-Basic. Both are inexpensive and have on-chip Basic interpreters for easy programming and debugging.

One category of embedded controllers straddles both worlds. The embedded PC has the architecture of a PC, but in a stripped-down form that may lack a full-screen display, keyboard, or disk drives. Embedded PCs are popular because they can use many of the PC's familiar programming tools.

The Programming

Each computer in a link must do each of the following:

- Detect communications intended for it.
- Send communications at appropriate times.
- Ignore communications intended for other nodes (if any).
- Carry out any other tasks the computer is responsible for on its own.

The computer's programming is responsible for each of these, with some assistance from the hardware.

Languages and Operating Systems

The program code may vary from one node to another, because the computer type and programming language may vary, and also because different nodes may have different functions.

On a PC, the program is software stored on disk. To run the program, the operating system loads it into the system's memory (RAM). In all but some embedded PCs, the user interface includes a keyboard and display.

On a microcontroller, the program is in *firmware*, which is program code stored in an EPROM or other nonvolatile memory chip. The microcontroller may run the program directly from where it is stored, without requiring an operating system to load the program into RAM or manage other operations.

The computers may use any programming language. The only requirement for communications is that all must agree on a format for data on the link.

Message Properties

Although there are many types of monitoring and control links, the communications in a link tend to have the following in common:

Messages are short, ranging from a byte or two in a very simple system to hundreds of bytes in others. A computer in this type of link isn't likely to send Megabytes of data at once.

Messages may require a quick response. In some links, a message may carry emergency information (*The motor is stuck! The door is open!*) and the receiving computer will need to respond quickly, either by taking direct action or by instructing another computer to handle the problem.

The frequency of messages may vary. In some links, a computer may send or receive many messages within a second. In others, a computer may go a day or a week without sending or receiving anything.

The communications protocol and message format are two ways that the programming ensures that each node recognizes and understands the messages directed to it.

Protocols

A protocol is a set of rules that defines how the computers will manage their communications. The protocol may specify how data is formatted for transmitting and when and how each node may transmit.

PCs and many microcontrollers have built-in components (UARTs) that handle many of the details automatically, or with limited program assistance.

When there are just two devices, the rules need to specify whether both ends can transmit at once, or whether they need to take turns. With three or more devices, things become more complicated. Because all nodes usually share the same path, each device has to know when it may transmit, as well as whether a received communication is meant for itself or another node.

Besides the data path, a link may use additional lines to indicate when a transmitter has data to send, when a receiver is able to accept new data, or other control or status information. The process of exchanging status information about a transmission is called *handshaking*. The control and status signals are handshaking signals. Hardware handshaking uses dedicated lines for the signals. Some links use software handshaking, which accomplishes the same thing by sending special codes in the data path.

Message Format

A message is a block of data intended for one or more receivers. The message format defines what type of data the message contains and how the data is arranged within the message. All nodes have to agree on a format.

When there is more than one receiver, the receivers need a way to detect which node is the intended receiver. For this reason, network messages usually include the receiver's address. In a very simple network, a message may consist of just two bytes: one to identify the receiver and another containing data.

Messages may include other information as well. To enable receiving nodes to detect the start and end of a message, the message may include codes to indicate these, or bytes specifying the length of the message. A message may also include one or more bytes that the receiving node uses in error-checking.

The Link

The physical link between computers consists of the wires or other medium that carries information from one computer to another, and the interface that connects the medium to the computers.

The requirements of a link help to determine which interface to use and what medium to use to connect the nodes. In the types of systems described in this book, the distance between computers may range from a few feet to a few thousand feet. The time between communications may be shorter than a second, or longer than a week. The number of nodes may range from two to over two hundred.

Most links use copper wire to connect computers, often inexpensive twisted-pair cable. The path may be a single data wire and a ground return, or a pair of wires that carry differential signals. Other options include fiber-optic cable, which encodes data as the presence or absence of light, and wireless links, which send data as electromagnetic (radio) or infrared signals in the air.

For most projects, there is a standard interface that can do the job. Most of the links described in this book use one of two popular interfaces: RS-232 for shorter, slower links between two computers, or RS-485 for longer or faster links with two or more computers.

An interface may use existing ports on the computers, or it may require added ports or adapters. Most PCs have at least one RS-232 interface, and an RS-232 or RS-485 interface is easily added to a PC or microcontroller.

Table 1-1 compares RS-232 and RS-485 to other interfaces that a monitoring or control system might use.

RS-232 is popular because it's widely available, inexpensive, and can use longer cables than many other options. RS-485 is also inexpensive, easy to add to a system, and supports even longer distances, higher speeds, and more nodes than RS-232.

The IrDA (Infrared Data Association) interface can use the same UARTs and data formats as RS-232 (with added encoding), but the data transmits as infrared energy over a wireless link. IrDA is useful for short, line-of-sight links between two devices where cabling is inconvenient.

MIDI (Musical Instrument Digital Interface) is used for transferring signals used by musical instruments, theatrical control equipment, and other machine controllers. It uses an optically isolated 5-milliampere current loop at 31.5 kbps.

Microwire, SPI, and I²C are synchronous serial interfaces that are useful for short links. Many microcontrollers have one or more of these interfaces built-in.

Table 1-1: Comparison of popular computer interfaces. Where a standard doesn't specify a maximum, typical maximums are listed.

Interface	Format	Number of Devices (maximum)	Length (maximum, feet)	Speed (maximum, bits/sec.)
RS-232 (EIA/TIA-232)	asynchronous serial	2	50-100	20k (115k with some drivers)
RS-485 (TIA/EIA-485)	asynchronous serial	32 unit loads	4000	10M
IrDA	asynchronous serial infrared	2	6	115k
Microwire	synchronous serial	8	10	2M
SPI	synchronous serial	8	10	2.1M
I²C	synchronous serial	40	18	400k
USB	asynchronous serial	127	16	12M
Firewire	serial	64	15	400M
IEEE-488 (GPIB)	parallel	15	60	1M
Ethernet	serial	1024	1600	10M
MIDI	serial current loop	2	15	31.5k
Parallel Printer Port	parallel	2, or 8 with daisy-chain support	10-30	1M

USB (Universal Serial Bus) and Firewire (IEEE-1384) are new, high-speed, intelligent interfaces for connecting PCs and other computers to various peripherals. USB is intended to replace the standard RS-232 and Centronics printer ports as the interface of choice for modems and other standard peripherals. Firewire is faster and designed for quick transferring of video, audio, and other large blocks of data.

Ethernet is the familiar network interface used in many PC networks. It's fast and capable, but the hardware and software required are complex and expensive compared to other interfaces.

The alternative to serial interfaces is parallel interfaces, which have multiple data lines. Because parallel interfaces transfer multiple bits at once, they can be fast. Usually there is just one set of data lines, so data travels in one direction at a time.

Over long distances or with more than two computers in a link, the cabling for parallel interfaces becomes too expensive to be practical.

The Centronics parallel printer interface predates the PC and just about every PC has included a Centronics-compatible interface. The IEEE-1284 standard defines new connectors, cables, and high-speed protocols for the port's 17 lines. Because the interface has been standard on all PCs, it's been pressed into service as an interface for scanners, external disk drives, data-acquisition devices, and many other special-purpose peripherals.

IEEE-488, which began life as Hewlett-Packard's GPIB (General-purpose Interface Bus) is another parallel interface popular in instrumentation and control applications.

Applications

This book focuses on what you need to design and program serial links. It doesn't get into application-specific details such as how to interface and access sensors, motors, and other devices that connect may to a computer in a monitoring or control link; these are topics for another time, and another book. But to give an idea of the possibilities, this section is an overview of the kinds of things you can do with these links.

One way to categorize links is by direction of data flow. In some systems all computers send and receive more or less equally. In others, most of the data flows to or from a central computer. For example, most of the activity in a link may relate a computer's collecting data from remote locations.

An everyday example of a system that collects data is a weather-watching network. A desktop PC may serve as a master that controls the activities of a variety of remote computers, which may simple microcontrollers. The master sends commands to the remote computers to tell them how often to collect data, what data to send to the master, and when to do it. The data collected may include temperature, air pressure, rainfall, and other variables. At intervals, each site sends its collected data to a master computer, which stores the data and makes it available for further viewing and processing.

This basic setup is adaptable to many other types of data-gathering systems. You can find a sensor to measure just about any property. Table 1-2 lists a variety of sensor types.

Other systems are mainly concerned with controlling external devices, rather than gathering data from them. A store-window display may include a set of mini-robots, each with switches and signals that control motors, lights, and other

Table 1-2: Types of Sensors

Acceleration	Flow	Moisture	Temperature
Chemical content	Force	Position	Thickness
Color	Level	Pressure	Velocity
Density	Light	Radiation	Vibration
Distance	Magnetic properties	Sound	Weight
Electrical properties	Mass	Strain	Wind

mechanical or electrical devices. Again, each device may have its own computer, with a master computer controlling the show by sending commands to each of the robot's computers. The robots may also return information about their current state to the master computer, but the main job of this type of system is to control the devices, rather than to collect information from them. This arrangement is typical of many other control systems.

An example of a system involved equally with monitoring and controlling is a home-control system, which may watch temperature, humidity, motion, switch states, and other conditions throughout a house. Control circuits hook into the house's heating, cooling, lighting, and alarm systems. When the master computer detects that a room has strayed from the set temperature, it causes more heated or cooled air to be pumped into the room. When alarm circuits are enabled and motion is detected, the system generates an alarm. The system may also control audio and video systems and outdoor lighting and watering.

In each of the examples above, one computer may act as a master that controls a series of slave computers whose actions are controlled by the master. A slave transmits only after the master contacts it and gives it permission.

It's also possible to have a system with no master. Instead, each computer has equal status with the others, and each can request actions from the others. For example, each computer may take turns transmitting to the others. Or one computer may send a message to another, which in turn can pass the same message, or a different message, to another computer. In some links, any computer may try to transmit at any time, and a protocol determines what happens if two try to transmit at once.

A simple link may use just two computers. One may gather data from or send commands to another. Or two computers may each be responsible for various monitoring and control functions, sharing information as equals.

These are just a few examples. By choosing components and writing programs to control them, you can put together a system to serve whatever purpose you have in mind. The rest of this book is devoted to presenting what you need to make this happen.

2

Formats and Protocols

The computers in a serial link may be of different types, but all must agree on conventions and rules for the data they exchange. This agreement helps to ensure that every transmission reaches its destination and that each computer can understand the messages sent to it.

This chapter introduces data formats and protocols used in serial links. The focus is on the asynchronous format used by most RS-232 and RS-485 links.

Sending Serial Data

In a serial link, the transmitter, or driver, sends bits one at a time, in sequence. A link with just two devices may have a dedicated path for each direction or it may have a single path shared by both, with the transmitters taking turns. When there are three or more devices, all usually share a path, and a network protocol determines when each can transmit.

One signal required by all serial links is a clock, or timing reference, to control the flow of data. The transmitter and receiver use a clock to decide when to send and read each bit. Two types of serial-data formats are synchronous and asynchronous, and each uses clocks in different ways.

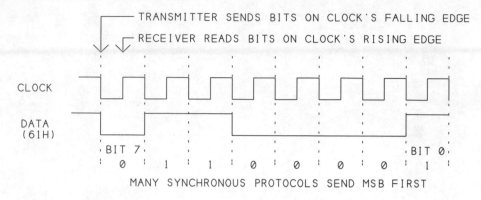

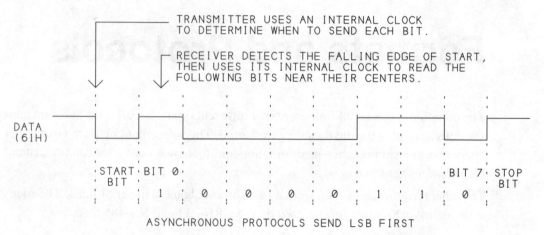

Figure 2-1: Typical synchronous and asynchronous transmissions.

Synchronous Format

In a synchronous transmission, all devices use a common clock generated by one of the devices or an external source. Figure 2-1A illustrates. The clock may have a fixed frequency or it may toggle at irregular intervals. All transmitted bits are synchronized to the clock. In other words, each transmitted bit is valid at a defined time after a clock transition (rising or falling edge). The receiver uses the clock transitions to decide when to read each incoming bit. The exact details of the protocol can vary. For example, a receiver may latch incoming data on the rising or falling clock edge, or on detecting a logic high or low level. Synchronous formats use a variety of ways to signal the start and end of a transmission, including Start and Stop bits and dedicated chip-select signals.

Synchronous interfaces are useful for short links, with cables of 15 feet or less or even between components on a single circuit board. For longer links, synchronous formats are less practical because of the need to transmit the clock signal, which requires an extra line and is subject to noise.

Asynchronous Format

In asynchronous (also called unsynchronous and non-synchronous) transmissions, the link doesn't include a clock line, because each end of the link provides its own clock. Each end must agree on the clock's frequency, and all of the clocks must match within a few percent. Each transmitted byte includes a Start bit to synchronize the clocks, and one or more Stop bits to signal the end of a transmitted word.

The RS-232 ports on PCs use asynchronous formats to communicate with modems and other devices. Although an RS-232 interface can also transfer synchronous data, asynchronous links are much more common. Most RS-485 links also use asynchronous communications.

An asynchronous transmission may use any of several common formats. Probably the most popular is 8-N-1, where the transmitter sends each data byte as 1 Start bit, followed by 8 data bits, beginning with bit 0 (the LSB, or least significant bit), and ending with 1 Stop bit. Figure 2-1B illustrates.

The N in 8-N-1 indicates that the transmissions don't use a parity bit. Other formats include a parity bit as a simple form of error checking. Parity can be Even, Odd, Mark, or Space. Table 2-1 illustrates Even and Odd parity. With Even parity, the parity bit is set or cleared so that the data bits plus the parity bit contain an even number of 1s. With Odd parity, the bit is set or cleared so that these bits contain an odd number of 1s. An example format using parity is 7-E-1. The transmitter sends 1 Start bit, 7 data bits, 1 parity bit, and 1 Stop bit. Here again, both ends of the link must agree on the format. The receiver examines the received data and informs the transmitter of an error if a result isn't the expected value.

Mark and Space parity are forms of *Stick* parity: with Mark parity, the parity bit is always 1, and with Space parity, it's always 0. These are less useful as error indicators, but one use for them is in the 9-bit networks described in Chapter 11. These networks use a parity bit to indicate whether a byte contains an address or data.

Other, less common formats use different numbers of data bits. Many serial ports support anywhere from 5 to 8 data bits, plus a parity bit.

Table 2-1: With Even parity, the data bits plus the parity bit contain an even number of 1s. With Odd parity, the data bits plus the parity bit contain an odd number of 1s.

Data Bits	Even Parity Bit	Odd Parity Bit
0000000	0	1
0000001	1	0
0000010	1	0
0000011	0	1
0000100	1	0
1111110	0	1
1111111	1	0

A link's bit rate is the number of bits per second transmitted or received per unit of time, usually expressed as bits per second (bps). Baud rate is the number of possible events, or data transitions, per second. The two values are often identical because in many links, including those described in this book, each transition period represents a new bit. Over phone lines, high-speed modems use phase shifts and other tricks to encode multiple bits in each data period, so the baud rate is actually much lower than the bit rate.

All of the bits required to transmit a value from Start to Stop bit form a *word*. The data bits in a word form a *character*. In some links, the characters actually do represent text characters (letters or numbers), while in others the characters are binary values that have nothing to do with text. The number of characters transmitted per second equals the bit rate times the number of bits in a word. Adding one Start and one Stop bit to a byte increases the transmission time of each byte by 25 percent (because there are 10 bits per byte instead of just 8). With 8-N-1 format, a byte transmits at 1/10 the bit rate: a 9600 bits-per-second link transmits 960 bytes per second.

If the receiver requires a little extra time to accept received data, the transmitter may stretch the Stop bit to the width of 1.5 or 2 bits. The original purpose of the longer Stop bit was to allow time for mechanical teletype machines to settle to an idle state.

There are other ways to generate Start and Stop bits without using a full bit width. The USB interface uses varying voltages to indicate start and stop. Of course, this requires hardware that supports these definitions.

System Support

Fortunately, the programming required to send and receive data in asynchronous formats is simpler than you might expect. PCs and many microcontrollers have a component called a UART (universal asynchronous receiver/transmitter) that handles most of the details of sending and receiving serial data.

In PCs, the operating system and programming languages include support for programming serial links without having to understand every detail of the UART's architecture. To open a link, the application selects a data rate and other settings and enables communications at the desired port. To send a byte, the application writes the byte to the transmit buffer of the selected port, and the UART sends the data, bit by bit, in the requested format, adding the Stop, Start, and parity bits as needed. In a similar way, received bytes are automatically stored in a buffer. The UART can trigger an interrupt to notify the CPU, and thus the application, of incoming data and other events.

Some microcontrollers don't include a UART, and sometimes you need more UARTs than the microcontroller has. In this case, there are two options: add an external UART, or simulate a UART in program code. Parallax's Basic Stamp is an example of a chip with a UART implemented in code.

A USART (Universal Synchronous/Asynchronous Receiver/Transmitter) is a similar device that supports both synchronous as well as asynchronous transmissions.

Transmitting a Byte

Understanding the details of how a byte transmits isn't strictly necessary in order to design, program, and use a serial link, but the knowledge can be useful in troubleshooting and selecting a protocol and interface for a project.

The Bit Format

Figure 2-1B showed how a byte transmits in 8-N-1 format. When idle, the transmitter's output is a logic 1. To signal the beginning of a transmission, the output sends a logic 0 for the length of one bit. This is the Start bit. At 300 bps, a bit is 3.3 milliseconds, while at 9600 bps, it's 0.1 millisecond.

After the Start bit, the transmitter sends the 8 data bits in sequence, beginning with bit 0, the least-significant bit (LSB). The transmitter then sends a logic 1, which functions as the Stop bit. The output remains at logic 1 for at least the width of one

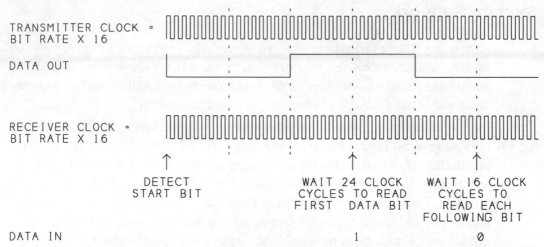

TRANSMITTER CLOCK =
BIT RATE X 16

DATA OUT

RECEIVER CLOCK =
BIT RATE X 16

↑   ↑   ↑
DETECT   WAIT 24 CLOCK   WAIT 16 CLOCK
START BIT   CYCLES TO READ   CYCLES TO
                                    FIRST   DATA BIT   READ EACH
                                                                   FOLLOWING BIT

DATA IN   1   0

Figure 2-2: Each end of the link uses a clock of 16 times the bit rate to determine when to send and read each bit.

bit. Immediately following this, or at any time after, the transmitter may send a new Start bit to announce the beginning of a new byte.

At the receiving end, the transition from logic 1 to the Start bit's logic 0 signals that a byte is arriving and determines the timing for detecting the following bits. The receiver measures the logic state of each bit near the middle of the bit. This helps ensure that the receiver reads the bits correctly even if the transmitting and receiving clocks don't match exactly.

Some interfaces, such as RS-232, use inverted voltages from those shown: the Stop bit is a negative voltage and the Start bit is positive.

The UART typically uses a receive clock that is 16 times the bit frequency: if the data rate is 300 bits per second, the receive clock must be 4800 bits per second. As Figure 2-2 shows, after detecting the transition that signals a start bit, the UART waits 16 clock cycles for the Start bit to end, then waits 8 more cycles to read bit 0 in the middle of the bit. It then reads each of the following bits 16 clock cycles after the previous one.

If the transmitting and receiving clocks don't match exactly, the receiver will read each successive bit closer and closer to an edge of the bit. To read all of the bits in a 10-bit word correctly, the transmit and receive clocks should vary no more than about three percent. Any more than this, and by the time the receiver tries to read the final bits, the timing may be off by so much that it will read the bits either before they've begun or after they've finished. However, the clocks only need to stay in sync for the length of a word, because each word begins with a new Start bit that resynchronizes the clocks.

Because of the need for accurate timing, asynchronous interfaces require a stable timing reference. Most are controlled by a crystal or ceramic resonator. For best results, the frequency of the reference should allow even division by the frequencies the receive clocks use for standard bit rates. In PCs, the standard UART clock frequency is 1.8432 Mhz. Division by 16 gives 115,200, which is the top bit rate the UART supports.

In a microcontroller, the chip's main timing crystal usually serves as a reference for hardware timers that control the UART's clock. In the 8051 family, the hardware timers run at 1/12 the crystal frequency. With a crystal of 11.0592 Mhz, the fastest UART time is 921,600 Hz, which allows a bit rate of 57,600 bps.

As a way of eliminating errors due to noise, some UARTs, like the 8051 microcontroller's, take three samples in the middle of each bit, and use the logic level that matches two or more of the samples.

Autodetecting the Bit Rate

The ultimate in user convenience is a link with autobaud ability, where the two ends automatically configure themselves to the same bit rate. There are two ways to do this. In each, one node (I'll call it the adjustable node) detects the bit rate of the other (the fixed node) and adjusts its bit rate to match.

The first method requires no special hardware or hardware-level programming. When the node wants to establish communications, it repeatedly sends a character, with a pause between each. The character may be a null (Chr(0)), or any ASCII character (through Chr(127), as long as the most significant data bit, which is the last one to transmit, is 0.

The adjustable node begins at its highest bit rate. When it detects that a byte has arrived, it waits long enough for a byte to transmit at the lowest expected bit rate (33 milliseconds at 300 bps), then reads the received byte or bytes.

If the receiver detects more than one character, its bit rate doesn't match the transmitter's, so it tries again, using the next lower bit rate. When it detects one and only one character, it has the correct bit rate. As an extra check, it can verify that the received character matches an expected value. The adjustable node then sends an acknowledgment to the fixed node, which stops sending the characters, and communications can begin.

Why does this routine work? When the receiver's bit rate is faster than the transmitter's, the receiver finishes reading the character while the final bits are still arriving. (The character will cause a framing error if the receiver doesn't see a logic 1 where it expects to find the Stop bit, but this is unimportant here.) After the receiver thinks the character has finished transmitting, any received 0 looks like a

Start bit. This causes the receiver to try to read another character. If the last transmitted bit is 0, the receiver will always detect more than one character if its bit rate is too high.

The other method requires code that can measure pulse widths as accurately as the UART's receive clock (16 times the highest expected bit rate). On receiving a character, the adjustable node measures the width of the received pulses. Because the node is expecting a particular character, it can calculate the bit rate from the measured widths and adjust its bit rate to match.

The 8052-Basic microcontroller uses this method to adjust its bit rate to match the rate of a terminal or other computer it connects to. On bootup, the 8052-Basic waits to receive a character at its serial port. At the terminal, the user presses the Space bar, which sends the character 20h. This method doesn't even require a particular crystal frequency at the 8052-Basic. The firmware just adjusts its bit rate relative to the received pulses.

Data Formats

The data bits in a serial transmission may represent anything at all, including commands, sensor readings, status information, error codes, or text messages. The information may be encoded as binary or text data.

Binary Data

With binary data, the receiver interprets a received byte as a binary number with a value from 0 to 255. The bits are conventionally numbered 0 through 7, with each bit representing the bit's value (0 or 1) multiplied by a power of 2. For example, in Visual-Basic syntax):

```
Bit0 = BitValue * (2^0)
Bit1= BitValue * (2^1)
Bit7= BitValue * (2^7)
```

A byte of 1111 1111 translates to 255, or FFh, and 0001 0001 translates to 17, or 11h. In asynchronous links, bit 0, the least-significant bit (LSB), arrives first, so if you're looking at the data on an oscilloscope or logic analyzer, remember to reverse the order when translating to conventional notation of most-significant-bit (MSB) first.

Text Data

Binary data works fine for many links. But some links need to send messages or files containing text. And for various reasons, a link may also send binary data encoded as text.

To send text, the program uses a code that assigns a numeric value to each text character. There are several coding conventions. One of the most common is ASCII (American Standard Code for Information Exchange), which consists of 128 codes and requires only seven data bits. An eighth bit, if used, may be 0 or a parity bit. ANSI (American National Standards Institute) text uses 256 codes, with the higher codes representing special and accented characters. In the IBM ASCII text used on the original IBM PC, many of the higher codes represented line- and box-drawing characters used by many DOS programs used to add simple graphics to text screens and printouts.

Other formats use 16 bits per character, which allows 65,536 different characters. The Unicode standard supports hundreds of additional alphabets, while DBCS (double-byte character set) is an earlier standard that supports many Asian languages.

The examples in this book use ANSI/ASCII text, which is the format used by Visual Basic's MSComm control.

ASCII Hex

Text mode is the obvious choice for transferring string variables or files that contain text. But you can also use text to transfer binary data, by expressing the data in ASCII Hex format. Each byte is represented by a pair of ASCII codes that represent the byte's two hexadecimal characters. (Appendix C has more on hexadecimal and other number systems.) This format can represent any value using only the ASCII codes 30h through 39h (for 0 through 9) and 41h to 46h (for A through F).

Instead of sending one byte to represent a value from 0 to 255, the sending device sends two, one for each character in the hex number that represents the byte. The receiving computer treats the values like ordinary text. After a computer receives the values, it can process or use the data any way it wants, including converting it back to binary data.

For example, consider the decimal number

```
163
```

Expressed as a binary number, it's

```
1010 0011
```

In hexadecimal, it's

A3h (or &hA3 in Visual-Basic syntax)

The ASCII codes for "A" and "3" are

41h, 33h

So the binary representation of this value in ASCII hex consists of these two bytes:

01000001 00110011

A serial link using ASCII Hex format would send the value *A3h* by transmitting these two bytes.

A downside of using ASCII hex is that each data byte requires two characters, so data takes twice as long to transfer. Also, in most cases the application at each end will at some point have to convert between ASCII hex and binary

Still, ASCII Hex has its uses. One reason to use it is that it frees all of the other codes for other uses, such as handshaking codes or an end-of-file indicator. It also allows protocols that only support 7 data bits to transmit any numeric value.

Other options are to send values as ASCII decimal, using only the codes for *0* through *9*, or ASCII binary, using just *0* and *1*. The Basic Stamp has built-in support for these as well as for ASCII Hex.

Preventing Missed Data

Most computers in serial links have other things to do besides waiting to receive data. For example, a data-acquisition unit may periodically collect and store data until another node requests it. Or a controller may be responsible for monitoring and controlling conditions, occasionally sending information or receiving instructions on the link.

A computer may want to transmit at a time when the receiving computer is occupied with something else. The design of a link should ensure that each receiver sees all of the data intended for it and that all of the data arrives without error.

There are many ways to ensure this, including handshaking, buffering, use of polling or interrupts to detect received data, error checking, and acknowledging of received data. A link may use one or more of these methods.

Handshaking

With handshaking signals, a transmitter can indicate when it has data to send, and a receiver can indicate when it's ready to receive data. The exact protocols, or rules, that the signals follow may vary, though many RS-232 and RS-485 links follow standard or conventional protocols.

In one common form of hardware handshaking, the receiver brings a line high when it's ready to receive data, and the transmitter waits for this signal before sending data. The receiver may bring the line low any time, even in the middle of receiving a block of data, and the transmitter must detect this, stop sending, and wait for the line to return high before finishing the transmission. Other links accomplish the same thing with software handshaking, by having the receiver send one code to indicate that it's ready to receive, and another to signal the transmitter to stop sending.

Buffers

Buffers are another way that receivers can ensure that they don't miss any data sent to them. Buffers can also be useful on the transmit side, where they can enable applications to work more efficiently by storing data to be sent as the link is available.

The buffers may be in hardware, software, or both. The serial ports on all but the oldest PCs have 16-byte hardware buffers built into the UARTs. In the receive direction, this means that the UART can store up to 16 bytes before the software needs to read them. In the transmit direction, the UART can store up to 16 bytes and the UART will take care of the details of transmitting the bytes bit by bit, according to the selected protocol.

When the hardware buffers aren't large enough, a PC may also use software buffers, which are programmable in size and may be as large as system memory permits. The port's software driver transfers data between the software and hardware buffers.

In microcontrollers, the buffers tend to be much smaller, and some chips have no hardware buffers at all. The smaller the buffers, the more important it is to use other techniques to ensure that no data is missed.

Polling and Interrupts

Events that may occur at a serial port include sending and receiving of data, changes in handshaking signals, and sending and receiving of error messages. There are two ways for an application to cause and detect these events.

One way is to have the program automatically jump to a routine when an event occurs. The application responds quickly and automatically to activity at the port, without having to waste time checking, only to learn that no activity has occurred.

This type of programming is called *event-driven* because an external event can break in at any time and cause the program's execution to branch to a particular routine.

In Visual Basic, MSComm's OnComm event performs this function. The OnComm routine executes in response to events such as a hardware interrupt at the serial port or a software buffer's count reaching a trigger value. Many microcontrollers have hardware interrupts for this purpose as well.

The other approach is to poll the port by periodically reading properties and signals to find out if an event has occurred. This type of programming is called procedural programming, and doesn't use the port's hardware interrupts. The application has to be sure to poll the port often enough so that it doesn't miss any data or events. The frequency of polling depends on buffer size and the amount of data expected (as well as the need for a quick response). For example, if a device has a 16-byte buffer and polls the port once per second, it can receive no more than 16 bytes per second or the buffer will overflow and data will be lost.

Polling is often appropriate for transferring short bursts of data, or when a computer sends data and expects an immediate reply. A polled interface doesn't require a hardware interrupt, so you can run this type of program on a port that has no assigned interrupt line. Many polled interfaces use a system-timer interrupt to schedule port reads at intervals.

Acknowledgments

Some links may have nodes that accept commands without responding, but usually it's useful for the receiving node to let the transmitter know that a message got through, even if the receiver has no other information to return. These acknowledgments are especially useful in networks, where multiple nodes share a communications path and a transmitter's switching on at the wrong time can block another transmitter's message.

The acknowledgment may be a defined byte, such as a value that identifies the receiver, or the transmitting node may assume that a node received its message when it receives requested data in reply. If the transmitting node doesn't receive the expected response, it should assume there is a problem and retry or take other action.

When transmitting to a node that has no input buffer, or a very small buffer, a transmitter can use an Acknowledgment to ensure that it has the node's attention before sending a block of data. The transmitting node begins by sending a byte to signal that it wants to send data. When the node sees the byte, it sends an acknowledgment and then devotes its full attention to watching its serial input. When the transmitting node sees the acknowledgment, it knows that it's OK to send the rest of the data.

Error-checking

A receiver can use error-checking to verify that all data arrived correctly. Ways to check a message for errors include sending redundant data and error-checking bytes.

A simple form of error-checking uses redundant, or duplicate, data. The transmitter sends each message twice and the receiver verifies that it's the same both times. Of course, this means that each message takes twice as long to transmit. Still, it can be useful when sending occasional, short bursts of data. Many infrared controllers use this method.

Another error-checking method is to send an error-checking byte along with the data. A checksum is calculated by performing an arithmetic or logical operation on the bytes in a message. A typical calculation adds the values of all of the bytes in the message and uses the lowest byte of the result as the checksum.

The receiving end repeats the calculation, and if it gets a different result, it knows that it didn't receive the same data that was sent. Since the checksum is typically just one byte, it doesn't add much to the message length, even when a message is very long. The checksum isn't foolproof; there is a small chance that the checksums will match even if the data doesn't. Intel Hex and Motorola S-Record are two data formats that include a checksum in each line of ASCII Hex data. Chapter 4 has routines that calculate and verify a checksum for a string.

Another type of error-checking byte is a CRC (cyclic redundancy code), which uses more complex math and is more reliable than a checksum. Some common error-checking protocols used in file transfers are Kermit, XModem, YModem, and ZModem.

When a node detects an error or receives a message it doesn't understand, it should try to notify the node that sent it so it can try again or take other action to remedy the situation. After a number of tries, if the transmitting node is unable to correct a problem or if the receiving node doesn't respond, the transmitting node should know enough to skip the node for the time being, display an error message, sound an alarm, or do something to notify the human operators of the problem, and then continue on with its other duties as best as it can.

The receiving node should also know what to do if a message is shorter than expected. Instead of waiting forever for a message to end, it should eventually time out and let the master know that it had a problem. The master may then resend or move on. Otherwise, the network may hang in an endless wait.

3

The PC's Serial Port from the Connector In

This chapter looks at serial ports inside the PC, between the connector and the CPU. You don't have to understand everything about the internal workings of a port in order to use it, but some background is useful, especially for links that use the port in unconventional ways.

Port Architecture

Serial ports have been a part of the PC from the beginning. Each COM, or Comm, (communications) port in a PC is an asynchronous serial port controlled by a UART. A COM port may have the conventional RS-232 interface, a related interface such as RS-485, or the port may be dedicated for use by an internal modem or other device. A PC may have other types of serial ports as well, such as USB, Firewire, and I²C, but these use different protocols and require different components.

Newer serial interfaces like USB and Firewire are fast and have other advantages. In fact, although Microsoft's PC 98 recommendations allow RS-232 ports, they recommend using USB in place of legacy (RS-232) serial ports whenever possible in new designs. And for many peripherals, the new interfaces are more appropriate.

But RS-232 and similar interfaces will continue to be popular in applications such as monitoring and control systems. These interfaces are inexpensive, easy to program, allow very long cables, and are easily used with inexpensive microcontrollers and older computers. As USB ports become more common, converters will become available to convert USB to RS-232 or RS-485. The converter will connect to the PC's USB port and translate between USB and the other interfaces. This setup will make it easy to add an RS-232 or RS-485 port to any system.

The UART

In the original IBM PC, the UART that controlled the serial port was the 8250, with a maximum speed of 57,600 bits per second. The UARTs in every PC since that time have continued to emulate this original chip, though the newer UARTs add buffering, higher speeds, and other features. These days, the UART in a PC is often part of a multifunction chip that contains one more UARTs along with support for a parallel port, disk drives, and other system components.

The UART translates between serial and parallel data. In one direction, the UART converts parallel data on the PC's system bus into serial data for transmitting. In the other direction, the UART converts received serial data to parallel data that the CPU reads on the system bus.

The PC's UART supports both full- and half-duplex communications. In a full-duplex link, the UART can send and receive at the same time. In half-duplex, only one device can transmit at a time, with control signals or codes determining when each can transmit. Half duplex is required if both directions share a path, or if there are two paths but one or both computers can communicate in just one direction at a time. And of course, the UART also supports one-way-only, or simplex, communications.

Another use of the terms full and half duplex is to describe which end of a link is responsible for echoing characters to a display. In this sense, full duplex means that the receiver echoes each character it receives back to the transmitter. Half duplex means that the receiver doesn't echo, so the transmitting software must cause the characters to display at the transmit end, if desired.

In addition to the data lines, the UART supports standard RS-232 handshaking and control signals such as *RTS, CTS, DTR, DCR, RI,* and *CD*.

Enhancements

An early improvement to the 8250 UART was the 16450, which supported speeds of up to 115,200 bps and added a scratch-pad register. The scratch pad is a byte of storage in the UART with no assigned function. The 16550 added transmit and receive buffers. New PCs have the equivalent of a 16550 or better.

Each of the 16550's buffers can store 16 bytes. The buffers are FIFOs (first-in, first-out), which means that data is read from the FIFO in the same order as it was received—the first byte in, or received, is the first one out, or read. (In contrast, a CPU's stack is often a LIFO (last in, first out): the last byte in is the first byte out.)

The buffers enable more efficient data transfers. On the receive side, the CPU doesn't have to worry about reading each byte before the next one arrives. If the CPU is busy, the buffer stores the received bytes and the CPU can read them at its convenience. The CPU's data bus is faster than the serial port's bit rate, so the CPU can read all 16 bytes in one operation, in a fraction of the time it took for them to arrive. On the transmit side, the CPU can write up to 16 bytes to the UART, and the UART will take care of the details of sending them out in the appropriate sequence.

New UARTs continue to build on the features of the 16550. Texas Instruments' TL16C750 has 64-byte FIFOs, can be powered at +5V or +3V, and has a low-power sleep mode. The chip supports bit rates of up to 1 Mbps when clocked by a 16-Mhz crystal. It also has built-in support for automatic RTS/CTS handshaking. In Auto-CTS mode, the UART transmits only when CTS is asserted, freeing the software from having to check its status. In Auto-RTS mode, the UART automatically asserts RTS when the receive FIFO has fewer than the defined threshold number of bytes. This signals the far end to send more data and helps to keep the FIFO from being empty.

Exar's ST16C50A is another example of a newer UART. It has 32-byte FIFOs, supports bit rates up to 1.5 Mbps, and includes an IrDA encoder/decoder for infrared links. It supports Auto-CTS/RTS handshaking as well as automatic software handshaking, and has the ability to detect a user-defined character.

However, the higher bit rates in the new UARTs are unavailable when the UART uses the PC's conventional 1.8432-Mhz clock, and the other advanced features go unused unless the software knows how to enable and use them.

Port Resources

Each serial port in a PC reserves a set of port addresses, and most also have an assigned interrupt-request (IRQ) line, or level. The ports are designated COM1, COM2, and so on up.

Finding Ports

To find out how many serial ports a computer has, you have to do more than count the RS-232 connectors on the back panel. Some serial devices use a COM port, but don't have an RS-232 interface. For example, the only external connector for an internal modem is the phone jack.

There are several ways to find information about the ports in a system.

Under Windows 95, you can view the ports' resources in the Control Panel: under *System, Ports,* select a COM port and click Properties. The *Port Settings* tab (Figure 3-1) shows the default bit rate and other settings, though these are easily changed by applications. If you want to disable the FIFOs for testing or some other reason, you can do so in the *Advanced Port Settings* window.

The *Resources* tab (Figure 3-2) shows the port's base address and assigned IRQ line. If the *Use Automatic Settings* box is checked, Windows has detected the port address and IRQ line. If the values shown don't match the hardware settings, you may be able to change them by unchecking *Use Automatic Settings* and selecting an alternate configuration from the list, or by typing new values. For some ports, Windows doesn't permit you to change the values at all from the Control Panel.

The configuration requires an IRQ (interrupt-request) line for each port. The window will display a message if Windows detects any conflicts with the settings you select.

Table 3-1 shows the four conventional base addresses for the ports and the IRQ lines usually assigned to them. Ports don't have to conform to this convention, however, and may use any addresses and IRQ lines supported by the hardware. Each port reserves eight sequential addresses beginning at the base address. So for example, a port at 3F8h reserves addresses from 3F8h through 3FFh.

The Window 3.x Control Panel also displays serial-port information. Under *Ports*, select a port, then *Settings*. Click *Advanced* to view or change the port's assigned address and IRQ line.

Because Windows stores the address and IRQ line for each port, applications don't have to keep track of them. An application can access ports using functions built into a programming language or the Windows API. The function call speci-

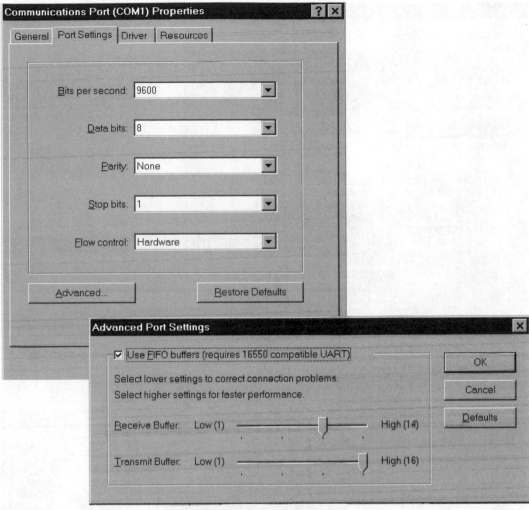

Figure 3-1: In Windows 95's Device Manager, the Port Settings tab for a serial port stores the default settings for the port and its buffers.

fies the port by name (COM1, COM2, etc.) and Windows knows where to find the port and how to use it.

Under DOS, you can find the COM port addresses in an area of memory called the BIOS data area. On boot-up, a routine in the PC's BIOS tests for the presence of serial ports at the following addresses, in order: 3F8h, 2F8h, 3E8h, 2E8h. It stores up to four 16-bit addresses beginning at address 40:00 in the BIOS data area. Some early BIOS's detected only the first two ports.

Chapter 4 shows how to find available ports in software.

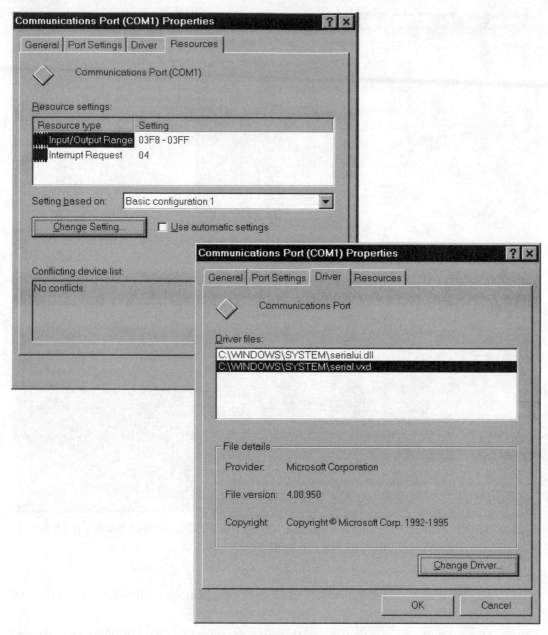

Figure 3-2: The Device Manager's Resources tab for a port show its reserved addresses and IRQ line. The Driver tab shows the port's software drivers.

Table 3-1: Conventional COM port addresses and IRQ lines.

Port	Address	IRQ
COM1	3F8h	4
COM2	2F8h	3
COM3	3E8h	4 or 11
COM4	2E8h	3 or 10

Port Information in the Registry

Windows' system registry stores the address and assigned IRQ line of each COM port. Listing 3-1 shows two serial ports listed under this registry key:

```
HKEY_LOCAL_MACHINE\Enum\Root\
```

If the configuration differs from the default entry under Bootconfig, the changes are stored under a `ForcedConfig` subkey.

Older, legacy serial ports are stored under this registry key:

```
HKEY_LOCAL_MACHINE\Enum\BIOS\
```

Windows 95 has an additional registry section that stores temporary configurations that are valid for a single session. Listing 3-2 shows the listings for the same two ports under these keys.

Windows' *Regedit* program enables you to examine the system registry and search for entries.

Configuring

Many serial ports have jumpers, switches, or configuration utilities that enable you to select a port address and IRQ line. The setup screens that you can access on bootup enable you to configure ports that reside on the main system board.

The amount of choice in the configuration varies. Some ports allow addresses and IRQ lines other than the conventional ones. Under Windows 95, the use of unconventional port addresses isn't a problem. When an expansion card with a port is installed, if Windows doesn't detect the port, you can add it manually. To do so, from the Control Panel, select *Add New Hardware*. When asked if you'd like it to search for the new hardware, select *No*. Select *Ports*, then *Communications Port*. Accept the address and IRQ line that Windows assigns—even if they're wrong—and click *Next* to complete the installation. Then if you need to change the address or IRQ line to match your hardware, do so from the Control Panel's Device Man-

```
[HKEY_LOCAL_MACHINE\Enum\Root\*PNP0500\0000]
"InfName"="MSPORTS.INF"
"DeviceDesc"="Communications Port (COM1)"
"Class"="Ports"
"HardwareID"="*PNP0500"
"DetFunc"="*:DETECTCOM"
"NoSetupUI"="1"
"DetFlags"=hex:00,00,00,00
"BootConfig"=hex:00,04,00,00,00,00,00,00,14,00,00,00,02,00,00,00,
  00,00,0c,00,f8,03,ff,03,00,00,00,03,10,00,00,00,04,00,00,00,01,0
  0,04,00,00,00,00,00,00,00,00,00,00
"VerifyKey"=hex:f8,03,00,00
"PortName"="COM1"
"Driver"="Ports\\0000"
"Mfg"="(Standard port types)"
"ConfigFlags"=hex:00,00,00,00
"FRIENDLYNAME"="Communications Port (COM1)"
"Settings"=hex:02,10,00,80
```

```
[HKEY_LOCAL_MACHINE\Enum\Root\*PNP0500\0001]
"InfName"="MSPORTS.INF"
"DeviceDesc"="Communications Port (COM2)"
"Class"="Ports"
"HardwareID"="*PNP0500"
"DetFunc"="*:DETECTCOM"
"NoSetupUI"="1"
"DetFlags"=hex:00,00,00,00
"BootConfig"=hex:00,04,00,00,00,00,00,00,14,00,00,00,02,00,00,00,
  00,00,0c,00,f8,02,ff,02,00,00,00,03,10,00,00,00,04,00,00,00,01,0
  0,03,00,00,00,00,00,00,\
  00,00,00
"VerifyKey"=hex:f8,02,00,00
"PortName"="COM2"
"Driver"="Ports\\0001"
"Mfg"="(Standard port types)"
"ConfigFlags"=hex:00,00,00,00
"FRIENDLYNAME"="Communications Port (COM2)"
"Settings"=hex:02,10,00,80
```

Listing 3-1: Registry keys that store port addresses and IRQ lines for COM ports. Under BootConfig, **f8,03** indicates a port address of 03F8h, and **f8,02** indicates a port address of 02F8h. The bold **04** and **03** are the assigned IRQ lines.

```
[HKEY_DYN_DATA\Config Manager\Enum\C119C24C]
"HardWareKey"="ROOT\\*PNP0500\\0000"
"Problem"=hex:00,00,00,00
"Status"=hex:cf,6a,00,00
"Allocation"=hex:00,04,00,00,00,00,00,00,14,00,00,00,02,00,00,00,
   00,00,0c,00,f8,03,ff,03,00,00,00,03,10,00,00,00,04,00,00,00,01,0
   0,04,00,00,00,00,00,00,00,00,00
```

```
[HKEY_DYN_DATA\Config Manager\Enum\C119C750]
"HardWareKey"="ROOT\\*PNP0500\\0001"
"Problem"=hex:00,00,00,00
"Status"=hex:cf,6a,00,00
"Allocation"=hex:00,04,00,00,00,00,00,00,14,00,00,00,02,00,00,00,
   00,00,0c,00,f8,02,ff,02,00,00,00,03,10,00,00,00,04,00,00,00,01,0
   0,03,00,00,00,00,00,00,00,00,00
```

Listing 3-2: COM port listings in Windows 95's registry branch for storing dynamic data.

ager, as described earlier. Once a port is installed, Windows remembers the configuration and programs should have no problem accessing it.

Under DOS, applications that depend on the BIOS for finding port addresses won't be able to access a port at an unconventional address, because the BIOS won't detect it. For example, I have an older serial card that assigns address 2E8h to COM3 and 2E0h to COM4 (assuming that the user already has two serial ports installed). When the BIOS doesn't find a port at COM3's normal address of 3E8h, it continues looking and assigns the next port it finds, 2E8h, as COM3. The port at 3E0h is never detected.

Under DOS, there are two ways to make use of a port at an unconventional address. One is to run a utility on bootup to store the address in the BIOS data area. This way, any application that reads port addresses in the BIOS data area will find it. Also, any application that enables users to enter a port address can use the port, assuming that the user knows the address to enter.

The BIOS data area doesn't store the IRQ lines assigned to a port, so DOS applications and serial-port drivers that use interrupts must either assume the default IRQ line, ask the user to select one, or try to detect which line is assigned. DOS and the BIOS also include some support for serial-port communications, but for better performance, most DOS programs use their own communications routines.

Other ways to view serial-port resources are to run the program *msd.exe* included with Windows 3.x and DOS, or similar diagnostic programs. The setup screens that you can access on bootup also contain information about the system's ports.

New Systems

Although Microsoft's recommendations for the PC 98 discourage the use of legacy COM ports, they do allow them, with the following requirements:

- The port must be equal to a 16550A UART or better, and must support bit rates of up to 115,200 bps.
- The port must be capable of being reconfigured and completely disabled in software.
- The port must support the conventional port addresses and IRQ lines.
- Each port must allow a choice of at least two IRQ lines. When there are two ports, the recommendation is to allow the choice of IRQ4 and IRQ11 for one port, and IRQ3 and IRQ10 for the other.
- An infrared adapter port may take the place of one serial port.

These are good, general recommendations for a flexible configuration on any system. Of course, users are free to install any serial port that their hardware supports. Older expansion cards should work fine in any computer with ISA slots, whether or not they meet the above requirements.

Adding a Port

A new PC typically has one or two RS-232 ports, though these are gradually being replaced in new systems by USB ports. Expansion cards are available with additional RS-232 ports, or you add a card with an RS-485 or other interface type.

For years, most expansion cards have plugged into the PC's ISA bus, which is the system bus of the original IBM PC. However, the ISA bus is gradually being phased out in favor of the much faster and more capable buses such as PCI. PCI expansion cards with serial ports are available. Before buying a card, be sure your PC has a free slot, and that you know what type it is. An 8-bit ISA slot has parallel rows of 31 contacts each. A 16-bit ISA slot adds an adjacent slot with rows of 18 contacts. A 32-bit PCI slot has parallel rows of 62 contacts each. Also be sure the card supports the IRQ line you want to assign to the port(s) on the card.

For an RS-485 port, you can add an expansion card, or use an existing RS-232 port and an external converter. Chapter 9 has more on this.

Figure 3-3: An older serial port expansion card. The two large 40-pin chips on the left are UARTs. The bottom UART is socketed for easy upgrading.

Using Older Hardware

In older systems and expansion cards that use 40-pin DIP sockets (Figure 3-3), you can upgrade an 8250 by replacing it with a 16450 or 16550. The pinouts of the 8250 and 16450 are identical. The 16550 adds two outputs, *TXRDY* and *RXRDY*, used in buffered DMA transfers, and eliminates one output, *CSOUT*, which indicates when the chip is selected. These aren't required for normal operation, however.

On reset, a 16550 acts like a 16450. Software has to enable the buffers. Windows detects the UART type and configures the UART to use the FIFOs. Under DOS, the application or serial-port driver must do these.

The part numbers of the early UARTs can be deceptive. For example, the 8250A has a scratch register like the 16450's, and the buffers on some early 16550s were unusable due to a product flaw.

One way to detect a 16450-type UART is to write to the scratch register and read back what you've written. If it matches, you have a 16450 or better. To detect a 16550-type UART, enable the buffers and try to use them.

Internal vs. External Devices

With modems and some other COM-port devices, you often have a choice between an internal and external device. Each has advantages.

Internal devices are usually a little cheaper and save desk space, or luggage room with portables. A PC may include an internal modem whether or not you want it.

If a PC has no free expansion slots and it does have a free RS-232 port, an external device may be the only option. If you use a device on more than one computer, it's easier to unplug and move an external device than to open up two enclosures to remove and install an internal card. When you upgrade, an external device is easy to recycle by moving it to another system. Because computers other than PCs also have RS-232 interfaces, you may be able to use an external device on other computer types as well.

External devices also make it easy to use multiple peripherals, one at a time, by using a switch box or just swapping the cable, without having to open up the enclosure or worry about finding a unique address or IRQ line for each.

IRQ Conflicts

One problem with using multiple serial ports is that there are only two IRQ lines reserved for use by all four ports. COM1 and COM3 conventionally use IRQ4, while COM2 and COM4 use IRQ3. However, assigning the same IRQ line to two ports can lead to problems. In some cases, even if you have four serial ports, you can use only two at a time.

Using Interrupts

Most serial-port applications use hardware interrupts because they enable faster data transfers by automatically detecting events at the port. The interrupt is a signal that tells the CPU that a task needs immediate servicing. The original IBM PC supported 8 interrupt lines. The PC model AT increased the number to 16, and this is where it has remained, even though the number of devices using interrupts continues to increase. Each IRQ line corresponds to a signal that connects the interrupt's source to the PC's interrupt controller.

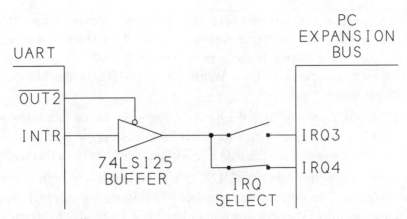

Figure 3-4: The UART's *-Out2* pin enables the serial-port interrupt on the PC.

A program that uses a hardware interrupt must provide an interrupt-service routine (ISR) that performs the desired actions when the interrupt occurs. For example, a serial-port ISR might read data from the port's receive buffer.

When a device sends an interrupt request by pulsing an IRQ line, the system's interrupt controller detects the request and informs the CPU that the request is pending. The CPU breaks away from whatever it was doing and executes the ISR. On exiting the ISR, the CPU returns to what it was doing when the interrupt occurred.

In Visual Basic, the MSComm control takes care of the details of installing and enabling the ISR. The application's OnComm routine contains the program code to execute on an interrupt. (Chapter 4 has more on this.)

Interrupt Circuits

The circuits associated with the interrupt lines explain why two ports can't share an interrupt. On the PC's ISA bus, interrupts are triggered by a rising edge.

Figure 3-4 shows the interrupt circuitry from an older serial-port expansion card. More recent serial ports use different components, but any ISA card should emulate the operation of these circuits. The chip that drives the IRQ line is a 74LS125 buffer. The user selects an IRQ line by closing a switch on the expansion card. This routes the buffer's output to one of two IRQ lines on the expansion bus.

The input to the buffer is the *INTR* output of the port's UART, which goes high to request an interrupt. The buffer also has an enable input, which is controlled by the UART's *-OUT2* output. This is a general-purpose output that the PC's architecture reserves for this function.

Before a program can use serial interrupts, the software must bring *-OUT2* low to cause the output of the buffer to follow its input. To make things confusing, the *-OUT2* pin on the UART is the complement of the *-OUT2* bit in the UART's modem control register (MCR). Writing 1 to *-OUT2* in the MCR brings the *-OUT2* pin low.

When the *-OUT2* pin is high, the buffer's output is off, or in a high-impedance state, and interrupt requests from the UART don't affect the IRQ line. This means that another device can use the IRQ line without conflicts from this serial port.

The problems begin when two 74LS125's are enabled and both connect to the same IRQ line. The outputs are totem-pole TTL type, where a high output has a low resistance to +5V, and a low output has a low resistance to signal ground. If two serial ports share the same interrupt line, if one output tries to go high and the other tries to go low, the result is unpredictable. Chances are good that the IRQ line won't go high enough to generate an interrupt request, and the resulting current may even damage the components involved.

Solutions for Multiple Ports

There are solutions to the shortage of IRQ lines. None is ideal, but you should be able to find something that works for a particular situation.

Limit the number of devices that use COM ports. If you never need to use more than two serial devices, use only COM1 and COM2, with IRQ4 assigned to COM1 and IRQ3 assigned to COM2. Don't assign these IRQ lines to any other devices.

Sometimes you can free up a serial port by using an alternate interface. A USB port can handle communications with multiple peripherals. Instead of requiring an IRQ line for each device, the USB driver polls the USB devices periodically to find out if any have a pending request.

Mice have used a variety of interfaces, including COM ports. These days, a mouse is more likely to be a PS/2-type, which uses a built-in mouse port that doesn't need a COM-port address, and typically uses IRQ 12. A bus mouse, which connects to a special mouse-interface expansion card, also doesn't normally use a COM-port address, though it may use IRQ3 or IRQ4. USB is the new recommended interface for mice.

Use a switch box. A switch box enables you to use multiple devices, one at a time. For example, you can have one internal device on COM1, with a switch box connected to multiple devices on COM2.

Use alternate IRQ lines. If you must use two even or two odd-numbered ports at once, see if you can assign a different IRQ line to one of the ports.

Possible available interrupts are IRQ7 and IRQ5, which are reserved for the parallel ports, but are sometimes unused. If your parallel port and the printer it connects to both support ECP mode, an assigned IRQ line will enable faster printer communications. The drivers for other parallel-port devices may be capable of using interrupts as well, though almost all parallel-port devices can operate without interrupts if necessary. Interrupts 10 through 12 may also be available, though not all serial ports allow these choices. Sound cards and other devices may be using any of these, however.

With a shared IRQ line, use one device at a time. If two ports must share an IRQ line, don't use both at the same time. This assumes that interrupts are disabled on the unused port. On exiting, a well-behaved application will disable any IRQ line it had enabled.

Use polling instead of interrupts. If you're writing your own software, you may be able to disable interrupts on the port and instead use a polled interface, where the software checks periodically for data or errors instead of relying on interrupts to signal them. Most commercial software uses interrupts because they are convenient and efficient. But if an application doesn't require fast response, doing without interrupts can be a solution.

Unfortunately, sometimes you have no choice except to enable the interrupt. In Visual Basic, opening a COM port with the MSComm control automatically enables the assigned IRQ line at -OUT2. The line remains enabled until the port is closed. So even if the program doesn't use interrupts, MSComm enables the buffer that drives the IRQ line, preventing other devices from using it.

However, if the IRQ line can be disabled at the port (by removing a jumper that enables an IRQ line, for example), -OUT2 will have no effect on the interrupt lines and the port can be used without interrupts.

Use a bus that allows interrupt sharing. The PCI bus found on most new PCs has four level-triggered, active-low, shareable interrupt lines. In a typical system configuration, a programmable interrupt router connects each PCI interrupt to one of the system's sixteen IRQ lines.

Two other earlier buses are the Micro Channel and EISA buses. On the Micro Channel bus introduced in IBM's model PS/2, the IRQ lines are active-low and shareable. On the EISA bus, the IRQ lines can have either configuration, with rising-edge interrupts for compatibility with ISA cards, and level-sensitive interrupts for EISA cards.

However, shareable IRQ lines require software that can identify which device requested an interrupt and jump to the appropriate ISR. The hardware for shareable lines usually uses open-collector or open-drain outputs (described in Chapter 5).

Use a multi-port card that allows IRQ sharing. Some cards with multiple ports allow interrupt sharing. This type of card should come with software drivers that read the UARTs' registers to detect which port was the source of an interrupt request and branches to the appropriate interrupt-service routine.

Use an RS-485 network. Another way to connect multiple serial devices to a PC is to use an RS-485 interface, which allows multiple devices to connect to one port. This is a solution for some monitoring and control systems. RS-485 expansion cards are available for PCs. Of course, all of the serial devices must also support RS-485, or use RS-485 adapters, and a multi-node RS-485 link requires programming to manage communications among the devices.

Inside the UART

The 16550 and similar UARTs contain twelve 8-bit registers. The registers hold the next byte to transmit, the last byte received, the bit rate and other port settings, and control and status information for handshaking, FIFO use, and interrupts.

Most of the time, there's no need to access the registers directly because the programming language or system API includes functions for configuring and using the port. But knowing how it all works can come in handy if you're tracking down problems or if you need to do something unusual with the port.

Although the UART has twelve internal registers and two FIFOs, it requires just eight port addresses. In some cases multiple registers share an address, and the register accessed depends on the value of a bit in another register or whether the operation is a read or write. The FIFOs are internal to the UART and require no port addresses.

Table 3-2 shows the functions and addresses of the internal registers of the three original UART types. Complete data sheets are available from National Semiconductor and other manufacturers.

The UART's addresses are relative to its base address. Address 0 is at the port's base address, with the others following in sequence. For example, on COM1, address 0 is usually at 3F8h, and address 7 is at 3FFh.

The base address has three registers. A write-only register holds the next byte to transmit and a read-only register holds the last byte received.

On reset, the DLAB bit (bit 7 of *base address* + *3*) is 0. Reading the base address (Receive Buffer) tells you the most recent data received at the UART's *SIN* pin. Writing a byte to the base address (Transmit Buffer) causes the byte to transmit in serial format at the *SOUT* pin.

Table 3-2: Register summary for 8250, 16450, and 16550 UARTs.

Address	Access	Name	Abbrev.	Bit Number							
				7	6	5	4	3	2	1	0
0	DLAB= 0, read only	receive buffer	RBR	received data							
	DLAB= 0, write only	transmit holding register	THR	transmit data							
	DLAB= 1, read/ write	divisor latch, low byte	DLL	baud rate divisor low byte							
1	DLAB= 0, read/ write	interrupt enable	IER	0	0	0	0	modem status	receiver line status	transmit holding register empty	received data available
	DLAB= 1, read/ write	divisor latch, high byte	DLM	baud rate divisor high byte							
2	read only	interrupt identify	IIR	FIFOs enabled**: 11 if FCR bit 0=1, 00 if FCR bit 0=0	0	0	Interrupt ID: 011=receive line status 010=received data avail. 110=character timeout 001=TR hold. reg empty 000=modem status				-Interrupt Pending
	write only**	FIFO control**	FCR **	receive FIFO trigger level:** 00=1 byte 01=4 bytes 10=8 bytes 11=14 bytes	reserved **	reserved **	DMA mode select**	transmit FIFO reset**	receive FIFO reset**	FIFO enable**
3	read/ write	line control	LCR	divisor latch access bit (DLAB)	break set	stick parity set	even parity set	parity enable	stop bits: 0=1 bit 1= 2 bits	word length: 00=5 bits 01=6 bits 10=7 bits 11=8 bits
4	read/ write	modem control	MCR	0	0	0	loop-back mode	-OUT2 (-IRQ enable on PCs)	-Out1	request to send (RTS)	data terminal ready (DTR)
5	read only	line status	LSR	error in receive FIFO	transmit buffer empty	transmit holding reg.	break interrupt	framing error	parity error	overrun error	data ready
6	read only	modem status	MSR	data carrier detect (CD)	ring indicator (RI)	data set ready (DSR)	clear to send (CTS)	change in CD	RS-232 falling edge at RI	change in DSR	change in CTS
7	read/ write	scratch*	SCR	scratch register, no designated function							

*16450 and 16550 only, **16550 only

Setting DLAB to 1 enables you to use the divisor latches at the base address and (*base address + 1*) to set a bit rate for the port. The divisor latches hold a 16-bit value that divides the UART's crystal frequency to the desired bit rate. Table 3-3 shows divisor-latch values for different bit rates, assuming the UART's standard 1.8432-Mhz crystal. Listing 3-3 is a Visual-Basic routine that calculates values for any bit rate.

On some older 8250's, the maximum bit rate is 57,600, with the divisor latch set to 2. Other UARTs can transmit and receive at up to 115,200 baud. With a faster crystal, new UARTs can handle higher speeds.

Setting or reading the bit rate is the only time you need to set DLAB to 1. After doing so, you should set DLAB to 0. On reset, the bit rate is 2400.

Interrupt Sources

When DLAB is 0, the Interrupt Enable register (IER, at *base address + 1*) can enable up to four interrupt sources. The interrupt sources provide a convenient way to detect errors or other situations that need attention. When an interrupt occurs, bits 1, 2, and 3 of the Interrupt Identify register (IIR, at *base address + 2*) reveal the source. Many of the interrupt sources correspond directly to the events detected by MSComm.

Many applications don't use all of the interrupt sources. The most commonly used source is bit 0, *Received Data Available*. With this bit set to 1, the UART will generate an interrupt when there is new data to be read. Reading the receive buffer clears the interrupt until the next byte arrives.

When bit 1 of IER is set, an interrupt occurs when the transmit buffer is empty, to signal the CPU that it should write more data to the buffer.

When bit 2 is set, an interrupt occurs when there is a transmission error, signaled by a change in bits 1-4 in register 5. These are the four errors detected:

Overrun: new data arrived at the receive buffer before the previous data was read.

Parity: with parity enabled, the parity bit of the byte at the top of the receive FIFO was incorrect.

Framing: a received character did not have a Stop bit. This error may also occur when the transmitter's and receiver's bit rates don't match.

Break interrupt: received data has been logic 0 for longer than the transmission time for one character.

When bit 3 of IER is set, an interrupt occurs when there is a change at one of the control inputs on the serial connector.

Table 3-3: Divisor-latch values for different bit rates on the PC's UART.

Bit Rate (bps)	High Byte (hex)	Low Byte (hex)
300	01	80
1200	00	60
2400	00	30
9600	00	0C
19,200	00	06
38,400	00	03
115,200	00	01

Bits 4–7 of the Modem Status register (MSR, at *base address + 6*) hold the status of the control inputs, and bits 0–3 signal which inputs have changed since the last time the register was read.

Bits 4–7 are inverted twice between the register and an RS-232 connector. The RS-232 interface inverts the signals once, and the inputs at the UART are the complements of the corresponding values in the register. So when bit 4 is 0, the *CTS* pin on the UART is a logic high, and the *CTS* pin on the RS-232 connector is negative, which is defined as Off, or False.

Control Registers

The Line Control register (LCR, at *base address + 3*) stores configuration information such as the number of stop, data, and parity bits used in each transmission. For example, for the popular settings of N,8,1, bits 5–0 would be 00111.

The Modem Control register (MCR, at *base address + 4*) has several important functions. Bit 3 (*-OUT2*) is a general-purpose output on the UART, but as explained earlier, in PCs, this bit enables the IRQ line at the port. Setting *-OUT2* to 0 turns off the output that generates interrupt requests for the port. Even if the UART detects an interrupt, the interrupt controller and CPU will never see it.

Bits 0 and 1 of MCR set and clear *DTR* and *RTS* on the serial connector, for applications that use these control signals. Bit 2 is another general-purpose output. This one has no defined function in PCs.

Setting bit 4 of MCR puts the UART in a loopback mode, which enables reading transmitted data at the receive buffer. Loopback allows you to test a port, or test for the presence of a port, by writing to it and reading back the result.

```
Public Sub FindDivisorLatchValues(BitRate As Long)
Dim LowByte As Long
Dim HighByte As Long
Dim Crystal As Long
Crystal = 1843200
HighByte = Crystal \ (&H1000 * BitRate)
LowByte = _
  (Crystal \ (BitRate * &H10)) - (HighByte * &H100)
Debug.Print "high byte: ", Hex$(HighByte)
Debug.Pinrt "low byte:  ", Hex$(LowByte)
End Sub
```

Listing 3-3: This Visual-Basic routine calculates UART divisor-latch values for a bit rate.

New Functions

Some of the registers and bits aren't in all versions of the UART. The 16450 and 16550 have a scratch register (*base address + 7*), which has no defined function. In your own programs, you can use this register any way you want.

Other bits control the 16550's FIFOs. Setting bit 0 of the FIFO Control register (*base address +2*) enables the FIFOs and also sets the register's bits 6 and 7. Setting bit 0 and then reading bits 6 and 7 is a quick way to test for the presence of the FIFOs. (A few early FIFOs fail this test.) On UARTs without FIFOs, bits 6 and 7 will always read 0.

4

PC Programming

Many programming languages for PCs support serial communications by including functions for configuring and reading and writing to serial ports. Serial-port controls are also available from other sources. Windows also has serial-communications functions in its API (Applications Programmer's Interface), and any programming language that can call API functions can use these.

This chapter focuses on Visual-Basic programming. A template application includes functions for detecting, opening, and transferring data with Visual Basic's MSComm control. The sample applications in the following chapters are based on this template.

Also included are descriptions of other ways to access ports, when MSComm is unavailable or doesn't have the needed abilities. These include using Windows API functions, direct port reads and writes, and access under DOS.

Although the syntax and other details vary, much of the information in this chapter also applies to serial-port programming in other dialects of Basic and other programming languages.

Using MSComm

MSComm is Visual Basic's custom control for serial communications. The control is included in Visual Basic's Professional and Enterprise editions, but not in the (lowest-cost) Learning edition. A custom control offers much easier programming and better performance than other methods of port access. If you're going to be doing much serial-port programming, it makes sense to invest in a version that includes MSComm or buy a serial-port control from another source.

Properties

Like other controls, MSComm has associated properties. The properties relate to configuring ports, transferring data, use of handshaking signals, and identifying the control. Visual Basic's documentation includes the syntax and other details required to use the properties, so I won't repeat them here. The following is quick reference, arranged by function.

Configuring

CommID. Returns a handle that identifies the device.

CommPort. Sets and returns the port number.

InBufferSize. Sets and returns the receive buffer's size, in bytes.

InputLen. Sets and returns the number of characters `Input` will read.

InputMode. Sets and returns the type of data (text or binary) returned by `Input` and accepted by Output.

NullDiscard. Determines whether null characters (`Chr(0)`) are transferred from the port to the receive buffer or dropped (ignored).

OutBufferSize. Sets and returns the transmit buffer's size, in bytes.

ParityReplace. Sets and returns the character that replaces an invalid character on parity error.

PortOpen. Sets and returns the state of the port. (`True` if open, `False` if closed.)

RThreshold. Sets and returns the number of characters to receive before triggering `comEvReceive`.

Settings. Sets and returns the bit rate, parity, and number of data and stop bits.

SThreshold. Sets and returns the minimum number of characters in the transmit buffer before triggering `comEvSend`.

Transferring Data

CommEvent. Returns the most recent event or error.

EOFEnable. Determines whether input will stop on receiving an *Eof* character.

InBufferCount. Returns the number of characters in the receive buffer.

Input. Returns and removes data from the receive buffer.

OutBufferCount. Returns the number of characters in the transmit buffer.

Output. Writes data to the transmit buffer.

Handshaking

Break. Sets or clears a break signal.

CDHolding. Returns the state of *CD*.

CTSHolding. Returns the state of *CTS*.

DSRHolding. Returns the state of *DSR*.

DTREnable. Sets or clears *DTR*.

Handshaking. Sets and returns the handshaking protocol.

RTSEnable. Sets or clears *RTS*.

Identification

Index. Sets and returns a number that identifies the control in a collection.

Name. Identifies the control. Example: `MSComm1`.

Object. Returns the control and/or a setting of a control's method or property.

Parent. Returns the form, object, or collection that contains the control.

Tag. Sets and returns an expression. User defined.

Text and Binary Transfers

Visual Basic 5 allows transferring of data in either text or binary format. The `InputMode` property determines which format MSComm uses.

Text Mode

With the `InputMode` property set to `comInputModeText`, MSComm sends and receives ANSI strings. To write a string to the port, set MSComm's `Output` property equal to the string:

```
Dim SampleText as String
'The text to send:
SampleText="ABC"
'Write the string to the port:
MSComm1.Output = SampleText
```

MSComm transmits an 8-bit ANSI code for each character in the string.

To read a string from the port, set a string equal to MSComm's `Input` property:

```
Dim SampleText as String
'Read the input into a string:
SampleText = MSComm1.Input
```

MSComm stores each received 8-bit ANSI code as a text character.

The `Output` property will also accept a variant containing a string, and MSComm will also read an input string into a variant.

Internally, Visual Basic stores strings as 16-bit Unicodes, but the conversion between Unicode and MSComm's 8-bit ANSI strings is automatic.

ASCII Hex Conversions

For applications that use ASCII Hex format, Visual Basic has functions that convert between ASCII Hex strings and the values they represent. The `Hex$` operator converts a number to an ASCII Hex string:

```
debug.print Hex$(165)
A5
```

The `Val` operator converts from ASCII Hex to the string's value:

```
debug.print Val("&h" & "A5")
165
```

Don't forget to add the *&h*, which tells Visual Basic to treat the value as hexadecimal.

Binary Mode

To transfer binary data, set MSComm's `InputMode` to `comInputModeBinary`.

Visual Basic 5 supports the Byte variable type for storing binary data. Bytes written to and read from the serial port are stored in variants that contain byte arrays. Even if there is just one byte, it must be in a byte array, not a simple byte variable.

Writing a byte array to the serial port is a two-step process. First assign the byte array to a variant, then send the data by setting the variant equal to the port's output property:

```
Dim BytesToSend(0 To 1) As Byte
Dim Buffer As Variant
'Store the data in a byte array:
BytesToSend(0) = &H4A
BytesToSend(1) = &H23
'Set a variant equal to the array:
Buffer = BytesToSend()
'Write the variant to the port:
MSComm1.Output = Buffer
```

To read bytes at the serial port, you do the same thing in reverse: read a variant at the port, then set a byte array equal to the variant:

```
Dim BytesReceived() As Byte
Dim Buffer As Variant
```

```
'Read the data from the port.
Buffer = MSComm1.Input
'Store the data in a byte array.
BytesReceived() = Buffer
```

There are two ways to convert between byte arrays and variants. You can set a variable equal to a variable of the desired type, and Visual Basic will do the conversion automatically:

```
Dim DimensionedByteArray(15) As Byte
Dim DynamicByteArray() As Byte
Dim Buffer As Variant
Dim Count As Integer

'Store a byte array in a variant:
'The array must be dimensioned.
Buffer = DimensionedByteArray()

'Copy the contents of a variant into a byte array:
'The array must be dynamic (undimensioned).
DynamicByteArray() = Buffer
```

Or you can use Visual Basic's type-conversion functions:

```
'Store a byte array in a variant:
Buffer = CVar(DynamicByteArray())

'Store the contents of a variant in a byte array:
For Count = 0 To (LenB(Buffer) - 1)
    DimensionedByteArray(Count) = CByte(Buffer(Count))
Next Count
```

Polled Communications

A polled data transfer just reads and writes to the port as needed with MSComm's `Input` and `Output` properties.

Sending

The `Output` property writes to the port:

```
Dim DataToWrite as Variant
MSComm1.Output = DataToWrite
```

When sending small blocks of data, set the `OutBufferSize` property to at least the largest number of bytes the program will transmit at once.

For very long transmissions, use `OutBufferCount` to ensure that the buffer doesn't overflow. Fill the buffer, then if you have more data to send, read Out-

BufferCount and subtract its value from OutBufferSize to find out how much room remains in the buffer. Refill the buffer by writing that number of bytes to the port. Or you can send the data in packets of a defined size, and send a packet only when OutBufferCount shows that there is enough room for it. For example, if OutBufferSize is 1024 and the packet size is 512, you can send a packet when OutBufferCount <= 512.

Receiving

To read incoming data, the application reads the InBufferCount property periodically. When the count shows that the desired number of characters are present, the application reads the data with the Input property.

```
Dim BytesToRead as Integer
Dim DataIn as Variant

'Set the number of bytes to read.
NumberOfBytesToRead = 512
MSComm1.InputLen = NumberOfBytesToRead

'Poll the input buffer.
Do
  DoEvents
Loop Until MSComm1.InBufferCount > NumberOfBytesToRead

'When the desired amount of bytes have arrived,
'read them.
DataIn = MSComm1.Input
```

The InBufferSize property should be large enough to handle the largest amount of data that may arrive before MSComm can read it. If the data will arrive in blocks of a fixed size, set InBufferSize to a multiple of the block size.

If the amount of incoming data is unknown, the application should read the input buffer even if it has just one byte. Waiting for multiple bytes can be futile because there's no way to know which byte is the last. If waiting for more than one byte, the code should include a timeout that eventually quits and reads what's there if all of the bytes don't arrive.

You can combine procedural and event-driven programming by using timers to determine when to access a port. For example, use a Timer event to trigger a port read once per second.

Using OnComm

MSComm has one associated Event: OnComm, which responds to various events at a port. OnComm eliminates the need to check for incoming data or to find out if the remote receiver is ready for new data. Instead, when any of 17 events occurs, the application automatically sets a CommEvent property and jumps to the control's OnComm subroutine. Inside the routine, a Select Case structure is a convenient way to decide what action to take. In response to an event, the routine may display a message, take other action, or just ignore the event entirely. Many of OnComm's events correspond directly to hardware events signaled by bits in the UART, as described in Chapter 3. Other events are software-triggered.

Receiving

In the receive direction, OnComm provides a simple and efficient way to detect when data has arrived at a port. MSComm's RThreshold property sets the minimum number of received characters required to trigger an OnComm event:

```
MSComm1.RThreshold = 1
```

When the receive buffer contains RThreshold or more characters, the application jumps to the OnComm subroutine. The routine is responsible for determining that the **ComEvReceive** event has occurred and reading the received characters:

```
Case ComEvReceive
Buffer = MSComm1.Input
```

Again, if RThreshold is greater than one, the last byte or bytes in a transmission may remain unread.

Setting RThreshold to 0 disables ComEvReceive; it will never trigger.

Sending

In the transmit direction, the reason to use OnComm isn't as obvious.

The CPU can write to the port faster than the port can send the serial data out. If the amount of data to send is larger than OutBufferSize, the application can't write all of the data to the buffer at once, or it will overflow. You can use OnComm to transfer large amounts of data efficiently, by ensuring that transmit buffer is never empty, yet never overflows.

MSComm's SThreshold property sets the number of characters in the Transmit buffer that will trigger an OnComm event:

```
MSComm1.SThreshold = 256
```

Use the Output property to fill the transmit buffer the first time:

```
MSComm1.Output = DataToSend
```

When the buffer drops from SThreshold + 1 to SThreshold number of characters, **comEvSend** causes a jump to the OnComm subroutine. The event signals that the transmit buffer has room for more data.

For example, if the transmit buffer is 1024 bytes and the port is transferring a 32k file, the application might set SThreshold at 256 bytes. To send the file, the application writes 1024 bytes to fill the transmit buffer, and the port begins transferring the data. When 256 bytes remain to be transmitted, the program's comEvSend routine can write 768 more bytes to refill the buffer. The process continues until the file has transferred.

If the amount of information to be transferred is less than OutBufferSize, there's no need to use OnComm in this way. The application can write the data directly to the transmit buffer, as described above. This is the simplest approach, if the system can spare the memory for the buffer. Setting SThreshold to 0 disables ComEvSend so that it will never trigger.

Even when comEvSend looks like it may be useful, it can be tricky to use. For example, if for some reason the CPU fills the output buffer more slowly than the bytes transmit, the buffer will never hold SThreshold number of bytes, and comEvSend will never fire. In many cases a polled interface is simpler and more reliable for sending data.

Handshaking Events

Another use for OnComm is to detect changes in the handshaking signals and other handshaking events:

comEvCTS. Change at the *CTS* input.

comEvDSR. Change at the *DSR* input.

comEvCD. Change at the *CD* input.

comEventRing. A Ring signal detected at *RI*. Visual Basic's Help warns that this event may not fire, so it's best to not rely on it and instead detect rings by scanning received data for a Ring code from a modem.

comEvEof. An *Eof* character was received. Used when the sending computer uses the *Eof* code to indicate end of file. The default *Eof* code is *1Ah* (Control+Z).

comEventBreak. The receive input has been logic 0 for longer than the time required to transmit one word. The break signal is a rarely used form of signaling that holds the output in a Space (0) condition even if data is written to the transmit buffer. When idle, the transmit output is normally a Mark (1), which is a negative RS-232 voltage. The Break signal provides a way to hold the transmit output positive.

Data Errors

OnComm also detects many data errors. In each of the following cases, the sending computer should resend the data that was missed.

comEventFrame. The receiver didn't detect a Stop bit. This error will occur if the transmitting node quits before sending a complete word, or if the bit rates or number of bits in the settings don't match.

comEventParity. The receiver's Setup property includes parity, and a received parity bit didn't match the expected value.

comEventOverrun. A character arrived when the UART's buffer was full.

comEventRxOver. A character arrived when the receive software buffer was full.

comEventTxOver. A character was written to the transmit software buffer when it was full.

DCB Errors

There is one other OnComm event:

comEventDCB. Error retrieving the DCB. The Device Control Block (DCB) is a structure used by Windows to store information about a COM port.

Disabling Events

Some of the OnComm events can be disabled, while others will fire whether or not the application needs to know. To disable ComEvReceive and ComEvSend, set their threshold properties to 0. To disable ComEventEof, set MSComm's EofEnable property to False. To disable ComEventParity, set parity to None in the Settings property.

The other events trigger OnComm whether the application needs to take action or not. If the event is of no importance, the OnComm routine should just end and return control to the main program.

Handshaking Options

MSComm offers a few options for automatic handshaking.

With the Handshaking property set to comRTS, MSComm uses *CTS* to determine when it's OK to transmit, and *RTS* to let the remote computer know when it's OK to send.

MSComm brings *RTS* false (a negative RS-232 voltage) when InBufferCount is nearly equal or equal to 80% of InBufferSize. (If the proportion doesn't fall exactly at 80%, *RTS* toggles early, when the next byte received will cause InBufferCount to be over 80% full.) The remote computer should stop transmitting when *RTS* is False. When enough bytes have been read from the input buffer so that `InBufferCount` has dropped to 20% full, MSComm brings *RTS* True (a positive RS-232 voltage) again.

In the other direction, MSComm transmits only when *CTS* is True. If *CTS* is False, the transmission will wait for it to go True, up to the time specified in `Set-CommTimeouts`, as described later in this chapter. If the wait times out, the transmit buffer clears and the data doesn't transmit.

Xon/Xoff provides software handshaking, which works in a similar way to hardware handshaking, except that the indicators are software codes rather than hardware signals. Software handshaking takes more time, and you can use it only on links that can dedicate codes for this use. The advantage is that there's no need for hardware handshaking lines in the link.

When `InBufferCount` is 80% of `InBufferSize`, MSComm transmits an Xoff character to tell the remote computer to stop sending. When `InBuffer-Count` has dropped to 20% of `InBufferSize`, MSComm sends an Xon character to tell the remote computer to resume transmitting. In the other direction, a received Xoff will cause MSComm to pause transmitting until receipt of an Xon character. The default XOn character is 11h (Control+Q); the default XOff is 13h (Control+S).

A third option, `comRTSXOnXOff`, uses both RTS/CTS and XOn/XOff handshaking.

Networks may use yet another type of handshaking. For example, a transmitting node may set *RTS* True (or False, depending on the hardware configuration) to enable a driver. When transmitting is complete, the node sets *RTS* to the opposite state to disable the driver and allow another node to transmit.

MSComm doesn't have the ability to do this type of handshake automatically, though it can be done by setting the `RTSEnable` property to the desired state in code, as the example network in Chapter 12 shows.

MSComm's documentation says that if `RTSEnable` and `DTREnable` are True, *RTS* and *DTR* will be set True on opening the port, and False on closing it. But in my experiments, on closing the port, these signals toggled False for just one word width, then returned True. So if you want to ensure that the signals are False when the port closes, set their properties to False before closing.

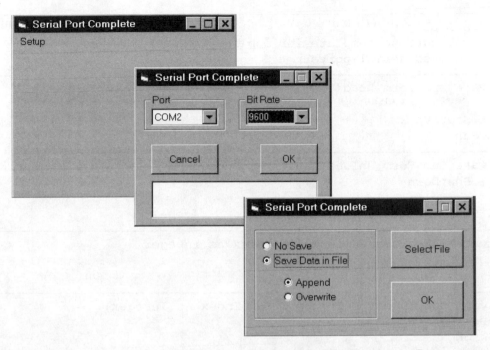

Figure 4-1: The template application has a blank main form and a Setup menu that brings up forms for selecting and configuring ports and selecting a file for storing data.

A Template Application

Figure 4-1 shows the windows included in a template application with various routines and forms that serial-port programs might use. The main form is blank except for a *Setup* menu with items that display windows for selecting a port and storing collected data in a file. You could also add button icons for these items. The example applications in later chapters use this template as a base, with application-specific command buttons, text boxes, and other elements added to the main form.

The application includes four code modules, one for the main form, two for the forms brought up by the Setup menu items, and a *.bas* module containing general serial-port routines.

The Main Form

Listing 4-1 is the program code for the applications's main window. The code contains little except an OnComm routine for the form's MSComm control and a routine to intialize the COM port.

```
Option Explicit
'General-purpose template for applications
'that access serial ports.

Private Sub Form_Load()
Show
Call Startup
End Sub

Private Sub Form_Unload(Cancel As Integer)
Call ShutDown
End
End Sub

Private Sub mnuDataFile_Click(Index As Integer)
frmDataFile.Show
End Sub

Private Sub mnuPortSettings_Click(Index As Integer)
frmPortSettings.Show
End Sub
```

Listing 4-1: Code for the template application's Main form. (Sheet 1 of 5)

```
Public Function fncInitializeComPort _
    (BitRate As Long, _
    PortNumber As Integer) _
    As Boolean
'Initializes the selected COM Port.
'All settings except BitRate are set explicitly in this routine.
'Some properties show alternate settings commented out.
Dim ComSettings as String
If MSComm1.PortOpen = True Then
    MSComm1.PortOpen = False
End If

MSComm1.CommPort = PortNumber
'Use BitRate, no parity, 8 data, and 1 stop bit:
ComSettings = CStr(BitRate) & ",N,8,1"
MSComm1.Settings = ComSettings

'Properties relating to receiving:
'Read entire buffer on Input:
MSComm1.InputLen = 0
'Read one byte at a time on Input:
'MSComm1.InputLen = 1

MSComm1.InBufferSize = 1024

'Generate no OnComm event on received data:
MSComm1.RThreshold = 0
'Generate an OnComm event on each character received:
'MSComm1.RThreshold = 1

'The Input property stores binary data:
'MSComm1.InputMode = comInputModeBinary
'The Input property stores data as text:
MSComm1.InputMode = comInputModeText

'Disable parity replacement"
'MSComm1.ParityReplace = ""
```

Listing 4-1: Code for the template application's Main form. (Sheet 2 of 5)

```
'Properties related to transmitting:

MSComm1.OutBufferSize = 1024

'Generate no transmit OnComm event:
MSComm1.SThreshold = 0
'Generate an OnComm event when the transmit buffer
'has SThreshold bytes or fewer:
'MSComm1.SThreshold = 512

'Handshaking options:
MSComm1.Handshaking = comNone
'MSComm1.Handshaking = comXOnXoff
'MSComm1.Handshaking = comRTS
'MSComm1.Handshaking = comRTSXOnXOff

'Open the port.
If MSComm1.PortOpen = False then
    MSComm1.PortOpen = True
End If
'Return success or failure
fncInitializeComPort = MSComm1.PortOpen
End Function
```

Listing 4-1: Code for the template application's Main form. (Sheet 3 of 5)

```
Public Sub MSComm1_OnComm()
'Handles all Comm events
Dim ComEventMessage As String
Select Case MSComm1.CommEvent
    'Handle each event or error by placing
    'code below each case statement
    'Events
    Case comEvCD
        ComEventMessage = "Change in the CD line."
    Case comEvCTS
        ComEventMessage = "Change in the CTS line."
    Case comEvDSR
        ComEventMessage = "Change in the DSR line."
    Case comEvRing
        ComEventMessage = "Change in the RI line."
    Case comEvReceive
        ComEventMessage = _
        "Receive buffer has RThreshold number of characters."
    Case comEvSend
        ComEventMessage = _
        "Transmit buffer has SThreshold number of characters."
    Case comEvEOF
        ComEventMessage = "EOF character (1Ah) received."
    'Errors
    Case comEventBreak
        ComEventMessage = "A Break was received."
    Case comEventCDTO
        ComEventMessage = "CD (RLSD) Timeout."
    Case comEventCTSTO
        ComEventMessage = "CTS Timeout."
    Case comEventDSRTO
        ComEventMessage = "DSR Timeout."
    Case comEventFrame
        ComEventMessage = "Framing Error"
    Case comEventOverrun
        ComEventMessage = "Overrun; data Lost."
    Case comEventRxOver
        ComEventMessage = "Receive buffer overflow."
    Case comEventRxParity
        ComEventMessage = "Parity Error."
    Case comEventTxFull
        ComEventMessage = "Transmit buffer full."
    Case comEventDCB
        ComEventMessage = "Unexpected error retrieving DCB."
End Select
```

Listing 4-1: Code for the template application's Main form. (Sheet 4 of 5)

```
'Use for debugging:
'Debug.Print ComEventMessage
End Sub
```

Listing 4-1: Code for the template application's Main form. (Sheet 5 of 5)

The OnComm routine uses a Select Case structure to detect the Comm event. An application can place whatever code is appropriate code under each event. For use in debugging, a ComEventMessage string variable contains a description of each error.

The fncInitializeComPort function opens the selected COM port and sets its properties. An application can use this routine to configure the port as needed.

General Routines

Listing 4-2 includes general routines that might be used by a program that accesses a serial port. Some of the routines access controls and variables on the forms in the template, but other than this, the routines are independent of a particular application.

The routines relate to finding ports, timing issues, and activities to perform on starting up and shutting down the application. The listing also includes many constant and API function declarations from the *win32api.txt* file included with Visual Basic.

Finding Ports

An application that uses MSComm doesn't have to know anything about a port except its name, which is simply COM1, COM2, and so on up. In most cases, the application doesn't have to know the port's address or the assigned IRQ line. because MSComm handles these details. But it is useful for an application to know what ports are available in a system, so it can offer users a choice. The routines offer two ways to find ports.

The FindPorts routine detects ports by trying to open all ports from COM1 through COM16. If the port opens or returns a *Port In Use* error, it exists. The routine adds the name of each port found to the Commports array.

The routine fncGetHighestComPortNumber accomplishes the same thing in another way, by using the EscapeComFunction API call to find the number of the highest installed port.

```
Option Explicit
'General routines used by applications
'that access the serial port.
'Some routines access forms and variables in template.vbp.

'The following constants are from win32api.txt:
'Constants used in DCB access
'Parity
Global Const NOPARITY = 0
Global Const ODDPARITY = 1
Global Const EVENPARITY = 2
Global Const MARKPARITY = 3
Global Const SPACEPARITY = 4
'Stop bits
Global Const ONESTOPBIT = 0
Global Const ONE5STOPBITS = 1
Global Const TWOSTOPBITS = 2

'Global Const IGNORE = 0
'Global Const INFINITE = &HFFFF

'Errors
Global Const CE_RXOVER = &H1
Global Const CE_OVERRUN = &H2
Global Const CE_RXPARITY = &H4
Global Const CE_FRAME = &H8
Global Const CE_BREAK = &H10
Global Const CE_CTSTO = &H20
Global Const CE_DSRTO = &H40
Global Const CE_RLSDTO = &H80
Global Const CE_TXFULL = &H100
Global Const CE_PTO = &H200
Global Const CE_IOE = &H400
Global Const CE_DNS = &H800
Global Const CE_OOP = &H1000
Global Const CE_MODE = &H8000
```

Listing 4-2: General-purpose routines for programs that access serial ports.
(Sheet 1 of 14)

```
Global Const IE_BADID = (-1)
Global Const IE_OPEN = (-2)
Global Const IE_NOPEN = (-3)
Global Const IE_MEMORY = (-4)
Global Const IE_DEFAULT = (-5)
Global Const IE_HARDWARE = (-10)
Global Const IE_BYTESIZE = (-11)
Global Const IE_BAUDRATE = (-12)

'CommEventMask bits
Global Const EV_RXCHAR = &H1
Global Const EV_RXFLAG = &H2
Global Const EV_TXEMPTY = &H4
Global Const EV_CTS = &H8
Global Const EV_DSR = &H10
Global Const EV_RLSD = &H20
Global Const EV_BREAK = &H40
Global Const EV_ERR = &H80
Global Const EV_RING = &H100
Global Const EV_PERR = &H200
Global Const EV_CTSS = &H400
Global Const EV_DSRS = &H800
Global Const EV_RLSDS = &H1000

'EscapeCommFunction values
Global Const SETXOFF = 1
Global Const SETXON = 2
Global Const SETRTS = 3
Global Const CLRRTS = 4
Global Const SETDTR = 5
Global Const CLRDTR = 6
Global Const RESETDEV = 7
Global Const GETMAXLPT = 8
Global Const GETMAXCOM = 9
Global Const GETBASEIRQ = 10
```

Listing 4-2: General-purpose routines for programs that access serial ports.
(Sheet 2 of 14)

```
'Bit rates
Global Const CBR_110 = &HFF10
Global Const CBR_300 = &HFF11
Global Const CBR_600 = &HFF12
Global Const CBR_1200 = &HFF13
Global Const CBR_2400 = &HFF14
Global Const CBR_4800 = &HFF15
Global Const CBR_9600 = &HFF16
Global Const CBR_14400 = &HFF17
Global Const CBR_19200 = &HFF18
Global Const CBR_38400 = &HFF1B
Global Const CBR_56000 = &HFF1F
Global Const CBR_128000 = &HFF23
Global Const CBR_256000 = &HFF27

Global Const CN_RECEIVE = &H1
Global Const CN_TRANSMIT = &H2
Global Const CN_EVENT = &H4
Global Const CSTF_CTSHOLD = &H1
Global Const CSTF_DSRHOLD = &H2
Global Const CSTF_RLSDHOLD = &H4
Global Const CSTF_XOFFHOLD = &H8
Global Const CSTF_XOFFSENT = &H10
Global Const CSTF_EOF = &H20
Global Const CSTF_TXIM = &H40
Global Const LPTx = &H80

'   DTR Control Flow Values.
Public Const DTR_CONTROL_DISABLE = &H0
Public Const DTR_CONTROL_ENABLE = &H1
Public Const DTR_CONTROL_HANDSHAKE = &H2

'   RTS Control Flow Values
Public Const RTS_CONTROL_DISABLE = &H0
Public Const RTS_CONTROL_ENABLE = &H1
Public Const RTS_CONTROL_HANDSHAKE = &H2
Public Const RTS_CONTROL_TOGGLE = &H3
```

Listing 4-2: General-purpose routines for programs that access serial ports.
(Sheet 3 of 14)

```
'DCB Bits values:
Public Const FLAG_fBinary& = &H1
Public Const FLAG_fParity& = &H2
Public Const FLAG_fOutxCtsFlow = &H4
Public Const FLAG_fOutxDsrFlow = &H8
Public Const FLAG_fDtrControl = &H30
Public Const FLAG_fDsrSensitivity = &H40
Public Const FLAG_fTXContinueOnXoff = &H80
Public Const FLAG_fOutX = &H100
Public Const FLAG_fInX = &H200
Public Const FLAG_fErrorChar = &H400
Public Const FLAG_fNull = &H800
Public Const FLAG_fRtsControl = &H3000
Public Const FLAG_fAbortOnError = &H4000

'End of win32api.txt constants.

Public Type COMMTIMEOUTS
    ReadIntervalTimeout As Long
    ReadTotalTimoutMultiplier As Long
    ReadTotalTimeoutConstant As Long
    WriteTotalTimeoutMultiplier As Long
    WriteTotalTimeoutConstant As Long
End Type

Public Type dcbType
        DCBlength As Long
        BaudRate As Long
        Bits1 As Long
        wReserved As Integer
        XonLim As Integer
        XoffLim As Integer
        ByteSize As Byte
        Parity As Byte
        StopBits As Byte
        XonChar As Byte
        XoffChar As Byte
        ErrorChar As Byte
        EofChar As Byte
        EvtChar As Byte
        wReserved2 As Integer
End Type
```

Listing 4-2: General-purpose routines for programs that access serial ports.
(Sheet 4 of 14)

```
'Global variables & constants used by the application:

Public Const ProjectName = "SerialPortComplete"

Public BitRate As Long
Public Buffer As Variant
Public CommDCB As dcbType
Public CommPorts() As String
Public OneByteDelay As Single
Public PortExists As Boolean
Public PortInUse As Boolean
Public PortNumber As Integer
Public PortOpen As Boolean
Public SaveDataInFile As Boolean
Public TimedOut As Boolean
Public ValidPort As Boolean
```

Listing 4-2: General-purpose routines for programs that access serial ports.
(Sheet 5 of 14)

```
'API declares:
Public Declare Function apiGetCommState _
    Lib "kernel32" _
    Alias "GetCommState" _
    (ByVal nCid As Long, _
    lpDCB As dcbType) _
    As Long
Public Declare Function apiSetCommState _
    Lib "kernel32" _
    Alias "SetCommState" _
    (ByVal hCommDev As Long, _
    lpDCB As dcbType) _
    As Long
Public Declare Function EscapeCommFunction _
    Lib "kernel32" _
    (ByVal nCid As Long, _
    ByVal nFunc As Long) _
    As Long
Public Declare Function GetCommTimeouts _
    Lib "kernel32" _
    (ByVal hFile As Long, _
    lpCommTimeouts As COMMTIMEOUTS) _
    As Long
Public Declare Function SetCommTimeouts _
    Lib "kernel32" _
    (ByVal hFile As Long, _
    lpCommTimeouts As COMMTIMEOUTS) _
    As Long
Public Declare Function timeGetTime _
    Lib "winmm.dll" () _
    As Long
Public Declare Function TransmitCommChar _
    Lib "kernel32" _
    (ByVal nCid As Long, _
    ByVal cChar As Byte) _
    As Long
```

Listing 4-2: General-purpose routines for programs that access serial ports. (Sheet 6 of 14)

```
Public Function fncAddChecksumToAsciiHexString _
    (UserString As String) _
    As String
'Calculates a checksum for a string containing
'a series bytes in Ascii Hex format.
'Places the checksum in Ascii Hex format
'at the end of the string.
Dim Count As Integer
Dim Sum As Long
Dim Checksum As Byte
Dim ChecksumAsAsciiHex As String
'Add the values of each Ascii Hex pair:
For Count = 1 To Len(UserString) - 1 Step 2
    Sum = Sum + Val("&h" & Mid(UserString, Count, 2))
Next Count
'The checksum is the low byte of the sum.
Checksum = Sum - (CInt(Sum / 256)) * 256
ChecksumAsAsciiHex = fncByteToAsciiHex(Checksum)
'Add the checksum to the end of the string.
fncAddChecksumToAsciiHexString = UserString & ChecksumAsAsciiHex
End Function
```

```
Public Function fncByteToAsciiHex _
    (ByteToConvert As Byte) _
    As String
'Converts a byte to a 2-character ASCII Hex string
Dim AsciiHex As String
AsciiHex = Hex$(ByteToConvert)
If Len(AsciiHex) = 1 Then
    AsciiHex = "0" & AsciiHex
End If
fncByteToAsciiHex = AsciiHex
End Function
```

```
Public Function fncDisplayDateAndTime() As String
'Date and time formatting.
fncDisplayDateAndTime = _
    CStr(Format(Date, "General Date")) & ", " & _
    (Format(Time, "Long Time"))
End Function
```

Listing 4-2: General-purpose routines for programs that access serial ports. (Sheet 7 of 14)

```
Public Function fncGetHighestComPortNumber() As Integer
'Returns the number of the system's highest COM port.
'Also shows how to use the EscapeCommFunction API call.
Dim ClosePortOnExit As Boolean
Dim PortCount As Long
Dim handle As Long
'The API call requires a CommID of an open port.
If frmMain.MSComm1.PortOpen = False Then
    frmMain.MSComm1.PortOpen = True
    ClosePortOnExit = True
Else
    ClosePortOnExit = False
End If
handle = frmMain.MSComm1.CommID
PortCount = GETMAXCOM
'Add 1 because EscapeCommFunction begins counting at 0.
fncGetHighestComPortNumber = _
    EscapeCommFunction(handle, PortCount) + 1
If ClosePortOnExit = True Then
    frmMain.MSComm1.PortOpen = False
End If
End Function
```

```
Public Function fncOneByteDelay(BitRate As Long) As Single
'Calculate the time in milliseconds to transmit
'8 bits + 1 Start & 1 Stop bit.
Dim DelayTime as Integer
DelayTime = 10000 / BitRate
fncOneByteDelay = DelayTime
End Function
```

Listing 4-2: General-purpose routines for programs that access serial ports. (Sheet 8 of 14)

```
Public Function fncVerifyChecksum _
    (UserString As String) _
    As Boolean
'Verifies data by comparing a received checksum
'to the calculated value.
'UserString is a series of bytes in Ascii Hex format,
'ending in a checksum.
Dim Count As Integer
Dim Sum As Long
Dim Checksum As Byte
Dim ChecksumAsAsciiHex As String
'Add the values of each Ascii Hex pair:
For Count = 1 To Len(UserString) - 3 Step 2
    Sum = Sum + Val("&h" & Mid(UserString, Count, 2))
Next Count
'The checksum is the low byte of the sum.
Checksum = Sum - (CInt(Sum / 256)) * 256
ChecksumAsAsciiHex = fncByteToAsciiHex(Checksum)
'Compare the calculated checksum to the received checksum.
If Checksum = Val("&h" & (Right(UserString, 2))) Then
    fncVerifyChecksum = True
Else
    fncVerifyChecksum = False
End If
End Function
```

```
Public Sub Delay(DelayInMilliseconds As Single)
'Delay timer with approximately 1-msec. resolution.
'Uses the API function timeGetTime.
'Rolls over 24 days after the last Windows startup.
Dim Timeout As Single
Timeout = DelayInMilliseconds + timeGetTime()
Do Until timeGetTime() >= Timeout
    DoEvents
Loop
End Sub
```

Listing 4-2: General-purpose routines for programs that access serial ports.
(Sheet 9 of 14)

```
Public Sub EditDCB()
'Enables changes to a port's DCB.
'The port must be open.
Dim Success As Boolean
Dim PortID As Long
PortID = frmMain.MSComm1.CommID
Success = apiGetCommState(PortID, CommDCB)

'To change a value, uncomment and revise the appropriate line:
'CommDCB.BaudRate = 2400
'CommDCB.Bits1 = &H11
'CommDCB.XonLim = 64
'CommDCB.XoffLim = 64
'CommDCB.ByteSize = 8
'CommDCB.Parity = 0
'CommDCB.StopBits = 0
'CommDCB.XonChar = &H11
'CommDCB.XoffChar = &H13
'CommDCB.ErrorChar = 0
'CommDCB.EofChar = &H1A
'CommDCB.EvtChar = 0

'Write the values to the DCB.
Success = apiSetCommState(PortID, CommDCB)

'Read the values back to verify changes.
Success = apiGetCommState(PortID, CommDCB)

Debug.Print "DCBlength: ", Hex$(CommDCB.DCBlength)
Debug.Print "BaudRate: ", CommDCB.BaudRate
Debug.Print "Bits1: ", Hex$(CommDCB.Bits1); "h"
Debug.Print "wReserved: ", Hex$(CommDCB.wReserved)
Debug.Print "XonLim: ", CommDCB.XonLim
Debug.Print "XoffLim: ", CommDCB.XoffLim
Debug.Print "ByteSize: ", CommDCB.ByteSize
Debug.Print "Parity: ", CommDCB.Parity
Debug.Print "StopBits: ", CommDCB.StopBits
Debug.Print "XonChar: ", Hex$(CommDCB.XonChar); "h"
Debug.Print "XoffChar: ", Hex$(CommDCB.XoffChar); "h"
Debug.Print "ErrorChar: ", Hex$(CommDCB.ErrorChar); "h"
Debug.Print "EofChar: ", Hex$(CommDCB.EofChar); "h"
Debug.Print "EvtChar: ", Hex$(CommDCB.EvtChar); "h"
Debug.Print "wReserved2: ", Hex$(CommDCB.wReserved2)

End Sub
```

Listing 4-2: General-purpose routines for programs that access serial ports. (Sheet 10 of 14)

```
Public Sub FindPorts()
'Find Comm ports by trying to open each.
'Each port must support the current settings (bit rate, etc.).
Dim Count As Integer: Dim NumberOfPorts As Integer
Dim SavedPortNumber As Integer: Dim SaveCurrentPort As Boolean
ReDim CommPorts(1 To 16)
On Error Resume Next
SaveCurrentPort = False: NumberOfPorts = 0
'If a port is already open, reopen it on exiting.
If frmMain.MSComm1.PortOpen = True Then
        frmMain.MSComm1.PortOpen = False
        SavedPortNumber = PortNumber
        SaveCurrentPort = True
End If
For Count = 1 To 16
    frmMain.MSComm1.CommPort = Count
    frmMain.MSComm1.PortOpen = True
    If Err.Number = 8005 Then
        'The port is already open & exists, so add it to the list.
        NumberOfPorts = NumberOfPorts + 1
        CommPorts(NumberOfPorts) = "COM" & CStr(Count)
        If SavedPortNumber = Count then
            frmMain.MSComm1.PortOpen = False
        End If
    ElseIf frmMain.MSComm1.PortOpen = True Then
        'If the port opens, it exists.
        'Close it and add to the list.
        frmMain.MSComm1.PortOpen = False
        NumberOfPorts = NumberOfPorts + 1
        CommPorts(NumberOfPorts) = "COM" & CStr(Count)
    Err.Clear
    End If
Next Count
On Error GoTo 0   'Disable the error handler
ReDim Preserve CommPorts(1 To NumberOfPorts)
If SaveCurrentPort = True Then
    PortNumber = SavedPortNumber
    frmMain.MSComm1.CommPort = PortNumber
    If frmMain.MSComm1.PortOpen = False Then
        frmMain.MSComm1.PortOpen = True
    EndIf
End If
End Sub
```

Listing 4-2: General-purpose routines for programs that access serial ports.
(Sheet 11 of 14)

```
Public Sub GetNewSettings()
'Read and store user changes in the Setup menu.
BitRate = Val(frmPortSettings.cboBitRate.Text)
PortNumber = Val(Right(frmPortSettings.cboPort.Text, 1))
Call frmMain.fncInitializeComPort(BitRate, PortNumber)
End Sub
```

```
Public Sub GetSettings()
'Get user settings from last time.
BitRate = GetSetting(ProjectName, "Startup", "BitRate", 1200)
PortNumber = GetSetting(ProjectName, "Startup", "PortNumber", 1)
'Defaults in case values retrieved are invalid:
If BitRate < 300 Then BitRate = 9600
If PortNumber < 1 Then PortNumber = 1
End Sub
```

```
Sub ImmediateTransmit(ByteToSend As Byte)
'Places a byte at the top of the transmit buffer
'for immediate sending.
Dim Success As Boolean
Success = TransmitCommChar(frmMain.MSComm1.CommID, ByteToSend)
End Sub
```

```
Public Sub LowResDelay(DelayInMilliseconds As Single)
'Uses the system timer, with resolution of about 56 milliseconds.
Dim Timeout As Single
'Add the delay to the current time.
Timeout = Timer + DelayInMilliseconds / 1000
If Timeout > 86399 Then
    'If the end of the delay spans midnight,
    'subtract 24 hrs. from the Timeout count:
    Timeout = Timeout - 86399
    'and wait for midnight:
    Do Until Timer < 100
        DoEvents
    Loop
End If
'Wait for the Timeout count.
Do Until Timer >= Timeout
    DoEvents
Loop
End Sub
```

Listing 4-2: General-purpose routines for programs that access serial ports.
(Sheet 12 of 14)

```
Public Sub SaveSettings()
'Save user settings for next time.
SaveSetting ProjectName, "Startup", "BitRate", BitRate
SaveSetting ProjectName, "Startup", "PortNumber", PortNumber
End Sub
```

```
Public Sub ShutDown()
'Close the port.
If frmMain.MSComm1.PortOpen = True Then
    frmMain.MSComm1.PortOpen = False
End If
Call SaveSettings
End Sub
```

```
Public Sub Startup()
Call GetSettings
PortOpen = frmMain.fncInitializeComPort(BitRate, PortNumber)
Call frmPortSettings.SetBitRateComboBox
Call frmPortSettings.SetPortComboBox
Call VbSetCommTimeouts(BitRate)
If ValidPort = False Then
    frmPortSettings.Show
Else
    frmPortSettings.Hide
End If
End Sub
```

Listing 4-2: General-purpose routines for programs that access serial ports.
(Sheet 13 of 14)

```
Public Sub VbSetCommTimeouts(BitRate As Long)
'The default timeout for serial-port operations is 5 seconds.
'This routine sets the timeout so that
'the requested number of bytes can transmit or be read
'at the current bit rate.
'Uses the GetCommTimeouts and SetCommTimeouts API functions.
Dim Timeouts As COMMTIMEOUTS
Dim Success As Long
Dim OneByteTimeout As Long
Success = GetCommTimeouts(frmMain.MSComm1.CommID, Timeouts)
OneByteTimeout = CLng(fncOneByteDelay(BitRate))
If frmMain.MSComm1.PortOpen = True Then
    'All values are milliseconds
    'Maximum time between two received characters:
    Timeouts.ReadIntervalTimeout = OneByteTimeout
    'Maximum time for a character to arrive:
    Timeouts.ReadTotalTimoutMultiplier = OneByteTimeout
    'Provide enough time for the bytes to arrive + 1 second.
    Timeouts.ReadTotalTimeoutConstant = 1000
    'Maximum time for a character to transmit:
    Timeouts.WriteTotalTimeoutMultiplier = OneByteTimeout
    'Provide enough time for the bytes to transmit + 1 second.
    Timeouts.WriteTotalTimeoutConstant = 1000
    Success = SetCommTimeouts(frmMain.MSComm1.CommID, Timeouts)
End If
'For debugging/verifying:
'Success = GetCommTimeouts(frmMain.MSComm1.CommID, Timeouts)
'Debug.Print Timeouts.ReadIntervalTimeout
'Debug.Print Timeouts.ReadTotalTimoutMultiplier
'Debug.Print Timeouts.ReadTotalTimeoutConstant
'Debug.Print Timeouts.WriteTotalTimeoutMultiplier
'Debug.Print Timeouts.WriteTotalTimeoutConstant
End Sub
```

Listing 4-2: General-purpose routines for programs that access serial ports. (Sheet 14 of 14)

Timing Routines

Many of the routines relate to timing issues. Applications that use serial communications may use timing to determine when a transmission is finished or when to quit waiting for a response from a remote computer. Windows also has timeout settings that an application may adjust.

General-purpose Delays. Two general-purpose routines are useful any time the code needs to time a specific delay. For example, an application may need to wait for an event but give up if nothing happens after a specified wait, or it may need to output a pulse of a specific width.

One routine uses an API call and has resolution of about 1 millisecond. The other uses Visual Basic's Timer function, with resolution of about 56 milliseconds.

The Delay routine waits the requested number of milliseconds. The routine uses the timeGetTime API function, which is part of Windows' multimedia subsystem. The function has a resolution of 1 millisecond. The accuracy of the routine isn't guaranteed, however, because Windows can cause delays that result in the timed delay being unpredictably longer than what was requested. Still, the routine is fine for generating delays that must be a minimum value, but don't have a rigid maximum.

The timeGetTime function returns the number of seconds since Windows was started. It overflows after 24 days, when the value increments from the maximum positive value, 7FFFFFFFh, to the negative value 80000000h. A delay that begins just before a rollover won't end as expected, so if you expect an application to run continuously, without rebooting, you should add code that handles rollovers. (The only problem is that you have to wait 24 days to test the code! While waiting, you can test by simulating timeGetTime's count with a software timer.)

An alternative timing routine is LowResDelay, which uses the system timer to generate a delay. The system timer operates at 18 cycles/second, so the resolution of this routine is about 56 milliseconds. As with the previous routine, Windows may cause delays that are longer than the specified time.

LowResDelay uses the Timer function, which returns the number of milliseconds since midnight. The code handles rollovers, which occur when a delay spans midnight. Another approach is to use a Timer control, which doesn't have midnight rollovers, but requires a cascading count for delays longer than 65 seconds.

One-byte Delay. The fncOneByteDelay routine calculates the time required to transmit one byte. This is useful in some half-duplex links, where the computer must switch off the transmitter after sending data, to allow another computer to transmit. The delay ensures that all of the bits in the byte have transmitted. The VbSetCommTimeouts routine also uses this delay time.

Handling Comm Timeouts. The SetCommTimeouts API function determines how long Windows' communications driver will allow to complete an Output or Input operation. The default for each is five seconds. When a timeout occurs, the operation quits, whether or not it has completed, and with no indication of failure. Received data will remain in the buffer until the application reads it, but in a transmit operation, the transmit buffer clears on timeout. This is not a desirable situation!

To prevent timeouts, use `SetCommTimeouts` to set values longer than the longest expected time the application will need to complete send and receive operations. The `VbSetCommTimeouts` routine can accomplish this by setting the timeouts to the amount of time required to transfer the data at the current bit rate, plus 1 second. To set the timeouts to a fixed value, set all of the parameters to 0 except `ReadTotalTimeoutConstant` and `WriteTotalTimeoutConstant`.

Hardware handshaking can slow the transfers as well, so don't forget to take that into account if necessary. For example, if the PC is communicating with a microcontroller that may take seconds to toggle a handshaking signal, add this time to the timeout.

Each `Input` and `Output` statement starts a new timeout clock, so if an application transfers small blocks of bytes and the receiving PC has no large handshaking delays, the default five-second timeouts should cause no problems.

When receiving, you can prevent timeout problems by checking the `InBufferCount` property and executing the `Input` statement only when the expected data is present. This is good a practice anyway, because Visual Basic returns an error on attempting to read an empty buffer.

To disable all timeouts, set all of the values to 0.

Time Formatting. The final routine relating to timing is `fncDisplayDateAndTime`, which formats date and time information. The application might use the formatting in displaying or storing the times of transfers.

Handling User Settings

Other routines in the module help to ensure a graceful startup and shutdown of an application. The `Startup` and `Shutdown` routines contain code that programs execute on starting or ending a program. These are called by the main form's `Load` and `Unload` routines.

`Shutdown` calls the `SaveSettings` routine, which stores user settings in the system registry. `Startup` calls the companion routine `GetSettings`, which retrieves the settings the next time the program runs. Using these routines will save users the tedium of re-selecting settings each time they run a program. The template application stores only the current bit rate and port number. You can add additional settings as appropriate. To save on registry clutter, all of the examples in this book stores settings under the same appname: *"SerialPortComplete"*.

The `GetNewSettings` routine stores changes made by the user in the Setup menu.

Auto-detecting the Port to Use

When there are multiple serial ports, selecting the port to use in software can be a hit-or-miss affair. Sometimes an application can free the user from having to know this information by automatically detecting which port connects to the link the program will access.

For example, when setting up a link, a computer can try to send a message on each of its COM ports. The computer at the other end of the link watches for the message and sends a reply to let the sending computer know when it's found the port. Or a link may use an unconventional handshake that's easily detected.

The Basic Stamp's editor software is an example of a link that autodetects which port is connected to a Stamp. The software also includes an option to specify the port manually, in the command line. This is always a good idea, for times when an autodetect doesn't work.

Error Checking

Two functions relate to calculating checksums for error checking. The function `fncAddChecksumToAsciiHexString` calculates a checksum for a string and appends it to the string. And `fncVerifyChecksum` compares a string to its checksum and returns true if the checksum is the expected value.

Selecting a Port

Listing 4-3 has the code for the *Port Settings* form in Figure 4-1, which enables users to select a port and bit rate. When the form loads, it calls `FindPorts` to detect the available ports and selects the user's previous port and bit-rate settings, if any. A text box displays status or error messages.

Saving Data

Listing 4-4 has the code for the *Data File* form in Figure 4-1, which enables users to select a file to store received data for later viewing or processing. The *Select File* command button brings up a Common Dialog box for the user to select or create a file. Option buttons determine whether the program overwrites or appends to existing data in the file.

Accessing Files

Visual Basic offers several ways to read and write to files. Table 4-1 summarizes the options. Which to select depends on how the data will be used. Data stored as

```
Option Explicit
'Enables users to select a serial port and bit rate.

Private Sub cboBitRate_Change()
Call VbSetCommTimeouts(BitRate)
End Sub

Private Sub cmdCancel_Click()
Hide
End Sub

Private Sub cmdOK_Click()
'The application's main form reads the new settings.
Call GetNewSettings
ValidPort = fncCheckForValidPort
If ValidPort = True Then
    Hide
End If
End Sub

Private Sub Form_Load()
Dim Count As Integer
Call FindPorts
'Set default values if a retrieved setting is invalid.
'Be sure the selected port exists.
PortExists = False
For Count = 1 To UBound(CommPorts())
    'Compare the selected port number with the names in CommPorts.
    If "COM" & CStr(PortNumber) = CommPorts(Count) Then
        PortExists = True
    End If
Next Count
'Display the Setup window if the retrieved port number is invalid,
'or if the port is unavailable.
ValidPort = fncCheckForValidPort
If ValidPort = False Then
    Show
End If
Call InitializePortComboBox
Call InitializeBitRateComboBox
End Sub
```

Listing 4-3: Code for the Port Settings form. (Sheet 1 of 3)

```
Private Sub InitializeBitRateComboBox()
cboBitRate.AddItem ("300")
cboBitRate.AddItem ("1200")
cboBitRate.AddItem ("2400")
cboBitRate.AddItem ("4800")
cboBitRate.AddItem ("9600")
cboBitRate.AddItem ("19200")
cboBitRate.AddItem ("57600")
cboBitRate.AddItem ("115200")
End Sub
```

```
Private Sub InitializePortComboBox()
Dim Count as Integer
For Count = 1 To UBound(CommPorts())
    cboPort.AddItem CommPorts(Count)
Next Count
End Sub
```

```
Public Function fncCheckForValidPort()
'Find out if the selected port exists and is available.
'If not, display the Setup window
'to enable the user to select another.
fncCheckForValidPort = True
If PortNumber < 1 Then
    Show
    cboPort.ListIndex = -1
    txtStatus.Text = "Please select a COM port."
    fncCheckForValidPort = False
    End If
If PortExists = False Then
    Show
    cboPort.ListIndex = -1
    txtStatus.Text = "COM" & PortNumber & " is unavailable. Please
  select a different port."
    fncCheckForValidPort = False
End If
End Function
```

Listing 4-3: Code for the Port Settings form. (Sheet 2 of 3)

```
Public Sub SetBitRateComboBox()
'Set the index of the BitRate combo box.
Do
    cboBitRate.ListIndex = cboBitRate.ListIndex + 1
Loop Until Val(cboBitRate.Text) = BitRate _
    Or cboBitRate.ListIndex = cboBitRate.ListCount - 1
End Sub
```

```
Public Sub SetPortComboBox()
'Set the index of the Port combo box.
'Read the numeric characters in the name of the selected port:
'"COM1", "COM2", etc.
Do
    cboPort.ListIndex = cboPort.ListIndex + 1
Loop Until _
    Val(Right(cboPort.Text, (Len(cboPort.Text) - 3))) = PortNumber
    _
    Or cboPort.ListIndex = cboPort.ListCount - 1
End Sub
```

Listing 4-3: Code for the Port Settings form. (Sheet 3 of 3)

strings is easy to view, while binary data is more compact and suited for calculations. Visual Basic's Help has more details on how to use each.

Other Ways to Access Serial Ports

MSComm isn't the only way to access serial ports in Visual-Basic programs.
Alternatives include using API functions or using a DLL or other driver that
enables reading and writing directly to the port registers.

API Functions

The Windows API includes functions for serial communications. For the most
part, these duplicate the abilities of MSComm. There are two situations when you
might use API functions for serial communications: when MSComm or a similar
control isn't available, or when you need to perform a function that MSComm
doesn't support.

Where MSComm (or a third-party control) is an option, it's almost always the
preferred choice. MSComm is simple to use because it's designed specifically for

```
Option Explicit
'Enables the user to select a file for storing data.
Dim DataFile As String
```

```
Private Sub cmdOK_Click()
Hide
If optDataFile(1).Value = True Then
    If optAppendOrOverwrite(0).Value = True Then
        Open DataFile For Append As #2
    Else
        Open DataFile For Output As #2
    End If
End If
End Sub
```

```
Private Sub cmdSelectFile_Click()
cdlDataFile.Filter = "All files (*.*)|*.*"
cdlDataFile.filename = DataFile
cdlDataFile.Flags = cdlOFNPathMustExist
cdlDataFile.Flags = cdlOFNOverwritePrompt
cdlDataFile.Flags = cdlOFNCreatePrompt
'Get the selected file from the common dialog box.
cdlDataFile.ShowOpen
If cdlDataFile.filename <> "" Then
    'Save the filename and path.
    DataFile = cdlDataFile.filename
    cmdOK.Enabled = True
Else
End If
End Sub
```

```
Private Sub Form_Load()
optDataFile(0).Value = True
End Sub
```

```
Private Sub GetSettings()
DataFile = GetSetting(ProjectName, "DataFile", "DataFile", "")
End Sub
```

Listing 4-4: Code for selecting a file for storing data. (Sheet 1 of 2)

```
Private Sub optDataFile_Click(Index As Integer)
'Configure the display elements.
If optDataFile(0).Value = True Then
    optAppendOrOverwrite(0).Enabled = False
    optAppendOrOverwrite(1).Enabled = False
    cmdSelectFile.Enabled = False
    frmMain.SaveDataInFile = False
    cmdOK.Enabled = True
Else
    optAppendOrOverwrite(0).Enabled = True
    optAppendOrOverwrite(1).Enabled = True
    optAppendOrOverwrite(0).Value = True
    cmdSelectFile.Enabled = True
    frmMain.SaveDataInFile = True
    cmdOK.Enabled = False
    'Bring up the dialog box to select a file.
    cmdSelectFile.Value = True
End If
End Sub
```

```
Private Sub SaveSettings()
SaveSetting ProjectName, "DataFile", "DataFile", DataFile
End Sub
```

Listing 4-4: Code for selecting a file for storing data. (Sheet 2 of 2)

use with Visual Basic, and its performance is as good or better than using API calls.

For situations that do require API calls, Visual Basic includes *win32api.txt*, a file that contains Visual-Basic declarations for API functions and the many constants they use. Each API call in an application must have a declaration.

But successful use of API functions requires knowing much more than you can glean from the declarations alone. Windows has precise and unyielding requirements relating to the size, structure, and location of the values passed to and from API functions. Variable types don't always correspond to Visual Basic's conventions, and the required syntax is often not at all obvious.

In this book, I provide only an overview of API functions relating to serial communications, plus a few examples of routines that do things that aren't available from MSComm. If you want to know more about API programming, the simplest way to get started is with a reference, such as Daniel Appleman's *Visual Basic 5.0 Programming Guide to the Win32 API,* which includes code for a serial link using API functions. Another excellent reference is Richard Grier's *Visual Basic Pro-*

Table 4-1: Visual-Basic options for reading and writing to files.

Syntax	Description	Use With
For Writing to Files:		
Print #	Can insert spaces or tabs between items.	Input, LineInput#
Put	Writes raw data to the specified record or byte number in the file.	Get
Write #	Adds comma delimiters, quotation marks around strings, and a carriage return/linefeed at the end of each output list.	Input #
For Reading from Files:		
Get	Reads a single record or byte into a variable	Put
Input	Returns a string.	Print #, Put
InputB	Returns byte data from a text file.	Print #, Put
Input #	Reads data into variables.	Write #
Line Input #	Reads one line and assigns it to a string.	Print #

grammer's Guide to Serial Communications, which includes serial-port routines using API functions and many other useful examples and tips for use with MSComm.

Table 4-2 lists 32-bit API functions that relate to serial communications. (The 16-bit API is somewhat different.) The functions relate to configuring a port, reading and writing to it, and setting and detecting events at a port.

Windows defines a structure called a device control block (DCB) that holds port settings. Table 4-3 lists the fields contained in the DCB and their functions. Table 4-4 lists the functions of the bits in the DCB's Bits field. Most of these correspond to MSComm's properties.

Editing the Device Control Block

Listing 4-2's EditDCB routine enables you to change the information in a port's DCB. The routine reads the current values into a DCB structure. A series of commented-out statements write to each element. To change a value, uncomment its statement and enter the desired value. The routine writes the values back to the port's DCB, then reads and displays them to verify any changes.

Quick Send

Another API function offers the ability to move a character to the front of the transmit buffer so it transmits next. This could be useful if an application discovers it needs to send a byte immediately, while in the middle of sending a large

Table 4-2: 32-bit Windows API functions related to serial communications.

API Function	Purpose
Opening and Closing Ports	
CreateFile	Opens a port.
CloseHandle	Closes the port.
Configuring	
BuildCommDCB	Loads a device control block with settings.
BuildCommDCBAndTimeouts	Loads a device control block with settings and timeouts.
CommConfigDialog	Displays a port-configuration dialog box.
CreateEvent	Creates an event object for an overlapped structure.
GetCommConfig	Retrieves configuration information in the DCB.
GetCommProperties	Retrieves available settings for a port.
GetCommState	Retrieves port configuration.
GetCommTimeouts	Retrieves timeout settings.
GlobalAlloc	Reserves a block of global memory for serial I/O.
GlobalFree	Frees a reserved block of global memory.
SetCommConfig	Configures a port.
SetCommMask	Determines which events to detect.
SetCommState	Sets configuration information in the DCB.
SetCommTimeouts	Sets port timeouts.
SetupComm	Sets recommended buffer sizes.
Transferring Data	
ClearCommBreak	Ends transmission of break signal.
ClearCommError	Clears error and sets GetLastError
EscapeCommFunction	Allows explicit control of handshaking signals.
GetCommMask	Retrieves status of requested events.
GetCommModemStatus	Retrieves status of handshaking signals.
GetLastError	Returns an error from a previous API call.
PurgeComm	Clears buffers and pending operations.
ReadFile	Reads data from a port.
SetCommBreak	Transmits break signal.
TransmitComChar	Places a character at the front of the output buffer.
WaitCommEvent	Waits for an event specified with SetCommMask.
WaitForSingleObject	Waits for an object to be signaled or timeout.
WriteFile	Writes data to a port.

Table 4-3: Serial port DCB fields.

Field	Type	Description
DCBLength	long	Size of the DCB structure (78 bytes).
BaudRate	long	Bit rate.
Bits	long	Specifies various parameters. (see Table 4-4.)
wReserved	integer	Reserved.
XonLim	integer	Send Xon when the number of characters in the receive buffer is less than this value.
XoffLim	integer	Send Xoff when the number of characters in the receive buffer is greater than this value.
ByteSize	byte	Bits per character (4-8).
Parity	byte	Constants: EVENPARITY, MARKPARITY, NOPARITY, ODDPARITY, SPACEPARITY.
StopBits	byte	Constants: ONESTOPBIT, ONE5STOPBITS, TWOSTOPBITS
XonChar	byte	Xon character. Usually 11h.
XoffChar	byte	Xoff character. Usually 13h.
ErrorChar	byte	Character to use on receive error.
EofChar	byte	Character to indicate end of data.
EvtChar	byte	Character to signal an error.
wReserved1	integer	Unused.

block of data. Listing 4-2's `ImmediateTransmit` routine performs this function by calling the `TransmitCommChar` API function.

Direct Port Access

The most low-level way to access a serial port is to write directly to the port's registers. Visual Basic doesn't include the ability to access ports directly, but you can add it. Under Windows 95 and 3.x, all you need is a DLL containing `Inp` and `Out` routines and declarations that enable you to access the routines.

The disk that accompanies this book includes DLLs for use under Windows 3.x and 95. Windows 95 programs can also use a VxD. Windows NT requires a kernel-mode driver for port access. There are several shareware and commercial sources for each of these.

Direct port access is useful if you want to do something that you can't do with MSComm or an API call, such as putting a port into loopback mode. You can also do many of the same things MSComm does, such as setting the bit rate, number of data bits, and parity type and sending and receiving data.

Table 4-4: Functions of bit flags.

Bit #	Name	Description
0	fBinary	Always 1 in W95. Indicates binary mode. Eof character does not signal end of data.
1	fParity	1=parity checking on. 0=parity checking off.
2	fOutxCtsFlow	1=no transmit when CTS=0. 0=CTS ignored.
3	fOutxDsrFlow	1=no transmit when DSR=0. 0=DSR ignored.
4–5	fDtrControl	DTR_CONTROL_DISABLE DTR_CONTROL_ENABLE DTR_CONTROL_HANDSHAKE
6	fDsrSensitivity	1=ignore received bytes when DSR=0. 0=DSR has no effect.
7	fTxContin-ueOnXoff	1=ignore Xoff. 0=stop transmitting after receiving Xoff.
8	fOutX	1=use XOn/XOff protocol when transmitting. 0=don't use transmit Xon/Xoff.
9	fInX	1=use XOn/XOff protocol when receiving. 0=don't use receive Xon/Xoff.
10	fNull	1=discard received Null characters (Chr(0)). 0=don't discard Null characters.
11–12	fRtsControl	RTS_CONTROL_DISABLE=RTS Off. RTS_CONTROL_ENABLE=RTS On. RTS_CONTROL_HANDSHAKE=RTS On if receive buffer < 1/2 full, Off if receive buffer > 3/4 full. RTS_CONTROL_TOGGLE=RTS On if bytes in the receive buffer, Off if receive buffer empty. (NT only)
13	fAbortOnError	1=abort Comm operations on error. 0=don't abort on error
14–31	fDummy2	Unused.

A system-level driver has the ability to prevent other applications from accessing a port. However, MSComm doesn't block direct access to a port's addresses, so reading and writing with a DLL is possible even if MSComm has opened the port.

To access a port directly, you need to know its base address. Although it's not an elegant way to do it, if you don't have access to MSComm, you can even use Inp and Out to read and write data at the port:

```
Dim BaseAdddress as Integer
Dim ByteToWrite as Integer
BaseAddress = &h2F8
ByteToWrite = &hA5
```

```
'Write a byte to the port:
Out BaseAddress, ByteToWrite
'Read a byte at the port:
ByteRead = Inp(BaseAddress)
```

Inp and Out pass integers, but read and write 8-bit values at the serial port.

You can also use the DLL to read and write to any of the UART registers described in Chapter 3.

Here is code to toggle the break signal from a port at 2F8h:

```
Dim LCR As Integer
Dim LCRAddress As Integer
Dim BaseAddress As Integer
BaseAddress = &H2F8
'Set Break is bit 6 of LCR (line control register).
LCRAddress = BaseAddress + 3
'Read the current value in LCR.
LCR = Inp(LCRAddress)
'Set bit 6 high.
Out LCRAddress, LCR Or &H40
'Set bit 6 low.
Out LCRAddress, LCR And &HBF
```

Using Older Basics

Most of this book concentrates on using version 5 of Visual Basic. However, Windows 3.x applications must use an earlier version. And many DOS systems use QuickBasic or a similar language. This book doesn't cover every nuance of using these languages in serial-port applications, but the following sections include some of the differences to be aware of.

Visual Basic Versions

Like other programming languages, Visual Basic has evolved over time. Many of the changes relate to the evolution of Windows itself. The switch from Windows 3.x to Windows 95 and NT included a switch from a 16-bit to 32-bit operating system.

Windows 3.x is 16-bit, which means that it can run on a PC with a 16-bit data bus. This includes machines with 80286 and higher CPUs. Windows 95, 98, and NT are 32-bit operating systems and require the 32-bit data bus found on the 80386 and higher CPUs.

A 16-bit program can run under Windows 3.x, 95/98, or NT. A 32-bit program requires a 32-bit operating system.

Version 3 of Visual Basic (VB3) creates 16-bit applications. Version 4 (VB4) was the first to support 32-bit applications. The Professional version of VB4 straddled both worlds, with the ability to create both 16- and 32-bit applications. The Standard version of VB4 created only the 32-bit applications. With Version 5 (VB5), support for 16-bit programming was dropped entirely.

If you need to support systems running Windows 3.x, you need to use VB3 or 16-bit VB4. If you're programming only for systems that use Windows 95 or later or NT, you can use any version of Visual Basic.

One difference between 16- and 32-bit programs is that each uses a different Windows API. A 16-bit application that uses API calls will probably require some changes when upgrading to 32 bits. In particular, the serial-communications API has many changes.

Changes in the String Variable Type

The 16- and 32-bit versions of Visual Basic each treat text characters differently. The change has little effect on serial links that transfer text. However, because 16-bit programs have traditionally used string variables to store binary data, the change does affect some applications that transfer binary data, especially if you're upgrading a 16-bit application to 32 bits.

In 16-bit Visual Basic (and other older Basics), the String is the only 8-bit variable type. Each String character is an 8-bit ANSI code. For this reason, string variables became the method of choice for storing binary data. Applications used `Mid` and similar string-manipulation statements and functions to store and retrieve bytes in strings.

For example, this routine creates a string containing 256 bytes with values from 0 to 255:

```
Dim TestString as String
Dim Count as Integer
For Count = 0 to 255
   Mid(TestString, Count) = Chr(Count)
Next Count
```

The `Chr` operator returns an ANSI code, which may be any value from 0 to 255. In a 16-bit program, you can use ANSI strings any time you want to store bytes, whether or not their values have anything to do with text strings. For example a series of readings from an analog-to-digital converter consists of numeric values, not text, but you can store the values as ANSI codes in a string.

In 32-bit Visual Basic, the String variable type stores text characters as 16-bit Unicodes, so storing binary data in strings is no longer convenient. The solution is to use the new Byte variable type, introduced in VB4 and described earlier in this chapter. However, VB4's MSComm doesn't have an `InputMode` property and reads and writes only strings, so VB5 is required for transferring byte arrays.

Although the 32-bit versions of Visual Basic use Unicode internally, MSComm continues to send and receive text as ANSI, and Visual-Basic programs automatically convert between the two. So even if one computer in a link uses ANSI and the other uses Unicode, you can transfer text between them without having to translate between formats. The only time a problem may arise is one computer uses DBCS strings, which use a different 16-bit code.

The ANSI/Unicode difference can cause problems when upgrading an application from 16-bit to 32-bit. If the 16-bit application stores binary data as string characters, each byte in the 32-bit version will use 16 bits rather than 8.

For compatibility, the characters for most of the first 128 and most of the next 128 Unicodes correspond to their matching ANSI codes (with the upper byte equal to zero). The exceptions are the codes 82h-8Ch, 91h-9Ch, and 9Fh. Listing 4-5 is a routine that compares the Unicode characters that correspond to the ANSI codes from 0 to 255 and displays the differences. Because of these differences, converting from Unicode to ANSI is more complicated than just dropping the higher byte.

If you need to work with ANSI strings in a 32-bit application, Visual Basic has functions and statements to help. `StrConv` converts a Unicode string to ANSI, or the reverse. And the various string-manipulation functions now have byte versions that treat the strings byte-by-byte: `LeftB`, `MidB`, `RightB`, `LenB`, and so on.

Accessing Ports under DOS

Some monitoring and control applications use DOS rather than Windows. A machine dedicated to collecting or sending data for a specific task may not need the abilities and features of Windows. Dedication to a single task means that there's no need for Windows' multitasking. An application that runs with very little or no operator intervention means that there's no need for Windows' visual interface. And the hardware requirements for a DOS system are much less than for Windows, so DOS is a good choice for older or simpler machines.

In these cases, you can access serial ports with Microsoft's QuickBasic or similar DOS Basics.

```
Dim Count As Integer
Dim AnsiValue As Integer
Dim UnicodeValue As Integer
For Count = 0 To 255
    AnsiValue = Count
    'Chr gets the ANSI character;
    'AscW gets its Unicode equivalent.
    UnicodeValue = AscW(Chr(Count))
    'Display codes that differ.
    If AnsiValue <> UnicodeValue Then
        Debug.Print Chr(Count) & " = ANSI " & Hex$(Count) _
        & " = Unicode " & Hex$(AscW(Chr(Count)))
    End If
Next Count
```

Listing 4-5: This routine displays the codes of characters whose ANSI codes and Unicodes differ.

Accessing serial ports under QuickBasic and Visual Basic is actually similar in many ways. QuickBasic's Open COM statement performs the functions of many of the properties in Visual Basic's MSComm. Instead of setting object properties to specify bit rate and other parameters, you set arguments in an option list. QuickBasic's On COM statement enables automatic detecting of incoming data, much like MSComm's comEvReceive event.

To find serial ports under DOS, you can read the addresses stored in the BIOS data area, as described in Chapter 3. The Peek operator will read the addresses.

Most commercial DOS software that accesses serial ports controls the UART directly. Another option is to use BIOS interrupt 14h, which has services to initialize, send to, receive from, and read the status of the serial port. MS-DOS's interrupt 21h, functions 03h and 04h will also send to and receive from a serial port. None of these options uses interrupts and all are limited in what they can control, so they're rarely used.

5

Microcontroller Serial Ports

PCs aren't the only computers that have asynchronous serial ports. Many micro-controllers and embedded controllers have them as well. Serial ports are a handy way for PCs and microcontrollers of all varieties to communicate with each other.

The features and abilities of microcontrollers' serial ports vary. On inexpensive 8-bit microcontrollers, the ports tend to be stripped to essentials, though they may include features that are useful in control circuits but not available in PCs. An embedded PC may have one or more UARTs identical to those in PCs.

This book includes examples that use two microcontrollers: Parallax's Basic Stamp II, based on Microchip's 16C57 PIC, and the 8052-Basic, based on the 8052 microcontroller. Their serial ports differ in features and abilities, so together they make a good introduction to microcontroller ports in general, even if these aren't what you end up using in a project.

The 8051 Family

The 8052-Basic is a member of the 8051 family, which has long been one of the most popular microcontroller families. The original 8051 has an 8-bit data bus and the ability to access 64 kilobytes each of program and data memory. The family now includes dozens of alternatives, including high-speed varieties and chips with more memory, a wider data bus, and other added features. From here on, I'll use 8051 to refer to the entire chip family.

The Serial Port

The 8051 includes an on-chip USART, which sends and receives both synchronous and asynchronous serial data. The asynchronous interface is full duplex, with dedicated transmit and receive pins on the chip. Each direction has a 1-byte buffer and the port has a hardware interrupt.

The input and output are 5V TTL logic levels, so a converter chip or other circuit is needed to convert to RS-232 or RS-485.

Unlike PCs, the 8051 doesn't have built-in support for control and handshaking lines, such as *RTS/CTS* and *DTR/DSR*. If you want to use these or other control signals, you can program their functions in firmware, using any available port bits.

Modes

The 8051's serial port has four modes. Mode 1 is basic asynchronous communications using 1 Start bit, 8 data bits, and 1 Stop bit. With a 12-Mhz clock, the bit rate can be as high as 62.5kbps.

Modes 2 and 3 support a ninth data bit that is especially useful for detecting addresses in a network. Chapter 11 has more details on 9-bit network protocols. The ninth data bit is an example of a feature found in many microcontroller ports, but not on PCs' serial ports. Mode 2 allows a faster bit rate, up to 1/32 of the clock rate, while Mode 3 supports more bit rates.

The final mode supported by the 8051, Mode 0, enables using the port in synchronous links. One line transmits a clock, and the other is used for both sending and receiving data.

Interrupts

If the serial-port interrupt is enabled, an interrupt occurs during the Stop bit whenever a byte is sent or received. The firmware must read internal flags to determine which event has occurred, and must clear the flag that was set. Instead of using interrupts, the firmware may check periodically for incoming data and ensure before transmitting that the transmit buffer is empty.

Registers

Several internal registers control and configure the serial communications. SBUF holds received data and data to send. SCON selects the mode, enables the receiver, holds the 9th data bit and interrupt flags, and determines how to use the 9th bit. A timer control register (TCON or T2CON) determines the bit rate. The IE register enables the serial-port interrupt.

Interfacing Options

The 8051's TX (serial transmit) output is weak, so even a short link will probably require an external driver and buffer. For RS-232 links, a MAX232 or similar chip will do the job, as described in Chapter 6.

The 8052-Basic

The 8052-Basic chip enables you to use Basic to write programs for the 8051 family. The chip is an 8052, which is an enhanced 8051 with more ROM program memory (8k), a second timer, and other enhancements. The 80C52-Basic is identical, except that it's based on a CMOS 80C52.

The chip's ROM contains a Basic-52 interpreter, a version of Basic designed for use in microcontroller projects. If you've programmed in other variants of Basic, the syntax of Basic-52 will be familiar in many ways. But Basic-52 is greatly simplified compared even to DOS QuickBasic, because the interpreter resides in just 8K of ROM. But the language does include features that PC Basics don't, such as commands for EPROM programming.

The interpreter includes console routines for communications with a computer terminal. These days, the terminal is most likely to be a PC running terminal-emulation software such as Windows 95's *HyperTerminal*. To use the terminal interface, you connect the 8052-Basic's serial port to the serial port of a PC or other computer running terminal-emulation software. The console routines enable you to use the PC's keyboard and video display to communicate with the chip, including writing, storing, running, and debugging programs. When debugging is complete, you can disconnect the PC and the 8052-Basic will run the program on its own.

If the application requires communications with a remote computer, you can keep the link to the PC or use the serial port to communicate with a different CPU. The remote computer can use terminal-emulation software, or it may use any custom programming that understands Basic-52's syntax rules.

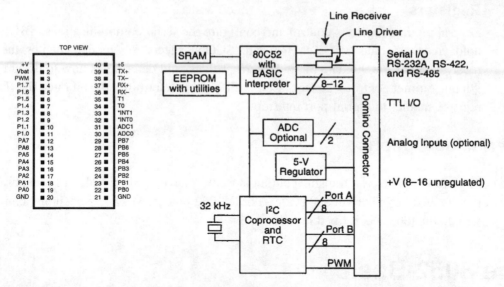

Figure 5-1: Micromint's Domino module contains a complete 8052-Basic system. (Images courtesy of Micromint.)

The interpreter also designates another port bit as a second, output-only serial port, intended for use with a serial printer.

An 8052-Basic system requires external RAM for temporary data storage and EEPROM, EPROM, or battery-backed RAM for program storage. Several vendors offer printed-circuit boards with the 8052-Basic chip along with program and data memory, an RS-232 interface, and other I/O bits. Some products use enhanced versions of the interpreter. Figure 5-1 and Figure 5-2 show examples of 8052-Basic systems. Micromint's Domino is a complete 80C52-Basic system in a 40-pin package. The Micro-485 from Blue Earth Research is another compact 80C52-Basic system. It resides on a small circuit board between two 25-pin D-sub connectors and has an RS-485 interface. The Micro-440e is similar, but with an RS-232 interface.

Basic compilers are also available for the 8051 family. Compiled programs are faster and allow the use of a cheaper, ROMless 8031 or 8032. Figure 5-3 shows Systronix's HSM/KISS board. The board holds Dallas Semiconductor's 80C320 High-Speed Microcontroller, which is an enhanced 8051 with two serial ports. The board comes with a serial program loader, and Systronix also offers a Basic compiler for the chip.

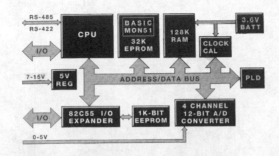

Figure 5-2: Blue Earth Research's Micro-485 and Micro-440e include both a Basic interpreter and a monitor program.(Images courtesy of Blue Earth Research.)

Communications Abilities

The Basic-52 language includes a variety of features for serial communications. These make it easy to write programs that exchange serial data without having to know the details of the chip's port registers. The statements enable the chip to communicate directly with a user via Basic-52's terminal interface, or to exchange information with another program running on a remote computer with or without user intervention.

Systronix's *Basic-52 Programming* manual has more details on Basic-52 programming, and my *Microcontroller Idea Book* covers hardware design and application examples for the 8052-Basic. The following section includes details that relate specifically to serial communications and the 8052-Basic.

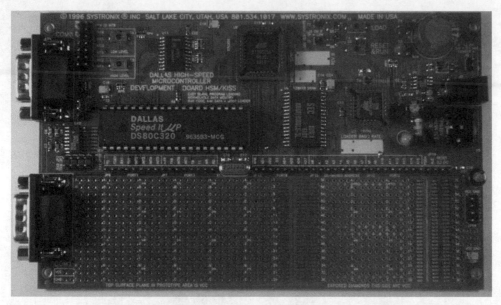

Figure 5-3: Systronix's HSM/KISS board contains an enhanced 8051 from Dallas Semiconductor. The chip has two serial ports. (Photo courtesy of Systronix.)

Sending Data

The `Print`, `PH0.`, and `PH1.` statements write to the serial port. With a terminal interface, the data displays on the video screen. You can use the same statements to send information to custom applications.

The statement and syntax determine whether or not Basic-52 adds a leading or trailing space (20h), leading zeros (30h), a trailing H (48h), or a carriage return (0Dh) and line feed (0Ah). These additions can be useful for displayed values, but in many cases they're unneeded when sending values directly to a program.

A Print statement can send text:

```
PRINT "456",
456

STRING 91,10
$(0)="123"
PRINT $(0),
123
```

or numeric values in ASCII format:

```
A=57
B-99
PRINT A,B
```

```
57  99
```

To send the character represented by an ASCII code, use the `Chr` operator:

```
A=57
PRINT CHR(A),
9
```

In the above example, Basic-52 writes 57 (01010111), which is the ASCII code for 9, to the serial port. The terminal translates 57 to the character 9.

`Print` adds both a leading and trailing space (20h) to numeric values, but not to strings.

Before using any string variables, the program must allocate memory for them with a String statement:

```
STRING TotalBytes, BytesPerString
```

where

BytesPerString = the largest number of characters a string will hold.

*TotalBytes = ((BytesPerString + 1) * NumberOfStrings) + 1*

To reserve space for ten strings with up to eight characters in each, use:

```
STRING 91,8
```

To reserve space for one string with two characters, use:

```
STRING 4,2
```

A `PH0.` statement sends values as ASCII Hex characters, with a leading space and a trailing *H*:

```
A=0F1H
PH0. A,
 F1H


B=16
PH0. B
 10H
```

`PH1.` is identical, except that it always sends four characters, filling with zeros as needed:

```
A=0F1H
PH0. A,
 00F1H


B=16
PH0. B
 0010H
```

A comma at the end of a `Print` or `PH0.` statement causes Basic-52 to send just the data. Otherwise, Basic-52 will follow the data with a carriage return and line feed. The receiving computer may use these codes as an end-of-value indicator, or it may ignore them if unneeded.

Receiving Data

For reading the serial port, there are two choices, each suitable for different uses.

Get reads the last character received at the serial port. If no character has arrived since the last Get statement, it returns zero. Get is a good way to receive single text characters, or to get the 8052-Basic's attention before sending more data. The program doesn't have to be watching the port when the character arrives. Instead, it can read Get periodically, and the byte will be waiting when the program gets to it.

This routine waits for a character to arrive, then displays it:

```
10 DO
20 G=GET
30 UNTIL G<>0
40 PRINT G, CHR(G)
RUN

  53 5
```

Get can read any text character. It clears the eighth bit, so values from 80h through FFh are the same as 0 through 7Fh.

You can read multiple bytes with multiple Gets, but the sending computer may have to add a pacing delay between bytes, to enable Basic-52 to read and store each byte before executing the next Get.

The other option for reading data is the Input statement, which reads up to a carriage return:

```
INPUT A
```

Input is useful for reading one or more bytes when the program is expecting incoming data. Unlike Get, Input doesn't remember data that arrives before the statement executes. One statement can read multiple values. Data sent to an Input statement must end in a carriage return or carriage return + line feed.

Basic-52 echoes all received Input data back out the serial port, ending with carriage return and line feed codes, even if the sending computer sent only a carriage return.

Unlike Get, Input doesn't discard the eighth bit. But as with Get, binary data is best sent in ASCII Hex format, because Basic-52 uses the carriage return as the end-of-input indicator, and also captures certain control codes, as described below.

Input data can be stored in one or more numeric or string variables. The responding computer must include a comma between numeric values and a carriage return after each series of values:

```
10 STRING 91,10
20 INPUT ,$(0),$(1),A,B
30 PRINT $(0),$(1),A,B
RUN

abc
987
43,76
abc987 43   76
```

If the carriage return arrives before the specified number of values, Basic-52 will send the message Try Again, and all data has to be re-entered from the beginning:

```
10 STRING 91,10
20 INPUT ,$(0),$(1),A,B
30 PRINT $(0),$(1),A,B
RUN

abc
987
43

TRY AGAIN

abc
987
43,76
abc987 43   76
```

The statement may also include a prompt:

```
10 INPUT "Please enter a value. ",A
20 PRINT A
RUN
Please enter a value. 900
  900
```

If there is no prompt, the statement uses a question mark as the prompt. To suppress the prompt entirely, place a comma after Input:

```
10 INPUT, A
20 PRINT A
RUN
49
  49
```

Processing Received Data

Basic-52's Asc operator can extract ASCII codes for the individual characters in received string. You can then convert the ASCII codes to the numeric values they represent, and combine them to find the value represented by the string.

Basic-52 has no Val operator to find the value of a string character, so programs must do this another way. The ASCII codes for 0 through 9 are 48–57, so the value of a numeric character equals (*ASCII code - 48*). ASCII Hex also uses the characters A–F. The codes for A through F are 65 -70, so each value equals (*ASCII code - 55*). Once you have the value of each digit, multiply each by the appropriate value (1, 10, 100) or (1, 16), and add the results. If you allow lower-case *a–f* (61h–66h) in ASCII Hex values, you'll need to test for those as well.

The following example reads a 3-character string, finds the value of each digit, and stores the result in *D*:

```
10 STRING 5,3
20 INPUT ,$(0)
30 D1=(ASC($(0),1)-48)*100
40 D2=(ASC($(0),2)-48)*10
50 D3=(ASC($(0),3)-48)
60 D=D1+D2+D3
70 PRINT D
RUN

123
 123
```

This routine finds the value of a 2-character ASCII Hex string:

```
10 STRING 4,2
20 INPUT ,$(0)
30 D1=ASC($(0),1)
40 IF D1>58 THEN D1=D1-55 ELSE D1=D1-48
50 D2=ASC($(0),2)
60 IF D2>58 THEN D2=D2-55 ELSE D2=D2-48
70 D=D1*16+D2
80 PH0. D
RUN

F1
 F1H
```

Any remote computer can communicate with an 8052-Basic as long as it obeys Basic-52's syntax rules. Most importantly, arriving data has to be able to co-exist with the interpreter's built-in communications routines (unless you install your own driver, as described below). This requires a few compromises.

The interpreter monitors all received serial data for three control codes: Control+C (03) ends the current program, Control+S (13h) pauses output to the serial port and Control+Q (11h) resumes output. When Basic-52 detects any of these, it removes the byte from the serial buffer and carries out the assigned function.

So, for example, when a byte with a value of 3 arrives at the serial port, the Basic-52 program will end and return the system to the bootup prompt. This will occur even if the program is in the middle of an Input statement. And whether or not Basic-52 is sending data to pause or resume, bytes with values of 11h and 13h will disappear from the serial buffer, and Get and Input won't detect them.

Because of these limits, the simplest approach is to send all data as text characters, with binary data in ASCII Hex format. You can also assign most of the remaining values from 0 to 255 to commands or other functions, as long as you avoid the codes with special meanings.

As an example, a remote computer may send a value from 0 to 7Fh to be read by a Get statement. Or the computer may send a series of bytes or strings separated by commas and followed by a carriage return, to be read by an Input statement. In the other direction, Basic-52 may use a Print statement to send a string ending in a carriage return, or multiple values separated by spaces, with a carriage return following the last value.

Basic-52 does offer a couple of workarounds if you don't want Control+C or error messages to stop the current program, including disabling Control+C and using a Run Trap mode to restart a program on Control+C or an error. The *Basic-52 Programming* manual has details on how to enable these modes. A remote computer can also restart a Basic-52 program by sending Control+C (if needed), then RUN and a carriage return.

Custom Communications

Basic-52 also includes the ability to replace its built-in communications routines with custom routines. These routines must be assembled or compiled and stored in external program memory. Bytes at 4030h and 4033h in external memory tell Basic-52 where to find the routines. Installing your own communications driver gives you the flexibility to program the communications exactly as you wish, while still using Basic-52 for other programming.

Figure 5-4: Two Basic Stamps: the BS1C (left) and BS2. (Photos courtesy of Parallax Inc.)

```
              BASIC STAMP II
 1                                           24
 ──  SOUT           (+5-+15VDC) PWR  ──
 2                                           23
 ──  SIN                       GND  ──
 3                                           22
 ──  ATN                    -RESET  ──
 4                                           21
 ──  GND                       +5V  ──
 5                                           20
 ──  P0                        P15  ──
 6                                           19
 ──  P1                        P14  ──
 7                                           18
 ──  P2                        P13  ──
 8                                           17
 ──  P3                        P12  ──
 9                                           16
 ──  P4                        P11  ──
10                                           15
 ──  P5                        P10  ──
11                                           14
 ──  P6                         P9  ──
12                                           13
 ──  P7                         P8  ──
```

Figure 5-5: Pinout of the Basic Stamp II.

The Basic Stamp

Another example of a microcontroller with a serial port is Parallax Inc.'s Basic Stamp. Like the 8052-Basic, the Stamp is a microcontroller with a Basic interpreter on-chip. There are two models. Each uses a microcontroller from Microchip's PIC family. The Stamp I uses a 16C56, and the Stamp II, a 16C57 (Figure 5-4).

Because of its enhanced features, the Stamp II is a better choice for many applications that use serial communications, especially with multiple nodes. The module has the footprint of a 24-pin DIP chip, with 16 pins of I/O, 2 kilobytes of EEPROM for storing user programs, and 24 bytes available for variable storage. For a power supply, it can use an unregulated DC supply from just over +5V to +15V (such as a 9V battery) or a regulated +5V supply.

Figure 5-5 shows the pinout. In some of the Stamp's documentation, *GND* is referred to as *Vss*, *Sin*, as *RX*, and *Sout*, as *TX*. *Sin* and *Sout* could stand for

SerialIn and *SerialOut*, but I prefer to think of them as *StampIn* and *StampOut*, because these more precisely describe the direction of data flow.

Like the 8052-Basic, the Stamp II uses an asynchronous serial interface for programming and debugging. To communicate with the Stamp, Parallax provides the Stamp2 host program, which runs under DOS and includes a text editor for writing programs, plus the ability to load Basic programs into the Stamp II and load and save programs on disk. You can also use the serial port to communicate with other devices.

The Stamp IC is a smaller and simpler version with 14 pins and 8 I/O bits. An earlier version resided on a larger circuit board and used through-hole rather than surface-mount components. Both versions have 256 bytes for storing user programs and 14 bytes of variable storage. Instead of connecting to a PC's serial port, The Stamp I uses a parallel-port interface for programming and debugging. (Serial-port software is available for the Macintosh, which has no parallel printer port.) As on the Stamp II, programs can use asynchronous serial communications to communicate with other devices.

Both Stamps use versions of Parallax's PBasic interpreter. Like Basic-52, PBasic has much in common with other Basics, yet is customized for use in a microcontroller. The Stamps' PIC microcontrollers are smaller and simpler in design than the 8052, so their interpreter is smaller and simpler to match.

Parallax offers carrier boards for both Stamps. Each includes a socket for the Stamp, a connector for PC communications, battery clip, reset button, and prototyping area. You can develop a project right on the carrier board or you can use a breadboard, your own perfboard, or any other method you prefer. Other vendors offer products with added features to make project development easy.

Serial Links

This chapter includes essential information for connecting a Stamp to a PC. Later chapters have more on the PC's RS-232 signals and how to use them.

The Stamp II may use as many as five serial-port signals plus a ground wire, though all of these aren't always needed. Table 5-1 lists the signal lines and their uses.

If you use the provided carrier board and cable, all you have to do is plug the cable into the board and a port on a PC (Figure 5-6A). The carrier board's connector is wired as a 9-pin RS-232 DCE device, so you don't need a null-modem cable or converter (as described in Chapter 7). The carrier board connects *DSR* and *RTS*. This connection enables the host software to detect which port connects to the Stamp.

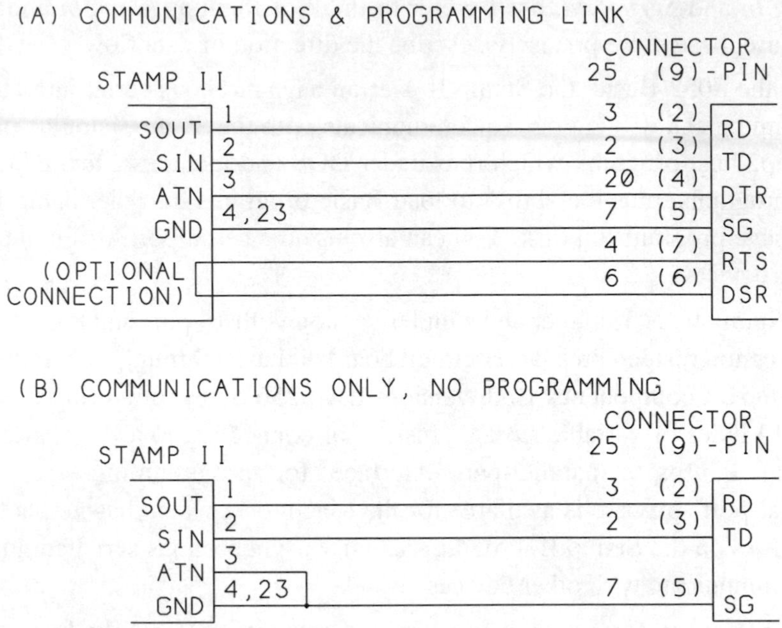

```
(A) COMMUNICATIONS & PROGRAMMING LINK
                                      CONNECTOR
       STAMP II                      25   (9)-PIN
      ┌───────┬─1                     3   (2)┌──────
 SOUT │       │ 2                     2   (3)│  RD
 SIN  │       │ 3                    20   (4)│  TD
 ATN  │       │ 4,23                  7   (5)│  DTR
 GND  │       │                       4   (7)│  SG
    (OPTIONAL │                       6   (6)│  RTS
  CONNECTION) └                             └  DSR


(B) COMMUNICATIONS ONLY, NO PROGRAMMING
                                      CONNECTOR
       STAMP II                      25   (9)-PIN
      ┌───────┬─1                     3   (2)┌──────
 SOUT │       │ 2                     2   (3)│  RD
 SIN  │       │ 3                                TD
 ATN  │       │ 4,23                  7   (5)│
 GND  │       │                             └  SG
```

Figure 5-6: Wiring for Basic Stamp II serial links.

If you don't use the carrier board, you can connect a power supply and serial cable directly to the Stamp. If you want the host to autodetect the port, connect *DSR* and *RTS* in your circuits. If you don't include this connection, you can specify a port in the command line when you run the host software: *Stamp2 /2*.

Instead of Parallax's provided cable, you can use any standard RS-232 cable that contains the needed wires. Standard serial cables may have 3, 9, or 25 wires. A standard cable with 9 or more wires will work fine. If you make your own cable, you can make the *DSR/RTS* connection at the PC's connector and eliminate two wires.

When a Stamp project is complete, the host software's autodetecting and program-downloading abilities are no longer needed (Figure 5-6B). *ATN* should be held low to prevent accidental resets. To defeat any handshaking enabled at the PC, you can tie *RTS* to *CTS* and tie *DTR, DSR*, and *CD* together in the serial cable or at the serial connector in your circuits. However, it's usually a simple matter to disable all handshaking at the PC, and then you don't need these connections.

When wiring your own circuits, be aware that the Stamp's *-Reset* pin connects to more than the PIC's *-MCLR* (reset) input. Additional circuits at *-MCLR* ensure a clean reset signal on power-up and enable the host software to reset the chip with *ATN*. Don't tie *-Reset* high if you need to communicate with the host software! If you do connect *-Reset* directly to +5V, the host software won't be able to reset or

Table 5-1: Serial-port connections between a Basic Stamp II and a PC.

Stamp II		PC Serial Port			Description
Pin	Signal	Signal	9-pin	25-pin	
2	Sin	TD	3	2	Carries data from the PC to the Stamp.
1	Sout	RD	2	3	Carries data from the Stamp to the PC.
-	On carrier board	RTS	7	4	Connects to *DSR* to enable the host software to detect which of a PC's serial ports connects to a Stamp.
-	-	CTS	8	5	No connection.
-	On carrier board	DSR	6	6	See *RTS*.
4, 23	Vss	SG	5	7	Signal ground.
-	-	CD	1	8	No connection.
3	ATN	DTR	4	20	Resets the Stamp. The PC's host software pulses *DTR* high to enable downloading of a new program.

communicate with the Stamp. *-Reset* may be left open or connected to a normally-open pushbutton with a pullup to +5V.

A Firmware UART

Although some PIC microcontrollers have hardware UARTs, the Stamps' microcontrollers don't. Instead, the Basic Stamps' UARTs are implemented in firmware, with the UART's functions programmed into the interpreter.

The serial ports on the Stamp IC and II are similar in many ways. Neither has any buffers at all. To read a byte at the serial port, the Stamp must execute a `Serin` statement and wait for a byte to arrive. If the byte arrives before `Serin` executes, the Stamp won't see it. If no byte arrives, the Stamp IC will wait forever. To prevent endless waits, the Stamp II allows use of a `Timeout` modifier that enables the Stamp to jump to a line label if a specified number of milliseconds pass with no activity at the port.

Because the Stamp's port is implemented in firmware, not hardware, it can include options that hardware ports don't normally have. The outputs can be inverted or not, so they're usable with or without inverting drivers and receivers. A Stamp can use any of its I/O bits for serial communications. It can even have multiple serial ports, using different bits for each (though it can use just one at a time). These abilities greatly simplify project development for Stamps used in serial links and networks. The Stamp can reserve *Sin* and *Sout* for PC communications for loading and saving programs, viewing debug messages, and other experimenting, and use other port bits for the network. When all is working fine, you can disconnect *Sin* and *Sout* and use the Stamp on its own in the network.

If you don't need 2-way communications, you can even have a 1-bit port. If you're connecting the serial ports of two Stamps, you can use the Stamp's open baudmode for 2-way communications over 1 bit.

If you want to know how to write a firmware UART, an excellent resource is Scott Edwards' *PIC Source Book,* which contains clearly commented assembly-code routines that emulate each of the Basic Stamp's instructions, including *Serin* and *Serout.*

Options and Features

Each read or write to the Stamp's serial port has to specify the bit rate, pin number, and other information. The values are easily stored in variables or constants, however, so each needs to appear just once in a program. The statement to read a serial port on the Stamp II is:

```
SerIn rpin {\fpin}, baudmode, {plabel,} {timeout,
tlabel,} [InputData]
```

To write, it's:

```
SerOut tpin{\fpin}, baudmode, {timeout, tlabel,}
[OutputData]
```

or

```
SerOut tpin, baudmode, {pace} [OutputData]
```

The parameters in the above statements are as follows:

`rpin` and `tpin` specify the pin to use for the serial input and output. Set these to 16 to use the Stamp's *Sin* or *Sout* pin, or 0–15 to select a port pin. `Serout` automatically configures the requested pin as an output and leaves it in that state after transmitting. In a similar way, `Serin` configures the requested pin as an input and leaves it in that state after receiving data or a timeout.

`\fpin` designates a pin for handshaking. On executing `Serin`, the Stamp sets *fpin* low (or high, if using inverted signals) to indicate that it's ready to receive data. `Serout` will wait for its designated *fpin* to be in the appropriate state before sending data.

`baudmode` is a 16-bit word that holds several settings. It specifies the bit rate, the number of data bits and parity, and the polarity of the bits to send and read. It can also enable the Stamp's open baudmode, described below. For most situations, you can select a baudmode value from the table in the Stamp's manual. Listing 5-1 is a Visual-Basic function that accepts a series of settings and returns a baudmode value to match. The value is calculated like this:

```
Public Function fncGetBaudMode _
    (BitRate As Long, _
    Parity As Boolean, _
    Inverted As Boolean, _
    OpenBaudMode As Boolean) _
As Long
'Returns the Basic Stamp's baudmode parameter
'for the requested settings.
Dim BitRateValue As Long
Dim ParityValue As Long
Dim InvertedValue As Long
Dim OpenBaudModeValue As Long
BitRateValue = 1000000 \ BitRate - 20
If Parity = True Then
    ParityValue = 8192
Else
    ParityValue = 0
End If
If Inverted = True Then
    InvertedValue = 16384
Else
    InvertedValue = 0
End If
If OpenBaudMode = True Then
    OpenBaudModeValue = 32768
Else
    OpenBaudModeValue = 0
End If
fncGetBaudMode = _
    (BitRateValue + ParityValue + InvertedValue + _
    OpenBaudModeValue)
End Function
```

Listing 5-1: This Visual-Basic routine calculates the baudmode parameter for the Basic Stamp's Serin and Serout statements.

Bits 0–12 equal the period of one bit in microseconds, minus 20. For example, 300 bps has a period of 3333 µsecs. Subtract 20 and the result is 3313. The top bit rate is 38,400 bps, though higher rates may require pacing between bytes, as described below.

Bit 13 is 0 for 8 bits, no parity, or 1 for 7 bits, Even parity.

Bit 14 is 0 for noninverted, 1 for inverted. When connecting two Stamps, both must have the same polarity. RS-232 uses inverted signals. When using RS-232, select inverted if the Stamp's interface doesn't use a MAX232 or other inverting driver, or non-inverted if it does.

Important tip: If you use inverted baudmode for RS-232 output on a pin other than *Sout*, write 1 to the bit on power up. This ensures that the bit will remain high (RS-232 idle state) until the Start bit of the first SerIn statement pulls it low. For example, if you're using bit 14 for serial output, place this statement near the beginning of the program:

```
high 14
```

For Serout, bit 15 is 0 for normal operation, and 1 for open baudmode, which enables connecting multiple Stamps to one line. (Chapter 12 has more on open baudmode.) Bit 15 is unused by Serin.

plabel names a label to jump to on parity error.

timeout is the number of milliseconds to wait for incoming data on SerIn, or for *fpin* to indicate ready on SerOut. Tlabel is the label to jump to on timeout.

pace gives a delay in milliseconds between bytes. Pacing allows time for the receiving device to process each byte before reading the next. Stamps may require pacing at 9600 bps or higher.

Data Formats

The final parameters, InputData and OutputData, lists the value or values to write or read at the serial pins. Both of these allow a variety of modifiers that automatically process data, either before sending it or on receiving it. The modifiers can save processing time and storage space in the Stamp and make it easy to communicate with devices that require specific formats.

The Dec modifier converts SerOut data to the ASCII codes that represent the value's decimal digits. For example, an OutputData of [Dec 5] writes 53, the ASCII code for 5, to the port. An OutputData of ["5"] accomplishes the same thing. Sending ASCII codes is useful if the receiver will display the values as ASCII text. Also, some networks send all data as ASCII text, reserving other values for node addressing, control codes, or other uses.

On the receive side, the Dec modifier causes SerIn to accept ASCII codes for characters 0–9 until receiving a code for a non-numeric character. SerIn then converts the codes to their numeric value, and stores the value in the indicated variable. This saves memory on the receiving end, because one byte can store a value represented by two or three characters. For example, input bytes of [50, 53, 53, 10] are the ASCII codes for 2, 5, 5, and linefeed. An InputData of [Dec A], where A is a byte variable, would accept the first three codes, quit on seeing the non-numeric linefeed character, and store the value 255 in A.

For Visual-Basic and QuickBasic programmers, `SerOut`'s `Dec` is equivalent to `CStr()`, and `SerIn`'s `Dec` is equivalent to `Val()`.

The `Dec1–Dec5` modifiers wait for the designated number of digits, so there's no need to send a non-numeric character with each value. In another variation, `SDec` and `SDec1–SDec5` enable sending signed values, with "–" preceding the digits of a negative value.

In a similar way, `Hex`, `Hex1–Hex4` and `SHex`, `Shex1–SHex4` send and accept hex characters 0–9 and A–F (or a–f). The `IHex ISHex` modifiers require $ preceding each value. The `Bin`, `SBin`, `IBin`, `ISBin` modifiers do the same for binary values, with binary characters *0* and *1* and a binary prefix of %.

Ensuring that the Stamp Sees Incoming Data

`SerIn` has two other modifiers: `Wait` and `Skip`, which can help to ensure that the Stamp sees the values intended for it while ignoring any others.

`Wait` causes the Stamp to ignore all data until it receives a value or values matching the `Wait` parameter(s). This can be useful in a network where a master node sends a node address followed by data intended for that node. If the receiving Stamps use the `Wait` modifier, they will automatically ignore bytes addressed to other nodes. Because a node will continue to wait until it recognizes its `Wait` modifiers, it won't miss any data intended for it.

However, there are limitations to using `Wait`. One is that the data following the node address can't include any bytes that equal another node's address. For example, if a master node sends a node address of 1 followed by a data byte of 7, when node 7 sees the data byte, it will think that master is addressing it. A way around this is to send all data with a `Dec`, `Hex`, or `Bin` modifier and send the node numbers as values (such as 0–7) that don't correspond to any ASCII codes used by these formats.

Another limitation to `Wait` is that nodes can waste a lot of time just watching for their address to come up. If using the timeout parameter, the timeout count quits on any received data, so `Wait` has little use as a data filter. Yet without a timeout, the node can't break out of a `SerIn` if the master fails to send the correct `Wait` modifier.

If a node is responsible for other activities, it may make more sense to have the program periodically read any incoming byte. Then if a byte doesn't match the node address, the program can move on instead of being stuck in a `Wait` statement.

Yet another modifier for `SerIn` is `Skip` L, which skips over *L* bytes of input. A network node might use this to send a series of bytes, with each byte intended for a different node. Node 1 can read the first byte; Node 2 can skip the first byte and read the next; Node 3 skips 2 bytes and reads the third, and so on.

The Stamp I also has SerIn and SerOut statements, which you can use with any port bits. These are similar to the Stamp II's statements, except that they don't support timeouts, parity, or pacing, and the maximum bit rate is 2400.

Hardware Handshaking

Another option for ensuring that the Stamp sees all data sent to it is to use the Stamp II's *fpin* parameter to designate a port bit for handshaking. Serout's *fpin* may connect to *CTS*, while Serin's *fpin* may connect to *RTS* on a remote PC. The PC transmits only when *CTS* is high, and the Stamp transmits only when *RTS* is high. The main drawback of this approach is the need to use additional port bits, cable wires, and possibly drivers and receivers.

Signal Levels

If the cable is short (15 feet), the Stamp II's Sin and Sout can connect directly to an RS-232 port. Because the port outputs on both the Stamp I and II have strong drivers, and because the Stamp is capable of inverting the signals, a short link between the port bits and an RS-232 port will also work in most cases, with only a current-limiting resistor at the RS-232 input. Later chapters have more on Stamp interfaces.

Stamp-to-Stamp Links

Basic Stamps can also use their serial ports to communicate with each other. If the distance between Stamps is short (15 feet or so), there's no need for added drivers or receivers. Just connect a serial output on each Stamp to a serial input on the other, and add a ground wire if the Stamps don't share a power supply.

Open Baudmode

Serout includes an *open baudmode* option that makes it easy for two or more Stamps to communicate over a single wire. If you're familiar with open-collector or open-drain outputs, open baudmode works in a similar way.

Figure 5-7 shows the circuits behind a Stamp's I/O pin. The CMOS output has complementary NMOS and PMOS transistors. The output has two driven, or active, states. For a logic high output, the PMOS transistor switches on, creating a low-resistance path from the output pin to +5V. For a logic low output, the NMOS transistor switches on, creating a low-resistance path from the output to ground.

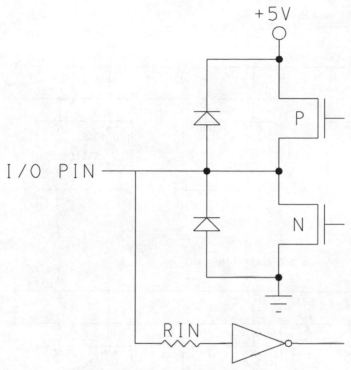

Figure 5-7: The circuits inside a Basic Stamp's I/O pin.

An input buffer enables programs to read the logic level at the pin. The resistor and diodes protect the chip by limiting input voltages and currents.

When the pin is being used as an input, neither transistor is on. The output is high impedance and has no effect on the circuits it connects to. The input buffer reads the logic level of whatever circuits connect to the pin. Other terms to describe this state are *off, open,* or *tristated.*

In normal operation, a pin being used as an output switches between active high and active low. In a full-duplex serial link, the serial output connects to an input pin on another Stamp or other device.

Because each pin can act as an output or input, why not make a 1-wire link by connecting bits on two or more Stamps? In fact, this is possible, as long as only one bit at a time is configured as an output. If two connected outputs are enabled at the same time, and if one output is high and the other low, the result is a low impedance path from +5V to ground that causes the bits' output transistors to draw high currents.

To prevent this from happening, all Stamps in the link but one must execute either a `Serin` to receive data or an `Input` statement configure the bit as input. For example, one Stamp sends data with `Serout`. After sending the data, and before

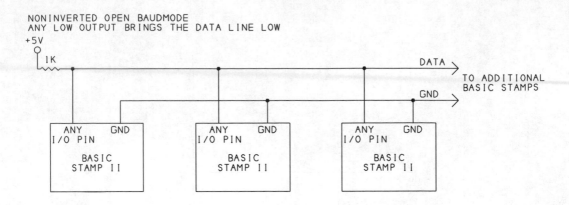

NONINVERTED OPEN BAUDMODE
ANY LOW OUTPUT BRINGS THE DATA LINE LOW

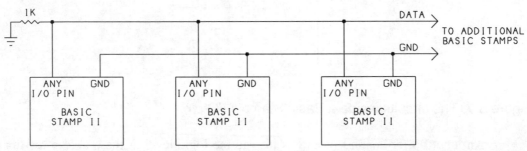

INVERTED OPEN BAUDMODE
ANY HIGH OUTPUT BRINGS THE DATA LINE HIGH

Figure 5-8: The Stamp II's open baudmode allows easy networking for short links.

another Stamp executes a Serout, the transmitting Stamp must execute a Serin or Input statement to configure the bit as an input.

Open baudmode provides a simpler and safer way to do this. Instead of switching between active high and active low, the open baudmode outputs switch between open and a driven state. A pullup or pulldown resistor determines the state of the line when all outputs that connect to the line are open, and whether the line uses inverted or noninverted data. Figure 5-8 illustrates.

If Serout sends noninverted data, the line uses a pullup to +5V. If all of the outputs are logic 1s, all are open and the pullup brings the line high. Writing 0 to any output pulls the line low because the resistance between that output and GND is much less than the resistance between the pullup and +5V.

If Serout uses inverted data, the line uses a pulldown to ground. If all of the outputs are open, the pulldown brings the line low. Writing 0 to any output bit results in a logic high at the pin, which pulls the line high.

With either configuration, an idle (not transmitting) pin is open. As long as only one Stamp transmits at a time, the data will arrive without errors. The Stamps that aren't transmitting can use `Serin` statements to read data on the line.

Open baudmode is for use only when connecting Stamps directly, without buffers or drivers, using any of I/O bits 0–15, with short cables. All connected Stamps must also share a ground connection. This type of link should handle 8 or more Stamps.

Adding a Hardware Serial Port

When a microcontroller doesn't have a serial port, or if a project requires an added port, an solution is to use an external UART.

Options

Conventional UARTs like the 8250 family require eight parallel data bits, plus read, write, and other control and status lines. Many microcontrollers don't have this many bits to spare. One chip that requires as few as three lines for a bidirectional link is Maxim's Max3100 SPI/Microwire UART.

An SPI/Microwire UART

The Max3100 converts between synchronous and asynchronous serial data. Figure 5-9 shows the pinout and Table 5-2 lists the pin functions. The DIP (through-hole package) has 14 pins, while surface-mount QSOP has 16 pins, though the package is actually much smaller. The synchronous data is compatible with SPI and Microwire formats, which require a clock line and a data line for each direction.

A microcontroller can communicate with the Max3100 by sending and receiving synchronous data. The microcontroller can toggle *SCLK* as needed, without worrying about maintaining a specific bit rate. The only restrictions on *SCLK*'s frequency are a minimum pulse width (high or low) of 100 nanoseconds, and a minimum clock period (high + low) of 238 nanoseconds.

The synchronous interface exchanges 16-bit words. In data transfers, eight bits are data, and the other bits may hold status and control information. The chip can also send and receive configuration data.

Table 5-2: Pin functions for the MAX3100.

Pin		Name	Description
QSOP	DIP		
1	1	DIN	SPI/Microwire data in.
2	2	DOUT	SPI/Microwire data out.
3	3	SCLK	SPI/Microwire clock in.
4	4	-CS	Chip select.
6	5	-IRQ	Interrupt request.
7	6	-SHDN	Power-saving shutdown.
8	7	GND	Ground.
9	8	X2	Crystal.
10	9	X1	Crystal or external clock input.
11	10	-CTS	RS-232 CTS or general-purpose input.
13	11	-RTS	RS-232 RTS or general-purpose output.
14	12	RX	Asynchronous in.
15	13	TX	Asynchronous out.
16	14	VCC	+2.7V to +5V
5,12	-	N.C.	No connection.

A crystal or ceramic resonator provides the timing reference for the UART's bit-rate generator. With a 1.8432Mhz crystal, the chip supports bit rates from 300 to 115,200. To double the available rates, double the crystal frequency.

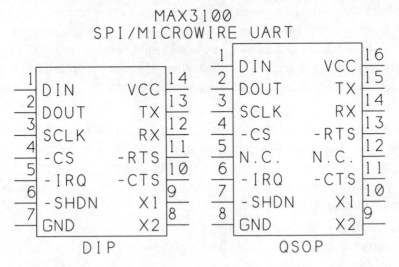

Figure 5-9: The MAX3100 converts between SPI or Microwire serial data and asynchronous format.

When the Max3100 receives synchronous data to transmit, it converts the byte to a standard UART format, including Start and Stop bits, and writes the bits to *TX*. The data may have 7 or 8 bits, plus an optional parity bit. The Max3100 doesn't calculate a parity bit; the sending device must set the parity as desired. This makes it easy to use the parity bit as an address/data identifier in 9-bit networks. The Max3100 can generate an interrupt request on receiving a parity bit of 1.

The chip has 8-byte FIFOs, so the interface doesn't have to worry about transferring each received byte before the next arrives.

Possible uses for the Max3100 include adding a second serial port to an 8052-Basic system. This enables sending and receiving serial data with another computer or a network, while leaving the dedicated serial bits available for Basic-52's console interface. You might also use a Max3100 to add a full-duplex, high-speed interface to a Basic Stamp. The UART's buffer frees the Stamp from having to watch for incoming data. Maxim has the complete data sheet.

6

Linking Two Devices with RS-232

RS-232 is one of the most popular computer interfaces of all time. It's the work-horse that has been built into just about every PC as well as many other types of computers from microcontrollers to mainframes, and the devices they connect to. RS-232's most common use is to connect to a modem, but other devices with RS-232 interfaces include printers, data-acquisition modules, test instruments, and control circuits. You can also use RS-232 as a simple link between computers of any type.

These days, there are faster and more sophisticated interfaces, but RS-232 contin-ues to be popular because the hardware and programming requirements are simple and inexpensive and because so many existing devices already have the interface built-in. Other choices include descendents of RS-232 that are faster or cheaper, while remaining compatible with RS-232 in many ways.

This chapter introduces RS-232 and similar interfaces, including their signals and interface chips. Later chapters discuss cables and other wiring concerns and pro-gramming.

About RS-232

RS-232 is designed to handle communications between two devices, with a distance limit of 50 to 100 feet, depending on the bit rate and cable type. Because RS-232 ports are so common, another popular use is to connect to an adapter that converts the interface to another type. For example, a simple circuit converts an RS-232 port to RS-485, which can connect to multiple devices and can use much longer links.

RS-232 links use *unbalanced* lines. Although a state of unbalance sounds like something to be avoided, in this context it just refers to electrical characteristics of the signals on the lines. In an unbalanced line, the signal voltage is applied to one wire, and all signal voltages are referenced to a common ground. Another term for this type of interface is single-ended. In contrast, in the balanced, or differential, lines described in Chapter 9, each signal uses two wires, with one wire carrying the inverse of the other.

Features

RS-232 has several advantages:

- It's ubiquitous. Every PC has one or more RS-232 ports. Newer computers are now supporting other serial interfaces such as USB, but RS-232 can do things that USB can't.

- On microcontrollers, interface chips make it easy to convert a 5V serial port to RS-232.

- Links can be 50 to 100 feet long. Most peripheral interfaces aren't intended to go long distances. USB links can be up to 16 feet, and the PC's parallel printer interface can go 10 to 15 feet, or 30 feet with IEEE-1284 Type B drivers. But RS-232 can use much longer cables. If each RS-232 port connects to a modem, you can use the phone network to transmit worldwide.

- You need just three wires for a 2-way link. A parallel link typically has eight data lines, two or more control signals, and several ground wires. The cost of all of the wires and larger connectors can add up.

The downside to RS-232 includes these:

- If the other end of the link requires parallel data, it will have to convert the serial data to parallel. This is easily done, however, with a UART.

- Serial ports are so useful that it may be hard to find a port that's free for use. PCs can have multiple serial ports, but a system may not have a unique interrupt-request line for each. Most microcontrollers have just one hardware serial port.

- There can be no more than two devices in a link.
- The specified maximum data rate is 20,000 bits per second. Many interface chips can exceed this, however, especially on shorter links.
- Very long links require a different interface.

For higher speeds, longer links, and multi-node links, RS-485's balanced interface is a solution.

Signals

In most respects, the standard serial port on PCs conforms to the RS-232 standard. The Telecommunications Industry Association (TIA) publishes the document that defines the signal functions, pin locations, and other characteristics of the interface. The standard has been through several revisions since its introduction in the 1960s, with the latest version, designated TIA/EIA-232-F, dated 1997. Previous versions were a product of the Electronics Industries Association (EIA), but TIA has taken over this function. A similar standard, V.28, is published by ITU (International Telecommunications Union) and CCITT (International Telegraph and Telephone Consultive Committee).

The original name for the interface was RS-232, and this is the name that has stuck in popular use. The *RS* stands for Recommended Standard. In this book, I'll continue to use RS-232 to refer to interfaces that are compatible with TIA/EIA-232.

The standard defines three things: the names and functions of the signals in the link, the electrical characteristics of the signals, and mechanical aspects, including pin assignments, of the interface. Earlier versions didn't include all of these. The new material, such as recommend connectors, was added to document what had become standard through popular use.

Although the standard designates 25 lines in the interface, PCs and many other devices rarely support more than the nine signals in Table 6-1. Some devices use only three lines (or even two, in a 1-way link). Appendix B lists all 25 lines and their functions. The additional signals are intended for use with synchronous modems, secondary transmission channels, and selecting a transmission speed on dual-rate modems. None of these are in common use today.

Table 6-1 uses mnemonic signal names that are basically abbreviations of the signals' functions. The standard document assigns completely different names for

Table 6-1: The PC's serial port and many other interfaces use only these nine signals (or fewer).

Pin (9-pin)	Pin (25-pin)	Signal	Source	Type	Description
1	8	CD	DCE	control	Carrier detect
2	3	RD	DCE	data	Received data
3	2	TD	DTE	data	Transmitted data
4	20	DTR	DTE	control	Data terminal ready
5	7	GND	-	-	Signal ground
6	6	DSR	DCE	control	Data set ready
7	4	RTS	DTE	control	Request to send
8	5	CTS	DCE	control	Clear to send
9	22	RI	DCE	control	Ring Indicator
-	1, 9-19, 21, 23-25	unused	-	-	-

the functions. For example, *TD* is *BA* and *RD* is *BB*. Appendix B lists both names. In this book, I use the more common mnemonics.

Much of the RS-232 terminology reflects its origin as a standard for communications between a computer terminal and a modem. A "dumb" terminal is little more than a keyboard, display, and communications port for accessing a remote computer. An RS-232 link connects the terminal to a modem, which in turn connects to the phone lines used to dial the remote computer. "Smart" terminals have some intelligence built-in, but have no disk storage or other features of a complete desktop computer.

With terminal-emulation software, such as Windows 95's *HyperTerminal*, PCs can emulate many types of computer terminals. These days, of course, RS-232 does many things besides terminal-to-modem communications. Instead of a terminal, you may find a complete computer, though it may be a tiny microcontroller. Instead of a modem, the other end of the link may connect to a mouse, printer, another PC or microcontroller, or just about anything you could imagine.

DTE and DCE

The standard calls the terminal end of the link the Data Terminal Equipment, or DTE. It calls the modem end the Data Circuit-terminating Equipment, or DCE. These names again reflect the original purpose of the interface.

It doesn't matter which device in a link is the DTE and which is the DCE, but a link must have one of each. The type determines which signals are inputs and which are outputs at the connector.

All of the signal names are from the perspective of the DTE. For example, *TD* (transmit data) is an output on a DTE and an input on a DCE, while *RD* (receive data) is an input on a DTE and an output on a DCE.

With few exceptions, serial ports on PCs are configured as DTEs, and all modems' serial ports are DCEs. Most other peripherals are DCEs, but there are exceptions, including many serial printers. When necessary, a simple adapter, described in Chapter 7, will convert one type of interface to the other.

The PC's Nine Signals

The three essential signals for 2-way RS-232 communications are these:

> *TD*. Carries data from the DTE to the DCE. Also called *TX* and *TXD*.
> *RD*. Carries data from the DCE to the DTE. Also called *RX* and *RXD*.
> *SG*. Signal ground. Also called *GND* and *SGND*.

The other signals are optional control signals intended for communicating about the readiness of a device, or the presence of a ringing or carrier signal on a phone line.

There are two pairs of handshaking signals: *DTR/DSR* and *RTS/CTS*. Each pair has uses defined by the standard.

There are several ways to describe the state of RS-232 and other control signals. A signal with a valid positive voltage may be described as *On, asserted*, or *True* to indicate that it's in its active state. For example, when *DTR* is True, the data terminal is ready. To bring the signal True, the controlling device *raises* the line. A signal with a valid negative voltage may be described as *Off, de-asserted*, or *False* to indicate that it's in its inactive state. For example, when *DTR* is False, the data terminal is not ready. To bring the signal False, the controlling device *lowers* the line.

In the following descriptions, I use *terminal* to refer to the DTE and *modem* to refer to the DCE.

The *DTR/DSR* handshake is intended for providing information about the status of the phone line or other communications channel connected to the modem. The terminal raises *DTR* (data terminal ready) to request the modem to connect to the communications channel. In response, the modem raises *DSR* (data set ready) to indicate that it's connected. *DSR* is False when the modem is not connected to the communications channel (on detecting a disconnect, for example) or on detecting a fault.

The terminal may also raise *DTR* in response to *RI* (ring indicator), to tell the modem to answer a call. In some links, *DTR* and *DSR* are raised on power-up and just indicate that the equipment is present and powered.

The *RTS/CTS* handshake provides additional information about whether a device is ready to receive data. There are two common uses for the signals.

In the first, and original, use, the signal pair provides a full handshake. When the terminal has data to send, it raises *RTS* (request to send). In response, the modem raises *CTS* (clear to send) to indicate that it's ready to receive. When the transmission is finished, the terminal may lower *RTS*. The modem should then continue processing whatever data it has received and lower *CTS* when it's ready to respond to the next *RTS*. When *RTS* is False, the terminal should wait for *CTS* to be False before raising *RTS* to request a new transmission. In the opposite direction, in a half-duplex link, the modem may transmit to the terminal only when *RTS* is False.

In the other protocol used by these signals, each device uses its output independently to let the other know when it's OK to send data. *CTS* has the same function: it indicates whether the DCE is ready to receive data. But *RTS* is redefined as the DTE's *Ready for Receiving*. Each device checks the opposite end's signal before transmitting. The latest version of TIA/EIA-232 includes this definition, which has long been in popular use.

RI (ring indicator) is True when a ringing signal is present on the communications channel. The signal is True when the audible ring is present, and False in the pauses between rings.

The final control signal is *CD* (carrier detect). The modem raises *CD* when it detects a signal of the expected frequency on the phone lines, indicating that a connection has been established to a remote modem.

SG (signal ground) is the common ground used by all of the signals.

Non-standard Handshakes

When a link doesn't need a control signal for its intended use, it may use the signal for another purpose.

One example is the Basic Stamp II, which has unconventional uses for three signals. Using a non-standard connection between *RTS* and *DTR* enables the Stamp software on the PC to detect which port connects to a Stamp. The Stamp uses *DTR* as a reset line. The PC toggles *DTR* to reset the Stamp and enable downloading of a user's Basic program into the Stamp.

Break Signaling

One rarely used form of signaling is the Break signal. Setting the break signal in the PC's UART causes the output to remain logic 0, which is a positive RS-232 voltage.

The break signal enables in-line signaling to a microcontroller or other device that has no input buffers or handshaking lines. It also provides a way to toggle the *TD* line as desired for any purpose.

Shield Ground

Pin 1 is a shield connection to allow grounding of a cable shield. This pin isn't always connected inside the device, and the 9-pin connector doesn't include it at all, so many shields instead use the connector shell to connect to a grounded chassis. The shield normally connects to only to the DTE's chassis (not the DCE's).

Earlier versions of the standard called pin 1 protective ground, and it was sometimes used to connect the chassis, or frames, of the equipment on both ends. Each chassis in turn connected to a safety ground at the equipment's power plug. The latest standard recommends using a separate wire (not one of the wires in the connector) to connect the two chassis' grounds, if needed.

Voltages

RS-232 logic levels are indicated by positive and negative voltages, rather than by the positive-only signals of 5V TTL and CMOS logic. At an RS-232 data output (*TD*), a logic 0 is defined as equal to or more positive than +5V, and a logic 1 is defined as equal to or more negative than -5V. In other words, the signals use negative logic, where the more negative voltage is logic 1.

The control signals use the same voltages, but with positive logic. A positive voltage indicates that the function is *On*, or asserted, and a negative voltage indicates that the function is *Off*, or not asserted.

RS-232 interface chips invert the signals. On a UART's output pin, a logic-1 data bit or an Off control signal is near 5V, which results in a negative voltage at the RS-232 interface. A logic-0 data bit or On control signal is near 0V, resulting in a positive voltage at the RS-232 interface.

Because an RS-232 receiver may be at the end of a long cable, by the time the signal reaches the receiver, its voltage may have attenuated or have noise riding on it. To allow for this, the minimum required voltages at the receiver are less than at the driver. An input more positive than +3V is a logic 0 at *RD*, or On at a control input. An input more negative than -3V is a logic 1 at *RD*, or Off at a control input. According to the standard, the logic level of an input between -3V and +3V is undefined.

The noise margin, or voltage margin, is the difference between the output and input voltages. RS-232's large voltage swings result in a much wider noise margin than 5V TTL logic. For example, even if an RS-232 driver's output is the minimum +5V, it can attenuate or have noise spikes as large as 2V at the receiver and still be a valid logic 0. Many RS-232 outputs have much wider voltage swings: ±9 and ±12V are common. These in turn give much wider noise margins. The maximum allowed voltage swing is ±15V, though receivers must handle voltages as high as ±25V without damage.

Two other terms used in relation to RS-232 are *Mark* and *Space*. Space is logic 0, and Mark is logic 1. These refer to the physical marks and spaces made by the mechanical recorders used years ago to log binary data.

Timing Limits

TIA/EIA-232 includes both minimum and maximum timing specifications. All of the many RS-232 interface chips meet these specifications.

The specified slew rate limits the maximum bit rate of the interface. Slew rate is a measure of how fast the voltage changes when the output switches and describes an output's instantaneous rate of voltage change. The slew rate of an RS-232 driver must be 30 Volts per microsecond or less.

The advantage of limiting slew rate is that it improves signal quality by virtually eliminating problems due to voltage reflections that occur on long links that carry signals with fast rise and fall times. Chapter 10 has more on this topic.

But the slew rate also limits a link's maximum speed. At 30 V/μs, an output requires 0.3 microsecond to switch from +5V to -5V. RS-232's specified maximum bit rate is 20 kbps, which translates to a bit width of 50 microseconds, or 166 times the switching time at the fastest allowed slew rate.

In reality, because UARTs read inputs near the middle of the bit, and because most timing references are very accurate, you can often safely use bit widths as short as 5 to 10 times the switching time. Taking these into account, some interface chips allow bit rates of 115 kbps and higher, even though this violates the standard's recommendations.

Besides having a maximum switching speed, RS-232 drivers must also meet minimum standards to ensure that signals don't linger in the undefined region between logic states. For the control signals and other signals of 40 bps and lower, the line must spend no more than 1 millisecond in the transition region between a valid logic 0 and logic 1. For other data and timing signals, the limit is 4% of a bit width, or 2 microseconds at 20 kbps. The signals' rise and fall times should also be as nearly equal as possible.

Converting between 5V Logic and RS-232

Many microcontrollers have asynchronous serial ports, but their inputs and outputs use 5V logic rather than RS-232 voltages. Interfacing 5V logic to an RS-232 port requires converting to and from RS-232 levels.

By 5V logic, I mean the logic levels used by TTL or CMOS logic chips powered by a single +5V power supply, with signal voltages referenced to ground. Table 6-2 illustrates. I also assume positive logic, where the more positive logic level, or logic-high, is logic 1.

With TTL logic, a logic-low output must be no higher than 0.4V, and a logic-low input must be no higher than 0.8V. A logic-high output must be at least 2.4V, while a logic-high input must be at least 2V. Using these levels, an interface may have 0.4V of noise without causing errors.

These logic levels are used by the original, standard 7400 series of TTL logic and its derivatives, including 74LS, 74F, and 74ALS TTL. Older microcontrollers made with NMOS technology also use these logic levels.

Most CMOS chips define logic levels differently and have wider noise margins. A logic-low CMOS output is no higher than 0.1V, and a logic-low input may be as high as 20% of the power supply, or 1V with a 5V supply. A logic-high output is at least 4.9V, and a logic-high input must be at least 70% of the power supply, or 3.5V with a 5V supply. Families that use these logic levels include the 4000 series, 74HC, and 74AC logic.

Some CMOS chips have TTL-compatible inputs and CMOS-compatible outputs. This enables direct interfacing with either CMOS or TTL logic. Chips that follow this convention include the 74HCT logic family and most microcontrollers.

The MAX232

A simple way to translate from 5V logic to RS-232 is to use one of the many chips designed for this purpose. Maxim Semiconductor was the first to offer RS-232 interface chips that require only a +5V power supply. Many other companies, including Linear Technology, Harris Semiconductor, Texas Instruments, Dallas Semiconductor, and National Semiconductor, now have similar chips, as well as dozens of derivatives for just about every conceivable configuration. The chips

Table 6-2: Voltages for 5V TTL and CMOS logic.

Parameter	TTL logic (volts)	CMOS logic (volts)	74HCT (volts)
logic-low output (maximum)	0.4	0.1	0.1
logic-high output (minimum)	2.4	3.5	3.5
logic-low input (maximum)	0.8	1	0.8
logic-high input (minimum)	2.0	3.5	2.0

may be listed in catalogs and data books under Linear, Interface, or Special Function ICs.

The original MAX232 (Figure 6-1) includes two drivers that convert TTL inputs to RS-232 outputs, and two receivers that accept RS-232 inputs and translate them to CMOS-compatible outputs. The drivers and receivers also invert the signals.

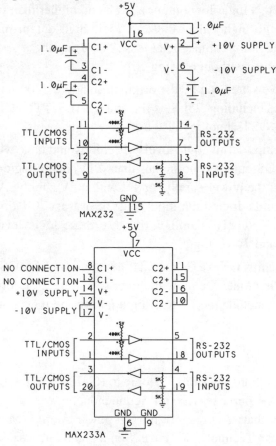

Figure 6-1: Chips like the MAX232 and MAX233 make it easy to interface 5V logic to RS-232.

The chip contains two charge-pump voltage converters that act as tiny, unregulated power supplies that enable loaded RS-232 outputs of ±7V or better. Four external capacitors store energy for the supplies. The recommended value for the capacitors is 1µF or larger.

If you use polarized capacitors, take care to get the polarities correct when you put the circuit together. The voltage at pin 6 is negative, so its capacitor's + terminal connects to ground. Because the outputs can be as high as 10V, be sure the capacitors are rated for a WVDC of at least 15V. (Most are.)

Other Interface Chips

Table 6-3 shows a selection of other RS-232 interface chips. The MAX232A was an early improvement, with the ability to operate at higher speeds and use smaller, 0.1µF capacitors. The MAX233 is even more convenient because it requires no external capacitors at all (but it costs more).

Many RS-232 links use only one driver and one receiver, yet interface chips with this configuration are rare. The Max3221 is one option.

Many newer chips include a power-saving shutdown feature. A Shutdown input places the chip in a reduced-power mode. Some chips have a separate Enable input to enable the receiver so a device won't miss incoming data even if in shutdown mode.

The Max3212 has two additional power-saving features. When the inputs aren't valid RS-232 voltages (which will occur if the remote driver is disabled), the chip automatically switches to a low-power mode. If the inputs are valid but idle, a transition-detecting output indicates when a transition occurs at an input. This signal is useful for waking up a microcontroller that is in sleep mode and needs to wake up to process incoming data.

Instead of requiring or generating their own negative voltage source, Dallas Semiconductor's DS275 and DS276 borrow voltages from the opposite end's interface.

Before the existence of the MAX232, many RS-232 interfaces used the MC1488/9 quad driver and receiver pair. The '1488 requires positive and negative supplies. The '1489 operates from a 5V supply, but accepts inputs as large as ±30 volts. If a circuit already has the required positive and negative supplies available, and especially if you need four drivers and four receivers, the 1488/89 pair is an alternative.

If you don't want to make your own converter, modules are available. Figure 6-2 shows an example.

Table 6-3: Selected RS-232 interface chips.

Source	Part Number	Features
Maxim Semiconductor	MAX232	original 5V-only chip; 120 kbps, 1 µF caps
National Semiconductor	DS14C232	
Maxim Semiconductor	MAX232A	0.1µF caps
National Semiconductor	DS14C202	
Maxim Semiconductor	MAX233	no external caps
Maxim Semiconductor	MAX220	22kbps
Linear Technology	LT1180A	200 kbps
Maxim Semiconductor	MAX232A	
Maxim Semiconductor	MAX232E	high ESD protection
Linear Technology	LT1137A	
National Semiconductor	DS14(C)88	4 drivers; requires dual supplies
Texas Instruments	MC1488	
National Semiconductor	DS14(C)89	4 receivers; complements 1488
Texas Instruments	MC1489	
Maxim Semiconductor	MAX3221	1driver, 1 receiver
Linear Technology	LTC1382	low-power shutdown mode
Maxim Semiconductor	MAX3212	autoshutdown on invalid inputs
Maxim Semiconductor	MAX242	low-power shutdown with separate receiver enable
Linear Technology	LTC1384	low-power shutdown with active receivers
Maxim Semiconductor	MAX223	
Dallas Semiconductor	DS276	low power, for links of 10 ft. or less
Maxim Semiconductor	MAX218	3V supply
Maxim Semiconductor	MAX252A	isolated interface

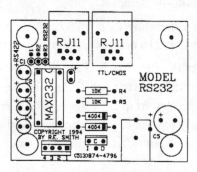

Figure 6-2: This module converts between RS-232 and TTL voltages. (Image courtesy of R.E. Smith.)

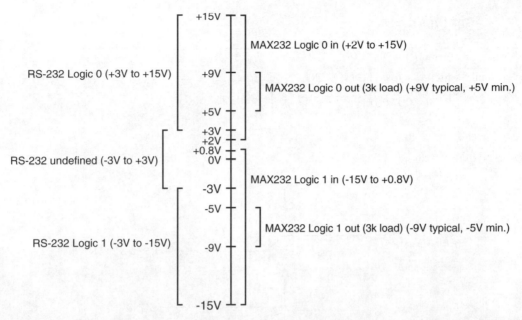

Figure 6-3: The MAX232 and other RS-232 interface chips accept TTL and 5V CMOS logic inputs.

Most of the example circuits in this book use a MAX232A or MAX233, but you can use any converter with the appropriate number of drivers and receivers.

Short-range Circuits

If you examine the data sheets for the MAX232 and similar chips, you'll see that the RS-232 inputs don't actually require RS-232 voltages. As Figure 6-3 shows, the input thresholds are identical to TTL logic, with a logic low defined as 0.8V or lower and a logic high defined as 2.0V or higher. The inputs of the '1489 also respond to TTL voltages, with 0.75V or less for logic lows, and 2.25V or more for logic highs.

This means that you can use any spare gates in a MAX232 or similar chip as low-speed inverters in a 5V circuit. It also means that in some cases you can use 5V logic to link to an RS-232 port.

Full Duplex

If your serial link is short (10 feet or less), you may be able to communicate with an RS-232 port by using an inexpensive interface that uses just 5V logic rather than RS-232 voltages.

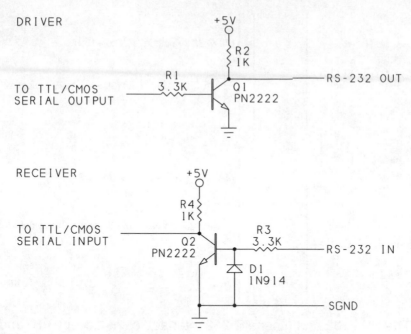

Figure 6-4: This 5V-only interface will work on many short links.

Figure 6-4 shows an option for connecting a 5V port to a remote RS-232 interface. This circuit is intended only for short links, because it doesn't meet RS-232's voltage and other requirements. But it's inexpensive and will do the job in some situations.

On the driver side, any inverted 5V logic can provide the interface. Figure 6-4 uses *Q1*, a PN2222 or other NPN general-purpose or switching transistor that acts as a simple inverter. A TTL/CMOS output drives the base of the transistor, with *R1* limiting its base current. When the TTL/CMOS output is low, *Q1* is off and *R2* pulls *RS-232 Out* near 5V. When the TTL/CMOS output is high, *Q1* switches on, and *RS-232 Out* is near 0V.

On the receiver side, an input designed for use with 5V logic can be damaged by RS-232 voltages, so it's important to protect the 5V inputs in any interface between the two.

Transistor *Q2* inverts and converts RS-232 voltages to 5V TTL/CMOS levels. *RS-232 In* drives the base of *Q2*. Resistor R3 limits *Q2*'s base current. Diode *D1* protects *Q2* by limiting its base voltage base to about -0.7V when *RS-232 In* goes negative. When *RS-232 In* is at or below 0V, *Q2* is off and R4 pulls the TTL/CMOS input to 5V. When *RS-232 In* goes positive, *Q2* switches on, bringing the TTL/CMOS input low.

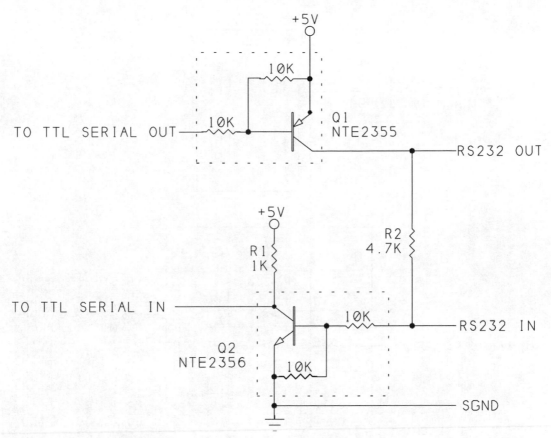

Figure 6-5: This half-duplex interface uses the RS-232 input's negative voltage to pull the RS-232 output below ground.

Half Duplex

Figure 6-5 shows an alternate 5V circuit. It has wider voltage swings than the previous circuit, but it's useful only in half-duplex links, which transmit in one direction at a time. The Basic Stamp II uses this type of interface. The negative output matches the negative transmitted voltage, and the positive output is near +5V.

The RS-232 receiver is much like the previous circuit's, but the driver's circuit is different. When *TTL Serial Out* is low, PNP transistor *Q1* is on and *RS-232 Out* equals the supply voltage, minus *Q1*'s collector-emitter voltage (a few tenths of a volt). When *TTL Serial Out* is high, *Q1* is off, and the RS-232 link loops back on itself through *R2*. *RS-232 Out* equals *RS-232 In*, minus a small voltage across *R2*. For this interface to work properly, *RS-232 In* must be idle (negative) whenever *TTL Serial Out* is transmitting.

The NTE2355 and NTE2356 transistors are designed for use as digital switches. They have built-in biasing resistors and a typical maximum frequency of 250 Mhz. Their emitter-to-base breakdown voltage is higher than most, at 10V.

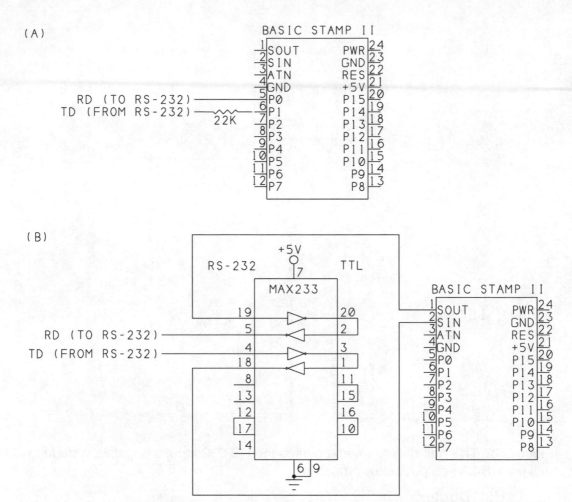

Figure 6-6: (A) For a short link to an RS-232 port, Basic Stamp I/O pins require only a series resistor at the input bit. (B) For a true RS-232 link at *Sin* and *Sout*, use a MAX233 or similar, with double inverters.

Other Options for Basic Stamps

Besides the Basic Stamp II's dedicated serial interface, the Basic Stamp I and II can use any other port bits for serial communications. The bits have TTL-compatible inputs and outputs.

A short-range interface from a Stamp's port bit to an RS-232 port requires just one resistor, as Figure 6-6A shows. This is because the Stamp's output drivers are strong enough to drive a short RS-232 link directly, and the inputs have protection diodes that limit voltages to +0.6V greater than chip's the power supply. The resistor provides additional protection by limiting input current. The Stamp's baudmode parameter must use inverted signals with this interface.

For a true RS-232 interface, you can connect a MAX232 or similar to any of the I/O port bits. If you want to use the Stamp's *Sin* and *Sout* pins, it's a little more complicated because of the Stamp's additional circuits at these pins.

The Stamp's hardware inverts the voltages at *Sin* and *Sout*, and RS-232 interface chips also invert the signals. This is no problem when using *SerIn* and *Serout* statements, because you can set baudmode to invert the signals in firmware. But when using the *Sin* and *Sout* pins for programming and debugging, there's no way to specify inverted signals. A solution is to add inverters to reinvert the signals. You can use ordinary 5V inverters, or spare MAX232 gates for this, as Figure 6-6B shows.

Port-powered Circuits

Some low-power circuits that connect to an RS-232 port don't need an external power supply. Instead, they draw all the power they need from the interface itself.

The power comes from unused outputs. To meet the standard, an RS-232 driver's output must be at least 5V with a 3,000-ohm load. From this, we can use Ohm's law to deduce that each output can source at least 1.6 milliampere at 5V. In practice, most RS-232 outputs exceed the minimum, but staying within the specification will ensure that a circuit will work on any port.

Using Signals as a Power Source

Figure 6-7 shows ways of using RS-232 outputs as a power source. When in the On state, *RTS* and *DTR* are between +5 and +15V. To set the signals to On in Visual Basic, set MSComm's RTSEnable and DTREnable properties to True.

Figure 6-7A shows a simple unregulated output. When an output is positive, it can serve as a positive voltage source. To double the output current, tie two lines together as shown, with a 1N5819 Schottky diode in each line. This prevents current from feeding back into the interface if the voltages differ. You can use any rectifier diodes, but Schottkys have a lower forward voltage than other silicon diodes.

You can even use the *TD* line as a power source by setting the Break signal, but of course this prevents you from using the line for data. However, this technique might be useful if you're using the port as a synchronous interface, using handshaking lines for the clock and data.

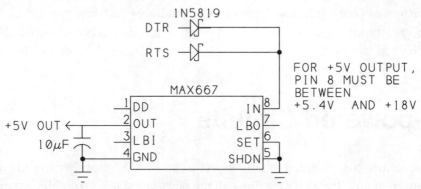

Figure 6-7: You can use spare handshaking outputs as a power source. Diodes enable using multiple outputs. For a regulated voltage, use a high-efficiency regulator like the Max667.

Regulating the Voltage

Adding a high-efficiency regulator results in a steady output voltage with little wasted power. Figure 6-7B shows a regulated 5V output using the MAX667 low-dropout, linear regulator. The input can be as high as 18V, and it needs to be just 10 millivolts greater than the output, so it will work with most ports. The regulator's quiescent current is under 100 microamperes with a load of several milliamperes.

For a circuit that will work even if the RS-232 output drops below 5V, use the MAX770, which is a switching regulator that has a 5V output with an input between 2V and 16V. The '770 requires several external components, including an inductor and output transistor. If you need only one or a few supplies, Maxim has an inexpensive evaluation kit containing a PC board with all of the components installed.

Another option for port power is to use a lower regulated voltage, either by connecting voltage-divider resistors between *Vout*, *Set*, and *Gnd* as described in the MAX667's data sheet, or by using a regulator with a lower fixed output such as the 3V MAX689.

Because you can count on getting at most a few milliamperes from the port, use care in choosing components that will use port power. Use the lowest-power components you can find, and use a 3V supply if possible.

Alternate Interfaces

If RS-232 doesn't meet your circuit's needs there may be an alternate interface that does. For some applications, a direct connection or simple 5V buffers and drivers are all that's needed. Or a different TIA/EIA interface may be more appropriate than RS-232.

Direct Connection

If the interface is between two microcontrollers or other chips whose serial ports use 5V logic, you may be able to connect the ports directly, output to input, without using RS-232 at all.

However, the outputs on many microcontrollers, such as the 8051, are quite weak. If this is the case, you can add a driver such as a 74LS240. These and similar chips can drive links up to 10 to 15 feet long. At the receiving end, a buffer with Schmitt-trigger inputs (74LS240, 74LS14) helps to reject noise. LSTTL buffer/drivers are cheaper than RS-232 interface chips. If you use inverters at the drivers, be sure to reinvert the signals at the receivers.

Other Unbalanced Interfaces

Table 6-4 compares RS-232 with other TIA/EIA interfaces that use unbalanced lines. Chapter 9 has details on TIA/EIA's balanced interfaces. (The titles of recent revisions begin with TIA/EIA, while earlier ones are EIA/TIA.)

EIA/TIA-562 defines an interface for transmitting at up 64kbps. The receiver sensitivity is identical to RS-232, but the output voltages are slightly lower, with a range from ±3.3V to ±13.2V. For data rates faster than 20 kbps, maximum capacitance must be 1000pF or less. Linear Technology's LTC1385 is an EIA/TIA-562 interface chip that operates from a single 3.3V supply.

Other alternatives use a combination of balanced and unbalanced signals. As Figure 6-8 shows, EIA/TIA-423 (commonly called RS-423) allows up to ten receivers and one transmitter. The drivers are unbalanced, like RS-232, but the receivers are balanced (and identical to RS-422's receivers, described in Chapter 9). The

Table 6-4: EIA/TIA unbalanced interfaces.

Specification	EIA/TIA-232-F	EIA-423-A	EIA/TIA-562	EIA/TIA-530-A
Cable length, max (feet), unshielded cable, 20pF/ft, 100kbits/sec	50	50	15 ft @ 64kbps	4000
Data rate, max (bits/sec)	20k	100k	64k	2.1M
Driver output (minimum, volts)	± 5	± 3.6	±3.3	± 3.3, ±2*
Driver output (maximum, volts)	± 15	± 6	±13.2	±6, ±10*
Receiver sensitivity (volts)	± 3	± 0.2	±3	±0.2
Maximum number of drivers	1	1	1	1
Maximum number receivers	1	10	1	10
Receiver input resistance (ohms)	3k-7k	450 (minimum)	3k-7k	450, 4k*

*Data and some control lines use a balanced interface. Other signals use an unbalanced interface.

receivers use the driver's output voltage and the link's signal-ground wire as the differential voltages.

EIA/TIA-530A uses balanced drivers and receivers for *TD*, *RD*, *RTS*, *CTS*, and *CD*, and unbalanced lines for *DTR*, *DSR*, and *RI*. This gives better performance

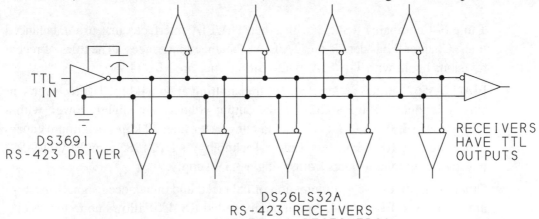

Figure 6-8: An RS-423 interface can have just one transmitter, but up to 10 receivers.

than RS-232, but requires more wires. This interface has largely replaced the earlier EIA-449, which used a 37-pin connector.

Another source for similar standards is ITU/CCITT.

7

Connectors and Cables for RS-232

An RS-232 link may use any of a number of connector types, pin configurations, and combinations of signals. Because of the many options, problems in serial links are often the result of miswired connections, so understanding this part of the link is important when designing or troubleshooting a link. This chapter discusses cables, connectors, and wiring configurations for RS-232.

Connectors

Figure 7-1 shows popular connectors used in RS-232 interfaces, and Figure 7-2 shows the pinouts of the connectors described in TIA/EIA-232. On most connectors, the pin or socket numbers are stamped near the pins or sockets, though you may have to look closely to see them.

25-pin Shells

Although the original RS-232 standard didn't recommend a connector, recent versions specify what had become a standard configuration by default. The recommended connector type is a 25-pin D-sub connector. The connector's shell is

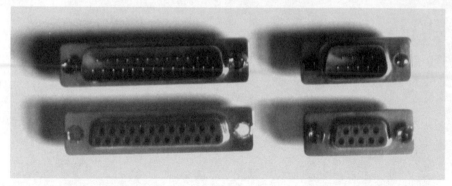

Figure 7-1: RS-232 D-sub connectors: clockwise from top left: 25-pin male, 9-pin male, 9-pin female, 25-pin female.

roughly in the shape of an upper-case D, which forces you to orient the connector correctly when you plug it in. The contacts are in two staggered rows, with the contacts in each row 0.109" apart. The DTE connector has male (pin) contacts, and the DCE has female (socket) contacts. Another name for this connector is DB-25, with the *B* indicating the shell size and *25* indicating the number of pins.

On a PC, don't confuse the parallel port's D-sub with the serial connector. On most PCs, the parallel ports use 25-pin female D-subs, while 25-pin serial ports use male connectors. Some SCSI interfaces also use a 25-pin female D-subs.

9-pin Shells

These days, most PCs use a 9-pin male D-sub connector for serial ports. These include only the nine signals described in Chapter 6. This smaller connector was introduced early in the PC's history, on IBM's model AT, probably because it leaves more room for other connectors on an expansion card's back panel. This connector is also called the DE-9, with the *E* indicating the shell size. Some sources call it the DB-9, probably because it replaced the DB-25 on the PC.

The 9-pin connector has different pin designations, even for the signals that are on pins 1–9 on the 25-pin connector. Especially confusing is that pins 2 and 3 are reversed, with pin 2 as *RD* and pin 3 as *TD*.

The Alt A Connector

For use when space is tight, the standard doesn't mention the DE-9 connector, but instead recommends a connector it calls Alt A. This connector has 26 contacts spaced 0.05" apart in each of two parallel rows, surrounded by a D-shell. The pin assignments are the same as for the 25-pin connector, with pin 26 unused. This

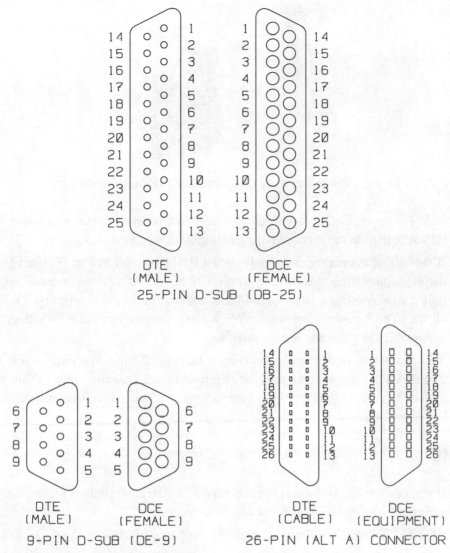

Figure 7-2: Pin locations for RS-232 connectors.

connector is the same for DTEs and DCEs. The cable always uses male connectors, and the equipment always uses female connectors.

Modular Connectors

Other connectors you may see are the modular plugs and jacks best known as the connectors on wall jacks for indoor telephone wiring (Figure 7-3). These are compact, reliable, and inexpensive solutions when there are no more than eight wires, and are commonly known by RJ codes, such as RJ-11. *RJ* stands for registered

Figure 7-3: Links with few wires may use modular phone connectors.

jack. However, the RJ codes actually refer to Universal Service Ordering Codes (USOC), that define specific wiring configurations on the jacks.

A 6-position connector commonly called RJ-11 is a WEW6 in Western Union's naming convention. (According to the USOC, an RJ-11 interface has wires on only the two middle contacts. RJ-14 uses the four middle contacts, and RJ-25 uses all six.) The 8-position connector, WEW8, is commonly called RJ-45, though this again refers to a specific 8-wire interface.

You can use 6- or 8-position connectors in RS-232 links that require few wires. The EIA/TIA-561 standard specifies a pinout for an 8-position jack (Table 7-1). It includes everything in the 9-pin interface except DSR. The 6-position connector has no recommended pinout.

Adapters

If you need to link different connector types, adapters and cables are available in a variety of configurations, or you can make your own.

All RS-232 inputs and outputs must be able to withstand a short circuit to any other RS-232 signal, including ground, without damage. This specification is very comforting when you accidently hook up a link incorrectly!

Connector Sizes

To connect a DTE to a DCE when both ends have the same size connector, the cable connects each wire straight across, pin 1 to pin 1, pin 2 to pin 2, and so on. Connecting a 9-pin to a 25-pin connector requires a cable or adapter that routes the signals correctly. Figure 7-4 illustrates.

If you do a lot with varied serial port configurations, it pays to invest in an assortment of connectors, cables, and adapters. One rule that always seems to hold true is that no matter how many types of connectors and cables you collect, you won't

SIGNAL	25-PIN CONNECTOR		9-PIN CONNECTOR
TD	2		3
RD	3		2
RTS	4		7
CTS	5		8
DSR	6		6
GND	7		5
CD	8		1
DTR	20		4
RI	22		9

Figure 7-4: Wiring for a 9-pin to 25-pin connection.

have what you need when you need it! Connectors with solder-cup or individual crimped connections are convenient because they enable you to wire connectors any way you want when necessary (Figure 7-5).

These are some of the unexpected obstacles you may face in cabling an interface:

You need to connect a 25-conductor cable to a PC with a 9-pin connector. But some 9-to-25-pin adapters are too wide to fit in the available space on the back panel. Solution: use an adapter with a short cable between the two connectors.

Figure 7-5: When making your own cables, there are several options for connecting the wires to the connector. From left to right: a ribbon cable clamps into an IDC (insulation displacement connector); individual wires solder onto solder-cup connectors; other connectors accept wires with crimp-on connectors.

Table 7-1: Recommended pinout for EIA/TIA-561 with an 8-position RJ-type connector.

Pin #	Signal
1	RI
2	CD
3	DTR
4	SG
5	RD
6	TD
7	CTS
8	RTS

Many connectors have a hex nut on either side of the D-shell, to enable the connector to screw onto the device it plugs into. Sometimes these hex nuts aren't removable, and if both connectors have them, the hex nuts keep the connectors from mating. Solution: avoid these connectors!

A 9-pin-to-9-pin cable works fine until you want to use a breakout box with 25-pin connectors. Solution: use a 9-to-25-pin adapter on each side of the breakout box.

Null Modems

Occasionally, a link will have two DTEs, or (less often) two DCEs. If you use a straight-across cable, the two *TD* outputs connect to each other, the two *RD* inputs connect to each other, and neither port sees anything sent by the other.

The solution is to use a null-modem cable or connector, which simulates a connection between a DTE and a DCE by swapping the complimentary signal and control lines. For example, each *TD* connects to the opposite end's *RD*. The name *null modem* refers to its origin as a cable that bypasses the computer-to-modem (DTE-to-DCE) connection and directly connects two computers (DTE-to-DTE).

There are several null-modem configurations (Figure 7-6).

The simplest is for 3-wire connections. The null modem swaps the *RD* and *TD* lines, so that each *TD* connects to the opposite *RD*. This is all you need if the devices don't use hardware handshaking.

The use of 25- and 9-pin connectors can lead to confusion when wiring even this simple null-modem, because it involves two sets of conversions. Use Figure 7-6's wiring to determine the null-modem connections for two connectors of the same size. Then if necessary, use Figure 7-4's wiring to convert between 9- and 25-pin connectors on one end. For example, if you're connecting a 25-pin DTE to a 9-pin

DTE, the *TD* and *RD* lines end up connected straight across, pin 2 to pin 2 and pin 3 to pin 3.

The full-handshake null modem allows hardware handshaking. Both the data and handshaking outputs connect to their corresponding inputs on the opposite device.

In a loopback null modem, the handshaking outputs are looped back to the corresponding inputs on the same device. This loopback handshaking gives the illusion of full handshaking, when in fact there is no handshake at all. The sending device just assumes that the receiving device is always ready. This is useful when one device requires handshaking signals but the other can't provide them. However, using this type of null modem will result in data errors if the receiving device can't keep up with the transmissions.

You can also use the loopback handshake in a DTE-to-DCE interface when only one device requires handshaking. In this case, the data lines connect normally, but

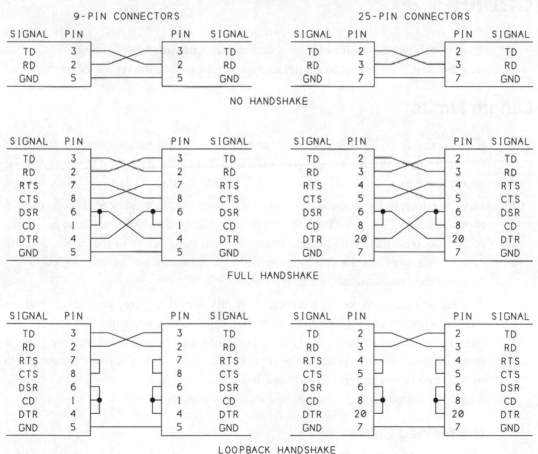

Figure 7-6: Null-modem connections for connecting two DTEs or two DCEs.

the handshaking outputs are looped back to their corresponding inputs. On a DTE, you would connect together *RTS, CTS, DSR,* and *CD.* In this way, whenever the DTE asserts *RTS*, it will also appear that the DCE is asserting *CTS, DSR*, and *CD*. A variation is to connect *RTS* to *CTS* and connect *DTR* to *DSR* and *CD*.

A final type of null modem is required for use with some serial printers. Serial printers are often configured as DTEs, so *TD* and *RD* must be swapped when connecting to a PC. Also, many printers use *DTR* as a handshaking signal, while some PC software assumes the use of *CTS*. When this is the case, the cable or an adapter must connect the printer's *DTR*, rather than *RTS*, to the PC's *CTS*.

A few older serial-port cards have jumpers that enable you to force the handshaking lines true. You can do the same thing in software.

Cables

RS-232 cables vary in number of wires and in amount and type of shielding. For long links, it's important to keep the cable length within the recommended limits.

Length Limits

Early versions of the RS-232 standard recommended limiting cable length to 50 feet, and this is still a good general guideline. For data rates of 20,000 bps or less, you can use just about any type of cable in links of up to 50 feet.

Later versions of the standard eliminate this limit and instead specify a maximum capacitance of 2500 picofarads at the receiver. This value includes the capacitance of the receiver, the mutual capacitance between conductors in the cable, and the capacitance between the conductor and the cable shield or, on unshielded cable, between the conductor and earth ground.

The capacitance has several effects. It limits the slew rate, or rate of voltage change when an output switches. A higher capacitance resulting in a lower slew rate and slower transitions. A higher capacitance also means that a voltage change requires more current to charge the capacitance, so the overall power consumption of the drivers is greater. Capacitance between wires can also result in crosstalk, where the signal on one wire also shows up on adjacent wires.

Unshielded Cable

Cable manufacturers often specify the capacitance of their products in picofarads per foot. For unshielded cable, an appendix to TIA/EIA-232 recommends adding

50 percent to the cable's capacitance to account for conductor-to-ground capacitance.

The formula to calculate cable length for unshielded cable is:

```
CableLength = _
(2500 - InputCapacitanceOfReceiver) / _
(CableCapacitance * 1.5)
```

Cable length is in feet, input capacitance in pF, and cable capacitance in pF/ft.

The standard doesn't recommend any particular cable type. Typical capacitance of ribbon cable is 15 pF/ft. Assuming that the receiver's input is 100 pF, the cable could be as long as 106 feet ((2500-100)/(15*1.5)). Typical capacitance for a single, unshielded twisted pair is 12pF/ft. Again assuming an input capacitance of 100 pF, maximum cable length is 133 feet.

Shielded Cable

Adding shielding to the cable shortens the maximum length, but shielding is sometimes required to block noise from coupling into or out of the cable. For shielded twisted-pair cable, the recommendation is to triple the value of the conductor-to-conductor capacitance to account for the conductor-to-shield capacitance.

So the formula to calculate cable length for shielded cable is:

```
CableLength = _
(2500 - InputCapacitanceOfReceiver) / _
(CableCapacitance * 3)
```

Cable length is in feet, input capacitance in pF, and cable capacitance in pF/ft.

This reduces the maximum length of shielded, twisted-pair cable to 66 feet.

If you want to use a link that exceeds the capacitance limit, you'll probably still be able to communicate, though at lower bit rates. Over short cables, with correspondingly lower capacitance, you should be able to communicate faster than 20,000 bps, if both the transmitting and receiving hardware support higher rates.

Twisted Pairs

For reduced crosstalk, you can use twisted-pair cable and multiple ground wires with RS-232. Each signal wire should be twisted with a ground wire. Chapter 10 has more on twisted pairs.

How Many Wires?

Whatever type of cable you choose, be sure that it has all of the wires your link needs! A cable with the nine wires supported by the 9-pin D-sub will handle most situations. Some serial cables have just three wires and don't support hardware handshaking. And of course, if you have 25-pin connectors on both ends, there's no harm in using a full 25-wire cable.

Many connectors are molded, with no easy way to visually inspect to find out what wires they contain. When in doubt, use an ohmmeter at the connectors to find out how many wires are in the cable.

Isolated Links

RS-232's large noise margins help to make the interface reliable and immune to data errors caused by external noise coupling into the wires. If a link's environment is electrically noisy, isolation can keep noise from coupling between the link and the circuits it connects to.

Isolation works by dividing a circuit into independent sections. The sections use optical and magnetic coupling to transfer power and data, while filtering out much of the noise.

The isolation may isolate the grounds, the data link, or both. Ground isolation makes a circuit immune to power surges and noise in the earth ground shared by nearby circuits. In long links, ground isolation also makes the link immune to differences in ground potential from end to end. Isolating the data link keeps noise from coupling between the link and the circuits it connects to.

Ways to Achieve Isolation

Most circuit connections use a direct method such as solder joints or mechanical connections such screw terminals or crimps. With galvanic isolation, a circuit's ground and signal wires have no ohmic path, or direct contact, with another circuit. Instead, the circuits may use optical or magnetic coupling to transfer power and signals. Isolation makes each circuit immune to noise in the other.

Common ways to achieve galvanic isolation include transformers to isolate power and optoisolators to isolate data. In a transformer, magnetic coupling between the windings causes current in the primary winding to induce a current in the secondary winding. Optoisolators transfer energy by means of phototransistors and photodiodes that emit and detect energy in the visible or infrared bands. In a similar way, a fiber-optic interface converts an electrical signal to light for transmitting in an optical fiber, and converts light to an electrical signal at the receiver.

For complete isolation, each end of an RS-232 link requires two things: an isolated power supply for the RS-232 interface and an isolated interface to transfer the signals across the isolation barrier.

About Grounds

Understanding isolation requires understanding the concept of ground. All current must eventually return to its source. A ground connection is any low-impedance path for this purpose. Different types of grounds include signal ground, analog and digital grounds, earth ground, and safety ground.

Signal Ground

Signal ground refers to the ground terminal of a power supply's output, and all points that connect to it. In RS-232 links, *SG* is the signal ground. Because RS-232 receivers measure voltages between the signal lines and *SG*, a noise spike on the *SG* line can cause a receiver to misread a logic level.

In digital logic, +5V is a shorthand way of saying 5 volts above signal ground. When a circuit uses more than one power supply, even if the supplies' grounds aren't isolated from each other, maintaining separate ground paths reduces the noise that couples from one path into another. The ground wires of each supply can use separate wiring and circuit-board traces, connecting together only at the supplies.

Circuits that contain both analog and digital circuits may provide a separate ground for each, connecting the two paths at only one point, near the power supply. Digital grounds tend to be noisy, because digital outputs draw high currents when they switch, so it makes sense to separate them from analog circuits, which may be sensitive to tiny voltage changes.

Safety Ground

Safety ground, or protective ground, is an earth-ground connection, which is commonly a large-diameter copper wire or copper-plated pipe partially buried underground. One of the three wires at an electrical outlet's wall socket connects to a safety ground.

The other wires at the outlet are the hot wire, which carries the 115VAC line voltage, and the neutral wire, which carries the 115VAC's return current. The neutral wire connects to the safety ground at the service entrance to the building. This means that the neutral wires of all of a building's circuits normally have a common connection at the service entrance.

The safety ground provides a low-impedance path to ground in case of a fault. For example, in many power supplies, a screw terminal connects the safety-ground wire to the supply's metal chassis. If the chassis isn't grounded and a loose wire or component failure causes a voltage source to contact the chassis, the chassis may carry a high voltage. This results in danger of electrical shock if someone touches the chassis while in contact with electrical ground. If the chassis is grounded, current instead follows the low-impedance path to earth ground until a fuse blows and the circuit opens, removing the danger.

The TIA/EIA-232 standard says that a DCE may have a removable strap to connect *SG* to safety ground. In reality, the *SG* line on both DCEs and DTEs often connects to a safety ground.

Earth Ground

Earth ground refers to the electrical potential of the earth itself. A safety ground is an earth ground. Because any electrical circuit may connect to earth ground, it's usually not a quiet, stable reference, but may carry huge amounts of noise of all types. Events that can cause ground noise include equipment switching on and off, power-system fluctuations, circuit malfunctions, lightning strikes, or anything that causes a surge in current. The noise may show up as dips, spikes, 60-Hz oscillations, or just about any other type of variation you can imagine.

Earth grounds at different locations may or may not connect electrically to each other. Whether or not they do, and how much the ground voltages vary, depends partly on how well the medium between the ground connections conducts electricity. Within a building, the electrical wiring provides a common connection to earth ground. Between buildings or over long distances, current will follow whatever path it can find. Wet soil is a better conductor than solid granite.

Effects of Common Grounds

If the two ends of an RS-232 link share a common earth ground and the *SG* line also connects to safety ground, ground currents from all sources will choose the path of least resistance: earth ground or the *SG* wire. This situation, where there are multiple return paths, is called a ground loop, and is not desirable! If the two devices are in different buildings, using different power systems, *SG* is likely to have lower impedance than other paths, and ground currents from other sources may find their way into the link's ground wire. The result is a noisy ground in the link. A link with isolated grounds avoids this problem.

Power Supply Grounds

An isolated interface requires a power supply for each side of the isolation barrier. Figure 7-7 shows two isolated RS-232 interfaces. Each uses a dual power supply, where a transformer steps 115VAC to lower voltages on two secondary windings. One winding provides voltage for the computer or other circuits that connect to equipment side of the optoisolator. The other winding provides the voltage for the RS-232 interface. Each supply has its own ground, and the grounds must have no common connection to an earth ground, the chassis, or signal ground. Instead of one supply with two windings, the interface may use two entirely separate power supplies or batteries whose outputs don't share a common ground.

How do you know if a DC supply isolated from earth ground? The answer requires knowing something about what's inside the supply.

In most DC supplies powered by line voltage, a transformer steps the line voltage to a lower value, and other components rectify, filter, and regulate the transformer's output to a steady DC value. The only connection required between the transformer's primary and secondary windings is the magnetic coupling induced when current flows in the primary. The transformer thus has the ability to isolate the power supply's outputs from the line-voltage wiring and safety ground.

In fact, the outputs of some power supplies for digital circuits have no connection to safety ground. There is little risk of electrical shock at the outputs because the voltages are low, the regulator limits the current, and a fuse opens the circuit if it tries to draw large currents.

In other supplies, the output's ground terminal connects to safety ground, breaking the isolation. The result is a shared ground with any other circuits that also connect to the safety ground, or earth ground. A connection may exist even if the circuits are in different buildings or thousands of feet apart.

The safest route is to assume that a supply's ground isn't isolated unless you can prove that it is. Don't assume that the *SG* pin on a PC's RS-232 or RS-485 port is isolated from earth ground; it may not be.

A supply with a 2-wire power plug may appear to have no safety-ground connection, but don't forget that the neutral wire connects to safety ground when the supply is plugged in. The supply's output is isolated only if its ground line doesn't connect to the neutral wire.

For supplies that contain a transformer, you can use an ohmmeter to find out if the output is isolated from safety ground. *With the supply unplugged from the wall socket,* measure the resistance between safety ground on the supply's AC power plug and the DC output's ground terminal. If the meter shows a connection,

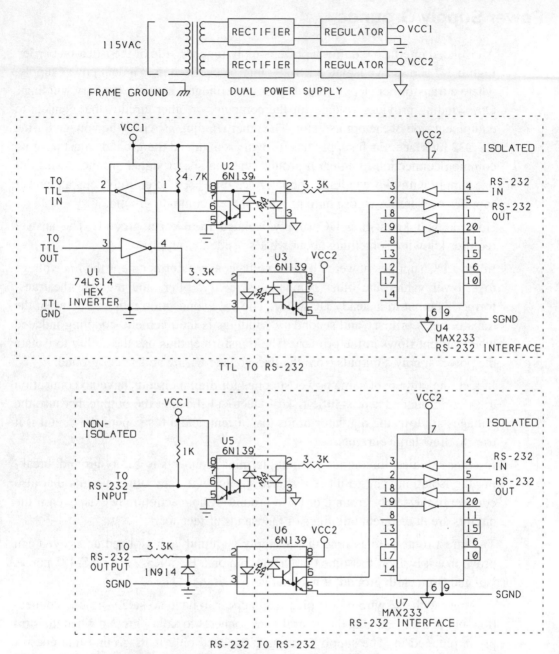

Figure 7-7: Optoisolators created an isolated interface from TTL to RS-232, or from an existing RS-232 interface to isolated RS-232.

there's no isolation. The neutral wire and safety ground should have no connection inside the supply. You can verify this with an ohmmeter as well.

Some supplies don't use transformers. They just rectify, reduce, and filter the line voltage directly. In this case, the output isn't isolated from earth ground. Even if the power plug has no safety-ground pin, the neutral wire connects to safety ground when the supply is plugged in.

Optoisolating

Optoisolators transfer signals across an isolation barrier. An optoisolator consists of a photodiode coupled to a phototransistor. Current through the photodiode causes it to emit energy in the visible or infrared band. The energy switches the phototransistor on, resulting in a low resistance between the transistor's emitter and collector. The phototransistor's base may be left unconnected. Adding a resistor from base to emitter results in faster switching but lower output current.

Figure 7-7's interfaces use 6N139 optoisolators, which are designed for direct interfacing to LSTTL logic. Their gain is high: 400% with a photodiode current of just 0.5 milliamp. In the TTL-to-RS-232 circuit, a logic low at pin 3 of the 74LS14 inverter causes current to flow through the photodiode. This switches on the corresponding phototransistor, bringing its collector low. The MAX233 inverts the signal and transmits a positive RS-232 voltage.

A logic high on pin 3 of the 74LS14 switches off the photodiode and phototransistor. The MAX233's internal pullup at pin 2 results in a negative RS-232 voltage.

The other direction works in a similar way. A negative RS-232 input causes the MAX233 to output a logic high. This switches on the photodiode and its phototransistor, resulting in a logic low at pin 1 and a logic high at pin 2 of the 74LS14. A positive RS-232 input causes the MAX233 to output a logic low. This switches the photodiode and its phototransistor off. A pullup brings pin 1 of the 74LS14 high, resulting in a logic low at pin 2.

The RS-232-to-RS-232 circuit shows how to isolate an existing, non-isolated RS-232 interface by using an RS-232 output to drive a photodiode directly. When the RS-232 voltage is positive, the photodiode is on, and the isolated RS-232 output is also positive. When the non-isolated output is negative, the photodiode is off and a diode clamps the voltage at about -0.7V. In the other direction, the circuits are similar to the top circuits, except that no 'LS14 inverter is needed because the non-isolated RS-232 interface inverts the signal.

For *VCC1* in the bottom circuit, you can use a positive output at *DTR* or *RTS*, if it's otherwise unused. The cable on the *VCC1* side of this circuit should be short.

Typical turn-on and turn-off times for phototransistors is several microseconds, which should cause no problems at data rates of 20kbps or less. For fast bit rates, look for a photodiode with switching times of 1/10 or less of the bit width.

Another way to achieve an isolated interface is to use separate, isolated ±12V supplies for the RS-232 side of the interface. This also enables you to use the cheaper 1488/9 drivers and receivers.

If you don't want to build your own isolation circuits, the Max252 is a complete, isolated RS-232 interface in a single package. The chip includes an oscillator and tiny transformer to generate an isolated supply from the chip's 5V supply. It also has two optoisolated driver/receiver pairs.

Fiber Optics

A completely different way to isolate a link is to use fiber optic cable in place of copper wire. Fiber optic cable carries signals in the form of the presence or absence of light, or it may use more complex encoding methods.

Fiber optics have several advantages. They are immune to ground noise and electromagnetic interference, and they generate no electromagnetic interface. A cable typically can run 1 to 2.5 miles before requiring a repeater.

The main disadvantage is expense, including the need for special tools and connectors.

Surge Protection

Another way to protect circuits from noise or damaging voltages and currents is surge protection. The ideal surge protection would absorb all voltages and currents outside the link's operating range, while not limiting the link's transmissions in any way. In real life, a variety of devices can protect a link from many disasters due to voltage surges, though all add some capacitance to the link, and thus limit the maximum bit rate.

In normal operation, the protection device presents a high impedance and is virtually invisible to the transmitting circuits. When the line sees a high-voltage surge, the protection device switches on, providing a low-impedance path to ground.

Two useful surge-suppression devices are TVS diodes and gas-discharge tubes. TVS (transient voltage suppression) diodes have low capacitance when off, respond quickly (1 picosecond), and are available in many breakdown-voltage ranges. Gas-discharge tubes are slower, but can protect against higher voltages. Some links use both. Each should connect through a ground strap or other low-impedance connection directly to an earth ground.

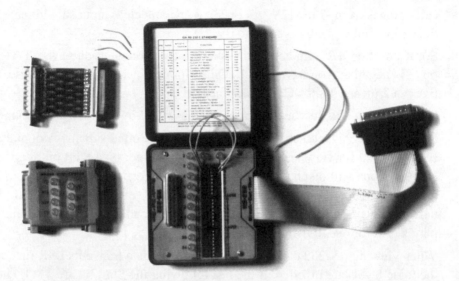

Figure 7-8: Breakout boxes may include LEDs that show the signal states and jumpers or switches to enable different wiring configurations.

Troubleshooting Tools

A breakout box, voltmeter, and oscilloscope are all helpful tools when you're setting up or troubleshooting a serial link.

A breakout box (Figure 7-8) connects in series with a serial cable, and displays the status of each line in the link.

LEDs indicate the logic states. Some boxes have separate red and green LEDs, while others use bicolor LEDs that can display both colors. Red indicates a negative voltage; green indicates positive. Some boxes also have jumper connections that enable you to rewire the interface in any configuration, for example, to determine what type of null modem the link requires.

If you lack a breakout box, you can monitor the lines one at a time with a voltmeter. If you're not sure whether a connector is wired as a DTE or DCE, a voltmeter is all you need to identify which of pins 2 and 3 is the data input, and which is the data output. An oscilloscope will also work for this, of course.

You can measure directly at the port connector, or on the connector at the end of the cable, whichever is more convenient. Measure on a port that is powered, but idle (not currently in use).

On the connector, measure the voltage from pin 2 to signal ground (pin 7 on a 25-pin connector, pin 5 on a 9-pin). Also measure from pin 3 to signal ground. On an idle port, an output should measure a negative voltage of at least -5V, and typically ranges from -7 to -12V. An open, or unconnected, input should measure less than +2V, and typically is close to 0V.

So, if pin 2 on a 25-pin connector is a negative voltage, you have a DTE, and if pin 3 is negative, you have a DCE. On a 9-pin connector, it's the reverse: a negative pin 2 means it's a DCE, while a negative pin 3 mean it's a DTE.

On a breakout box, just see which of *TD* and *RD* shows the negative voltage.

Sometimes there's no substitute for watching the actual signals. A digital oscilloscope is ideal for viewing serial data. You can trigger on a Start bit or control line and the scope will display and preserve the waveform to examine at your leisure. You can save a waveform and compare it to waveforms captured later. If the timebase has a variable control, you can simplify the reading of bits by setting the display's grid for one division per bit.

When viewing RS-232 data, don't forget that the data transmits LSB first, and that the logic levels are inverted. If the bits following the Start bit are 1111 1110 from left to right on the screen, their byte value is 80h, not FEh or 7Fh.

A logic analyzer is another good tool for viewing serial data. Many logic analyzers have eight or more channels, which enables you to view multiple data and handshaking lines at once. Also available are hardware and software tools designed specifically for debugging serial links, including triggering on specific characters and other functions for detecting and analyzing signals.

8

RS-232 Applications

This chapter shows examples of RS-232 links, including an application that enables a PC to exchange data with another PC or a microcontroller, ways to use RS-232 for direct control and monitoring of remote signals, and tips on using the built-in communications tools in Windows and DOS.

Linking Two Computers

Figure 8-1 is the user screen for an application that uses a serial link to enable a local computer to communicate with a remote computer. Listing 8-1 is the program code for the application, which builds on the template application introduced in Chapter 4. You can use the code as a starting point for programming a monitoring or control link between PCs, or between a PC and a Basic Stamp or 8052-Basic system. You can modify it as needed for use with other CPUs.

A 2-PC Link

Connecting two PCs' RS-232 ports is usually just a matter of hooking up the cable. Both ports will almost certainly be configured as DTEs, so you'll need a null-modem cable or adapter, as described in Chapter 7. The application also works fine with a full-duplex RS-485 link, as described in Chapter 9.

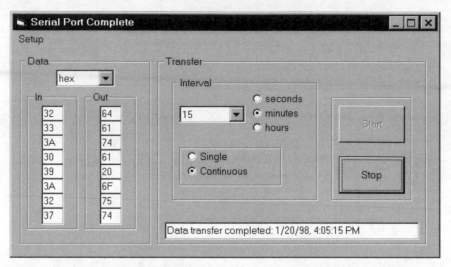

Figure 8-1: This program exchanges blocks of eight bytes with a remote computer.

Basic Operation

The PCs exchange blocks of eight bytes. The bytes may contain commands, data, or other information. The local PC sends eight bytes, then waits for the remote PC to send eight bytes in return.

An option button selects Single or Continuous data transfers. In Single mode, clicking *Start* causes the PC to transfer data once. In Continuous mode, the PC transfers data repeatedly, at the selected interval. Option buttons and a combo box select the interval length in seconds, minutes, or hours.

Text boxes display the bytes sent and received. A Status text box indicates the date and time of each transfer and whether it succeeded or failed.

You can program the remote computer in Visual Basic, QBasic, or a different language entirely. A Visual Basic program for the remote PC would be similar to Listing 8-1's, but simpler, because the remote PC just waits to receive data, then replies. This book's program disk includes DOS QuickBasic code for a remote PC.

The example program exchanges simple test data. In an application, the data may consist of readings or settings for I/O ports, commands, or anything else the computers need to exchange. Instead of blocks of eight bytes, the programs may exchange blocks of any size, or entire files.

```
Option Explicit
'This program uses a serial port to
'exchange blocks of 8 bytes with a remote computer.
Private Type typDataTransferFormat
    SingleOrContinuous As String
    IntervalUnits As String
    IntervalValue As Single
End Type
Dim DataOut(7) As Byte
Dim DataIn(7) As Byte
Dim DataTransferFormat As typDataTransferFormat
Dim PreviousTime As Date
Dim TimeOfTransfer As String
Dim Timeout As Boolean
Dim TransferInProgress As Boolean
Public RemoteCPU As String
Public SaveDataInFile As Boolean
```

```
Private Sub cboDataFormat_Click()
'Change the display to match the selected format.
Dim Count As Integer
Select Case cboDataFormat.Text
    Case "text"
        For Count = 0 To 7
            txtDataOut(Count).Text = Chr$(DataOut(Count))
            txtDataIn(Count).Text = Chr$(DataIn(Count))
        Next Count
    Case "decimal"
        For Count = 0 To 7
            txtDataOut(Count).Text = CStr(DataOut(Count))
            txtDataIn(Count).Text = CStr(DataIn(Count))
        Next Count
    Case "hex"
        For Count = 0 To 7
            txtDataOut(Count).Text = Hex$(DataOut(Count))
            txtDataIn(Count).Text = Hex$(DataIn(Count))
        Next Count
End Select
End Sub
```

Listing 8-1: Code for the PC's main form. (Sheet 1 of 13)

```
Private Sub cboIntervalValue_Click()
'Store the selected interval.
DataTransferFormat.IntervalValue = Val(cboIntervalValue.Text)
'With shorter intervals, check elapsed time more often.
Select Case DataTransferFormat.IntervalUnits
    Case "seconds"
        tmrTransferInterval.Interval = 100
    Case "minutes", "hours"
        tmrTransferInterval.Interval = 1000
End Select
End Sub
```

```
Private Sub cmdStart_Click()
'Initiate data transfer in the selected format.
Select Case DataTransferFormat.SingleOrContinuous
    Case "single"
        'Transfer data once.
        Call TransferData(DataTransferFormat)
    Case "continuous"
        cmdStart.Enabled = False
        cmdStop.Enabled = True
        cmdStop.SetFocus
        PreviousTime = Now
        tmrTransferInterval.Enabled = True
        'Do one transfer immediately, then let the timer take over.
        Call TransferData(DataTransferFormat)
End Select
End Sub
```

```
Private Sub cmdStop_Click()
'Stop transferring data.
tmrTransferInterval.Enabled = False
cmdStop.Enabled = False
cmdStart.Enabled = True
End Sub
```

Listing 8-1: Code for the PC's main form. (Sheet 2 of 13)

```
Private Sub DisplayDataToSend()
Dim Count As Integer
Select Case cboDataFormat.Text
    Case "text"
        For Count = 0 To 7
            txtDataOut(Count).Text = Chr$(DataOut(Count))
        Next Count
    Case "decimal"
        For Count = 0 To 7
            txtDataOut(Count) = DataOut(Count)
        Next Count
     Case "hex"
        For Count = 0 To 7
            txtDataOut(Count) = Hex$(DataOut(Count))
        Next Count
    End Select
End Sub
```

```
Private Sub DisplayReceivedData()
Dim Count As Integer
Select Case cboDataFormat.Text
    Case "text"
        For Count = 0 To 7
            txtDataIn(Count).Text = Chr$(DataIn(Count))
        Next Count
    Case "decimal"
        For Count = 0 To 7
            txtDataIn(Count) = DataIn(Count)
        Next Count
     Case "hex"
        For Count = 0 To 7
            txtDataIn(Count) = Hex$(DataIn(Count))
        Next Count
    End Select
End Sub
```

```
Private Function fncDisplayDateAndTime() As String
'Date and time formatting.
fncDisplayDateAndTime = _
    CStr(Format(Date, "General Date")) & ", " & _
        (Format(Time, "Long Time"))
End Function
```

Listing 8-1: Code for the PC's main form. (Sheet 3 of 13)

```
Private Function fncGet8052sAttention() As Boolean
'Send a byte to the 8052-Basic & wait for a response.
'Give up on timeout.
Dim ByteArray(0) As Byte
Dim OutputBuffer As Variant
Dim InputData() As Byte
'Use Control+A to signal the 8052:
Const Attention = 1
'Use Control+F for Acknowledge.
Const Acknowledge = 6
Timeout = False
tmrTimeout.Interval = 2000
ByteArray(0) = Attention
OutputBuffer = ByteArray()
'Send the byte.
MSComm1.Output = OutputBuffer
'Wait for the 8052 to reply.
tmrTimeout.Enabled = True
Do
    DoEvents
Loop Until (MSComm1.InBufferCount > 0) Or (Timeout = True)
If Timeout = False Then
    tmrTimeout.Enabled = False
    'Read the received byte.
    Buffer = MSComm1.Input
    InputData() = Buffer
    'The 8052 returns an Acknowledge.
    If InputData(0) = Acknowledge Then
        fncGet8052sAttention = True
        'Short delay to enable the 8052
        'to execute an Input statement.
        Call LowResDelay(0.2)
    Else
        fncGet8052sAttention = False
        txtStatus.Text = _
          "Incorrect response from 8052, " & fncDisplayDateAndTime
    End If
Else
    txtStatus.Text = _
      "No response from 8052, " & fncDisplayDateAndTime
End If
End Function
```

Listing 8-1: Code for the PC's main form. (Sheet 4 of 13)

Serial Port Complete

```
Private Function fncGetStampsAttention() As Boolean
'Send a byte repeatedly until the Stamp responds or timeout.
'Give up on timeout.
Dim ByteArray(0) As Byte
Dim OutputBuffer As Variant
Dim DelayBetweenBytes As Single
Const Attention = &HA5
Const Acknowledge = &HA6
Timeout = False
tmrTimeout.Interval = 2000
'Delay 2 byte widths between bytes
'to make it easier for the Stamp to detect the Start bit.
DelayBetweenBytes = fncOneByteDelay(CSng(BitRate)) * 2
'The Stamp watches for the Attention byte.
ByteArray(0) = Attention
'Wait for the Stamp to send a byte in reply.
tmrTimeout.Enabled = True
Do
    OutputBuffer = ByteArray()
    MSComm1.Output = OutputBuffer
    Call Delay(DelayBetweenBytes)
Loop Until (MSComm1.InBufferCount > 0) Or (Timeout = True)
If Timeout = False Then
        tmrTimeout.Enabled = False
        'Read the received byte.
        Buffer = MSComm1.Input
        'The Stamp returns an Acknowledge.
        If Buffer(0) = Acknowledge Then
            fncGetStampsAttention = True
            'Short delay to enable Stamp _
            'to execute Serin statement.
            Call LowResDelay(0.2)
        Else
            fncGetStampsAttention = False
            txtStatus.Text = _
                "Incorrect response from Stamp, " & _
                    fncDisplayDateAndTime
        End If
Else
    txtStatus.Text = _
        "No response from Stamp, " & fncDisplayDateAndTime
End If
End Function
```

Listing 8-1: Code for the PC's main form. (Sheet 5 of 13)

```
Private Sub Form_Load()
Show
Call Startup
Call GetSettings
TransferInProgress = False
Timeout = False
tmrTimeout.Interval = 3000
tmrTransferInterval.Enabled = False
Call InitializeDisplayElements
SaveDataInFile = False
Load frmRemoteCPU
End Sub
```

```
Private Sub Form_Unload(Cancel As Integer)
Call SaveSettings
Call ShutDown
Close #2
Unload frmRemoteCPU
Unload frmDataFile
End
End Sub
```

```
Private Sub GetDataToSend()
'Collect the 8 bytes to send to the remote computer
'and store them in DataOut()
'Dummy data for testing:
DataOut(0) = AscB("d")
DataOut(1) = AscB("a")
DataOut(2) = AscB("t")
DataOut(3) = AscB("a")
DataOut(4) = &H20      'space
DataOut(5) = AscB("o")
DataOut(6) = AscB("u")
DataOut(7) = AscB("t")
End Sub
```

```
Private Sub InitializeDataFormatComboBox()
cboDataFormat.AddItem "text"
cboDataFormat.AddItem "decimal"
cboDataFormat.AddItem "hex"
End Sub
```

Listing 8-1: Code for the PC's main form. (Sheet 6 of 13)

```
Private Sub InitializeDisplayElements()
Dim Count As Integer
Call InitializeDataFormatComboBox
optSingleOrContinuous(0).Value = True
optIntervalUnits(0).Value = True
cboIntervalValue.ListIndex = 0
cboDataFormat.ListIndex = 0
txtStatus.Locked = True
For Count = 0 To 7
    txtDataIn(Count).Locked = True
Next Count
txtStatus.Text = ""
DataTransferFormat.IntervalValue = 1
cmdStop.Enabled = False
End Sub
```

```
Private Sub mnuDataFile_Click(Index As Integer)
frmDataFile.Show
End Sub
```

```
Private Sub mnuPortSettings_Click(Index As Integer)
frmPortSettings.Show
End Sub
```

```
Private Sub mnuRemoteCPU_Click(Index As Integer)
frmRemoteCPU.Show
End Sub
```

Listing 8-1: Code for the PC's main form. (Sheet 7 of 13)

```
Private Sub optIntervalUnits_Click(Index As Integer)
'Configure the interval combo box to match the units selected.
Dim Maximum As Integer
Dim Count As Integer
cboIntervalValue.Clear
Select Case Index
    Case 0
        Maximum = 59
        DataTransferFormat.IntervalUnits = "seconds"
    Case 1
        Maximum = 59
        DataTransferFormat.IntervalUnits = "minutes"
    Case 2
        Maximum = 24
        DataTransferFormat.IntervalUnits = "hours"
End Select
For Count = 1 To Maximum
    cboIntervalValue.AddItem CStr(Count)
Next Count
End Sub
```

```
Private Sub optSingleOrContinuous_Click(Index As Integer)
Select Case Index
    Case 0
        DataTransferFormat.SingleOrContinuous = "single"
        'Disable interval selection:
        optIntervalUnits(0).Enabled = False
        optIntervalUnits(1).Enabled = False
        optIntervalUnits(2).Enabled = False
    Case 1
        DataTransferFormat.SingleOrContinuous = "continuous"
        'Enable interval selection:
        optIntervalUnits(0).Enabled = True
        optIntervalUnits(1).Enabled = True
        optIntervalUnits(2).Enabled = True
End Select
End Sub
```

Listing 8-1: Code for the PC's main form. (Sheet 8 of 13)

```
Private Sub ReceiveData()
'Receive and display data from the remote computer.
Dim InputBuffer As Variant
Dim Count As Integer
Dim ByteArray() As Byte
Dim BytesIn As Integer
Dim ByteCount As Integer


'Time out if no response
tmrTimeout.Enabled = True
Timeout = False
'8052-Basic echoes the received data, plus CR+LF.
'So the PC receives 10 additional bytes from an 8052.
If RemoteCPU = "8052-Basic" Then
    ByteCount = 18
Else
    ByteCount = 8
End If
'Wait for the bytes to arrive
Do
    DoEvents
    BytesIn = MSComm1.InBufferCount
Loop Until (BytesIn >= ByteCount) Or (Timeout = True)
If Timeout = True Then
    Timeout = False
    txtStatus.Text = _
        "Remote computer not responding: " & _
            fncDisplayDateAndTime
Else
    tmrTimeout.Enabled = False
    'Get and display received data.
    InputBuffer = MSComm1.Input
    'Assign the variant's contents
    'to a variable-length byte array.
    ByteArray() = InputBuffer
    'Store the byte array's contents in DataIn.
    'For 8052-Basic, ignore the first ten bytes.
    For Count = 0 To 7
        DataIn(Count) = ByteArray(Count + ByteCount - 8)
    Next Count
    Call DisplayReceivedData
End If
End Sub
```

Listing 8-1: Code for the PC's main form. (Sheet 9 of 13)

```
Private Sub SendData()
'Send data to the remote computer.
Dim OutputBuffer As Variant
Dim CarriageReturn(0) As Byte
'The 8052-Basic's Input statement requires a carriage return.
CarriageReturn(0) = &HD
'Get the data to send, display it, & write it to the serial port.
Call GetDataToSend
Call DisplayDataToSend
'Assign the byte array to a variant.
OutputBuffer = DataOut()
'Write the variant to the serial port.
MSComm1.Output = OutputBuffer
If RemoteCPU = "8052-Basic" Then
    OutputBuffer = CarriageReturn()
    MSComm1.Output = OutputBuffer
End If
End Sub
```

```
Private Sub StoreReceivedData()
'Save received data and time in a file.
Write #2, _
    TimeOfTransfer, _
    CStr(DataIn(0)), _
    CStr(DataIn(1)), _
    CStr(DataIn(2)), _
    CStr(DataIn(3)), _
    CStr(DataIn(4)), _
    CStr(DataIn(5)), _
    CStr(DataIn(6)), _
    CStr(DataIn(7))
End Sub
```

```
Private Sub tmrTimeout_Timer()
tmrTimeout.Enabled = False
Timeout = True
End Sub
```

Listing 8-1: Code for the PC's main form. (Sheet 10 of 13)

Serial Port Complete

```
Private Sub tmrTransferInterval_Timer()
'See if it's time to do a transfer.
Dim CurrentTime As Date
Dim Units As String
CurrentTime = Now
Select Case DataTransferFormat.IntervalUnits
    Case "seconds"
        Units = "s"
    Case "minutes"
        Units = "n"
    Case "hours"
        Units = "h"
End Select
'If elapsed time since the last transfer is more than
'the selected seconds, minutes, or hours, do a data transfer.
If DateDiff(Units, PreviousTime, CurrentTime) >= _
        DataTransferFormat.IntervalValue Then
    PreviousTime = CurrentTime
    'But don't start a new transfer if one is in progress.
    If TransferInProgress = False Then
        Call TransferData(DataTransferFormat)
    End If
End If
End Sub
```

Listing 8-1: Code for the PC's main form. (Sheet 11 of 13)

```
Private Sub TransferData _
    (DataTransferFormat As typDataTransferFormat)
Dim ClearToSend As Boolean
TransferInProgress = True
txtStatus.Text = ""
MSComm1.InBufferCount = 0
'If necessary, get the remote CPU's attention.
Select Case RemoteCPU
    Case "PC"
        ClearToSend = True
    Case "Basic Stamp"
        ClearToSend = fncGetStampsAttention
    Case "8052-Basic"
        ClearToSend = fncGet8052sAttention
End Select
If ClearToSend = True Then
    Call SendData
    Call ReceiveData
    TimeOfTransfer = fncDisplayDateAndTime
    If txtStatus.Text = "" Then
        txtStatus.Text = _
            "Data transfer completed: " & TimeOfTransfer
    End If
    If SaveDataInFile = True Then
        Call StoreReceivedData
    End If
End If
TransferInProgress = False
End Sub
```

Listing 8-1: Code for the PC's main form. (Sheet 12 of 13)

```
Public Function fncInitializeComPort _
    (BitRate As Long, PortNumber As Integer) As Boolean
'BitRate and PortNumber are passed to this routine.
'All other properties are set explicitly in the routine.
Dim ComSettings$
If MSComm1.PortOpen = True Then
    MSComm1.PortOpen = False
End If
ComSettings = CStr(BitRate) & ",N,8,1"
    MSComm1.CommPort = PortNumber
    ' bit rate, no parity, 8 data, and 1 stop bit.
    MSComm1.Settings = ComSettings
    'Set to 0 to read entire buffer on Input
    MSComm1.InputLen = 0
    MSComm1.InBufferSize = 256
    'Input and output data are the contents of a byte array
    'stored in a variant.
    MSComm1.InputMode = comInputModeBinary
    'MSComm does no handshaking.
    MSComm1.Handshaking = comNone
    MSComm1.OutBufferSize = 256
    MSComm1.EOFEnable = False
    'No OnComm event on received data.
    MSComm1.RThreshold = 0
    'No OnComm transmit event.
    MSComm1.SThreshold = 0
    MSComm1.PortOpen = True: fncInitializeComPort = True
End Function
```

Listing 8-1: Code for the PC's main form. (Sheet 13 of 13)

Selecting a Remote CPU

An added menu item to the template application is *Remote CPU*, which brings up Figure 8-2's form. Listing 8-2 is the code for this form, which sets the Remo-

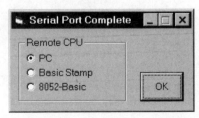

Figure 8-2: The application can communicate with several CPU types.

```
Option Explicit
'Enables the user to specify the type of remote computer.
'Each has different communication requirements.
```

```
Private Sub cmdOK_Click()
Dim Index As Integer
Index = -1
Do
    Index = Index + 1
Loop Until optRemoteCPU(Index).Value = True
Select Case Index
    Case 0
        frmMain.RemoteCPU = "PC"
    Case 1
        frmMain.RemoteCPU = "Basic Stamp"
    Case 2
        frmMain.RemoteCPU = "8052-Basic"
End Select
Hide
End Sub
```

```
Private Sub Form_Load()
optRemoteCPU(0).Value = True
Call GetSettings
End Sub
```

```
Private Sub Form_Unload(Cancel As Integer)
Call SaveSettings
End Sub
```

```
Private Sub GetSettings()
Dim Index As Integer
Index = -1
frmMain.RemoteCPU = _
  GetSetting(ProjectName, "Startup", "RemoteCPU", "PC")
Do
    Index = Index + 1
Loop Until optRemoteCPU(Index).Caption = _
  frmMain.RemoteCPU Or Index = 2
optRemoteCPU(Index).Value = True
End Sub
```

Listing 8-2: Code for Figure 8-2's form.

```
Private Sub SaveSettings()
SaveSetting ProjectName, "Startup", "RemoteCPU",
 frmMain.RemoteCPU
End Sub
```

Listing 8-2: Code for Figure 8-2's form.

teCPU variable to the appropriate value. The main application uses this information to handle specific needs of different CPUs.

PC-to-Basic Stamp Link

Figure 8-3 shows a link between a PC and a Basic Stamp II. The link uses a true RS-232 interface to link two of the Stamp's port pins to a PC's serial port. A MAX233 converts to RS-232 voltages. This circuit leaves the Stamp's *Sin* and *Sout* pins unused, though you can connect them to another PC's serial port for development and debugging.

The Stamp communicates with the PC as in the previous example, exchanging blocks of eight bytes. Listing 8-3 is the Stamp's program code.

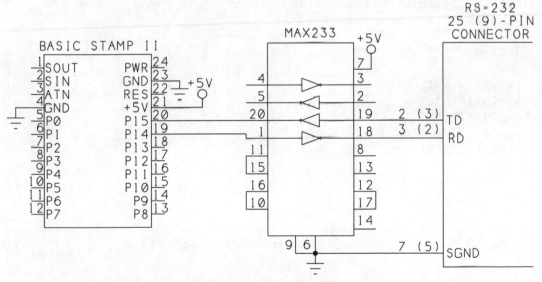

Figure 8-3: A link between a Basic Stamp and a PC.

```
'StampII RS-232 link to PC.
'The PC and Stamp exchange blocks of 8 bytes.
'All debug statements are for troubleshooting & may be removed.

'Variables:
DataIn var byte(8)
DataOut var byte(8)

Constants:
'Serial I/O bits:
'serial transmit output
SerialOutput con 14
'serial receive input
SerialInput con 15

Attention con $A5
Acknowledge con $A6

'Serial transmissions are at 2400 bps, noninverted, 8-N-1
BaudMode con 396

'Timeouts are 2 seconds.
TimeOut con 2000

'Bits 0-13 are undefined (free for any use).
'Bits 14-15 are for serial link:
dir14=1
dir15=0

'Default test data:
DataOut(0)="1"
DataOut(1)="2"
DataOut(2)="3"
DataOut(3)="4"
DataOut(4)="5"
DataOut(5)="6"
DataOut(6)="7"
DataOut(7)="8"
```

Listing 8-3: Basic Stamp II code for an RS-232 link. (Sheet 1 of 2)

```
'main program loop:
debug "Waiting to receive data...",cr
begin:
gosub NodeActivities
'Wait for a byte or timeout.
'Skip the first byte received. (It may be a partial byte.)
'If the expected byte is received, send a reply
serin serialinput,baudmode,timeout,Begin,[Skip 1, DataIn(0)]
debug "received ",dec DataIn(0),cr
if DataIn(0)=Attention then TransferData
goto begin
end

NoData:
debug "No data received.",cr
GoTo Begin

TransferData:
'Send acknowledge byte.
debug "sending ack",cr
serout SerialOutput,BaudMode, [Acknowledge]
'Wait to ensure PC has stopped sending Attention byte.
pause 100
'Read incoming bytes.
Serin SerialInput,baudmode,timeout,NoData,[DataIn(0), DataIn(1),
  DataIn(2), DataIn(3), DataIn(4), DataIn(5), DataIn(6), DataIn(7)
  ]
debug "Received: ",DataIn(0), DataIn(1), DataIn(2), DataIn(3),
  DataIn(4), DataIn(5), DataIn(6), DataIn(7),cr
'Send 8 bytes
serout SerialOutput,Baudmode,[DataOut(0), DataOut(1),
  DataOut(2), DataOut(3), DataOut(4), DataOut(5), DataOut(6),
  DataOut(7) ]
debug "Sending: ",DataOut(0), DataOut(1), DataOut(2), DataOut(3),
  DataOut(4), DataOut(5), DataOut(6), DataOut(7),cr
goto begin

NodeActivities:
'Use this routine for any activities the Stamp is responsible for
  on its own.
'Set one output byte to match port bits 0-7.
'DataOut(0)=InL
return
```

Listing 8-3: Basic Stamp II code for an RS-232 link. (Sheet 2 of 2)

Exchanging Data

The biggest difference between communicating with a Stamp and a PC is that the Stamp's serial port has no input buffer. Because of this, the PC first sends a byte to get the Stamp's attention (in `fncGetStampsAttention`). Because the Stamp might be busy doing something else when the PC sends its byte, the PC sends the byte repeatedly until it either sees a response or decides that the Stamp isn't going to respond at all.

The PC adds a delay of at least one byte width between the bytes. This is to help the Stamp identify the Start bit. Otherwise, if `SerIn` begins reading in the middle of a byte, it will misread the value. The Stamp's `SerIn` statement skips the first byte it detects, in case it's a partial byte, and waits for the next Start bit. Figure 8-4's waveforms show a PC signaling a Stamp until the Stamp responds.

The Stamp alternates between watching for incoming serial data and carrying out its own duties. With each `Serin` statement, the Stamp spends an allotted time waiting for incoming data. When the Stamp detects a byte, it branches to a subroutine that sends a byte back to the PC to acknowledge that it has received the byte.

The Stamp then executes a `SerIn` statement and waits for the expected eight bytes. The PC sends the bytes, and the Stamp stores them and sends eight bytes back to the PC. The PC reads the received bytes and the communication is complete.

If the Stamp sees no data, it jumps to the beginning of its program.

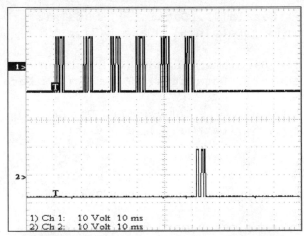

Figure 8-4: Trace 1 shows a byte sent repeatedly by a PC to a Basic Stamp. When the Stamp responds (trace 2), the PC stops sending.

In the example code, the initial bytes exchanged to get and acknowledge the Stamp's attention are specific values, but otherwise have no particular meaning. However, these bytes could contain data or commands as well.

Ensuring that the Stamp Sees Incoming Data

If the Stamp has little else to do except watch for incoming data, it will detect incoming bytes without problems. If the Stamp spends most of its time in other activities, the timing of the communications is more critical.

To guarantee that the Stamp will see a byte sent by the PC, two conditions must be met. First, the interval between bytes sent by the PC should be shorter than the Stamp's `Serin Timeout` value. And the total time that the PC spends trying to get the Stamp's attention should be longer than the interval between `SerIn` statements at the Stamp.

In the example code, the PC sends the byte continuously for up to two seconds, and the Stamp watches its serial port for one second at a time. The PC could delay up to one second between sending each pair of bytes, but sending the bytes continuously ensures the quickest response from the Stamp. The Stamp must execute `SerIn` at least once every two seconds, to ensure that the PC doesn't time out before the Stamp detects an incoming byte. If the PC sees no response after two seconds, it displays a message and moves on.

You can adjust the timing values as needed. For example, if the Stamp may delay as much as 5 seconds between `SerIn` statements, the PC's timeout limit should be greater than 5 seconds.

PC-to 8052-Basic Link

The application also supports a link between an 8052-Basic and a PC. Use a Max233 or similar interface at the 8052's *Serial In* and *Serial Out* pins, as described in Chapter 5.

Like the other CPUs, the 8052-Basic sends and receives blocks of eight bytes. Listing 8-4 shows the Basic-52 program code.

Ensuring that the 8052-Basic Sees Incoming Data

As with the Stamp, when the PC wants to send data, it first gets the 8052's attention by sending a byte and waiting for a reply (in `fncGet8052sAttention`). Because Basic-52's `Get` statement can retrieve the last byte received, the PC

```
10 REM 8052-Basic link
20      REM reserve room for two 8-byte strings
30      STRING 19,8
40      REM Attention and Acknowledge bytes:
50      ATT=1
60      ACK=6
100     REM main program loop
110     DO
120     REM perform other activities
130     GOSUB 500
140     REM check for incoming byte
150     G=GET
160     REM if a received byte matches
170     REM the expect value,
180     REM jump to a subroutine
190     IF G=ATT THEN GOSUB 1000
200     WHILE 1=1
210     END

500     REM node activities
510     REM dummy test data
520     $(0)="12345678"
590     RETURN

1000    REM send acknowledge
1010    PRINT CHR(ACK)
1020    REM store incoming bytes in a string.
1030    REM The bytes end with a carriage return.
1040    INPUT ,$(1)
1050    REM Send 8 bytes back in a string
1060    PRINT $(0),
1070    RETURN
```

Listing 8-4: Basic-52 code for an RS-232 link.

sends the *Attention* byte only once, then waits a set amount of time for a reply before giving up.

Like the Stamp, the 8052 alternates between performing its normal duties and watching for serial input. A Get statement periodically reads the last byte that arrived at the serial port.

If Get matches the expected value, the program jumps to a subroutine. The 8052-Basic sends a byte back to the PC and then executes an Input statement that waits for a line of text followed by a carriage return.

Exchanging Data

When the PC sees the byte returned by the 8052, it sends eight bytes, followed by a carriage return (*0Dh*).

When the 8052 has detected and stored the eight bytes, it sends eight bytes back to the PC, which reads and displays the bytes. Because Basic-52 echoes back the received `Input` characters plus a carriage return and linefeed, the PC skips the first ten bytes received. Figure 8-5 shows waveforms for a PC and 8052-Basic exchanging data.

The data bytes from the PC can be text or anything except certain control codes or a carriage return or linefeed, as explained in Chapter 5. Basic-52's `Asc` operator can extract individual bytes from a received string. After executing an `Input` statement, the 8052 will wait forever for a carriage return, so if for some reason it misses it, sending another will send the program on its way. A program error will stop the program, unless one of the options described in Chapter 5 is enabled.

Simple I/O

Some applications don't need to transfer bytes of data, but only require a few bits of input and output. RS-232's handshaking lines are a simple solution that doesn't even require even a UART at the remote end. Most ports have four inputs (*CTS, DSR, CD*, and *RI*) and two outputs (*RTS, DTR*) available for this use.

Figure 8-5: Trace 1 shows a PC sending eight bytes to an 8052-Basic. Trace 2 shows the 8052-Basic echoing the received data, then sending eight bytes back to the PC.

Because the signals are RS-232, the cable can be 50 feet or more. If you need TTL levels at the far end, a MAX232 will do the conversion. An obvious use is to control or read simple switches, but interfacing to any other TTL-level signals is possible.

If you want to use the RS-232 levels directly, remember that the outputs may range from ±5V to ±15V. For example, if you use an output to drive an LED, the current through the LED, and thus its brightness, will vary with the output voltage. Buffer any signals that carry high currents or that drive relay coils or other inductive loads.

Accessing the Signals

Visual Basic's MSComm control has Boolean properties that enable you to read and write to the each of the signals except *RI:*

```
'Open the port with no handshaking
Dim CTS as Boolean
Dim DSR as Boolean
Dim CD as Boolean
'To read the inputs:
CTS = MsComm1.CTSHolding
DSR = MSComm1.DTRHolding
CD = MSCOMM1.CDHolding

'To write to the outputs:
MSComm1.RTSEnable = True
MSComm1.DTREnable = False
```

Setting a signal True brings it positive at the RS-232 interface, while False brings it negative. In the same way, a positive input reads True, and a negative input reads False.

If you need to use *RI* as well, you can read its status by directly reading bit 6 in the UART's Modem Status Register (at the port's base address + 6). To do so, you'll need to know the port's base address and use a DLL or other driver as explained in Chapter 4.

For DOS programmers, QuickBasic doesn't include functions for reading and writing to the handshaking lines, but you can do so by reading and writing directly to the registers in the port's UART.

Connecting to a Stand-alone UART

If you want to control or read many parallel I/O bits from a serial port, an alternative is to use a stand-alone UART. The Harris/RCA 6402 is an older UART that is convenient for basic monitoring and control links because it has separate parallel transmit and receive pins. Other UARTs, such as the 8250 series used in most PCs, are designed for interfacing to a computer's data bus, and have a single set of bidirectional data lines.

The chip requires a counter or bit-rate generator such as the MC14411, but requires no programming beyond selecting a setup in hardware. A MAX232 will convert the UART's serial bits to RS-232. You can connect this UART to a microcontroller's serial port or, with an RS-232 interface, to a PC's serial port.

Controlling Synchronous Interfaces

Another use for a port's handshaking lines is to control a synchronous serial interface. These interfaces have a clock line and one or two data lines. Devices with synchronous interfaces include serial EEPROMs, analog-to-digital converters, shift registers, or any device that supports an SPI, I²C, or Microwire interface. The easiest devices to use have no minimum clock frequency and allow the clock to toggle as needed.

The 74LS299 universal shift register is a synchronous device whose eight parallel bits can be configured as inputs or outputs.

If you're short on outputs to use to control a synchronous interface, you can even use *TD* as a clock. MSComm's `Break` property enables setting *TD* True and False as desired. The `OnComm` event `comEventBreak` detects a break signal equal to at least one character width. Or, to cause a positive pulse equal to 1 bit width (the Start bit), write a single byte of *FFh* to *TD*. For a positive pulse equal to 9 bits (8 data bits plus Start), write a byte of 0. In a similar way, you can use *RD* to detect a change from a negative to positive RS-232 voltage as a Start bit. MSComm will generate a framing error if the input pulse's width doesn't match MSComm's settings, but your program can ignore this.

Operating System Tools

MS-DOS and Windows 95 have built-in ways to link PCs via their serial (or parallel) ports. For file transfers or even simple networks, these may be all you need.

Direct Cable Connection

Windows 95 has PC-to-PC communications abilities with its *Direct Cable Connection* (DCC). DCC creates a simple network between two computers. Both computers must be running Windows 95.

With DCC, one computer is the host, and the other is the guest. The guest has access to the resources of the host, including accessing the host's files, drives, and printers and even running applications on the host. If the host is connected to a network, the guest can access the network, and the host can access shared resources on the guest.

DCC works with either serial or parallel ports. Serial ports require a null-modem cable or adapter. For parallel connections, DCC can use a nibble-mode (Laplink-type) bidirectional cable, or a special Direct Parallel Universal Cable from Parallel Technologies. The Universal cable is useful if the ports on both computers are capable of bidirectional, EPP, or ECP data transfers. The cable automatically detects the port types at each end and configures itself for the fastest data transfers possible. The parallel link is faster, but the serial link is handy if you don't have parallel ports to spare, if the computers are too far apart for a parallel link, or if you don't have the required parallel cable handy.

To use DCC, both computers must have Dial-up Networking and Direct Cable Connect installed. To find out if these are installed, go to *Control Panel, Add/Remove Programs, Windows Setup, Communications, Details.* To add an item, click the appropriate check box, then *OK*, and follow the instructions.

Establishing a Connection

To establish a Direct Cable Connection, click on the *Start* menu, *Programs, Accessories, Direct Cable Connection.* At each computer, on-screen prompts guide you through selecting a port and selecting host or guest. If the connection fails, Windows Help includes a *DCC Troubleshooter* that helps resolve many common problems.

The host must specify which resources it wants to share, and what type of sharing to enable. You can choose to share individual files, folders, or drives. The shared access can be read-only or full (read/write). To enable sharing, in *My Computer,* right-click the file or drive to share and select *Properties, Sharing* (Figure 8-6). Click on *Shared As* and enter a name, which can be the same as the drive or file name, and select an *Access Type.* When a resource is shared, its icon changes to include an outstretched hand, so the shared resources are easy to identify in a list.

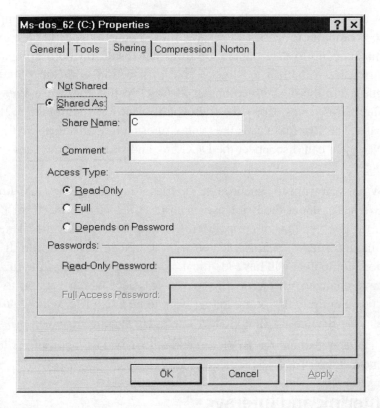

Figure 8-6: Use the Sharing Tab to specify drives that PCs can share under a Direct Cable Connection.

When the DCC is established, the *View Host* button on the DCC window enables you to view and access the shared resources on the host. To select a folder, click on it as usual.

Another way to view and access the host is to map a drive to an unused drive letter on the guest. The host must have a name, which you specify in its Control Panel under *Network, Identification, Computer Name.* In *My Computer,* click the *Map Network Drive* icon. Select an unused drive letter, and type the path of the drive you want to access. A double backslash (\\) preceding the path tells the system that the path is on the remote system. Don't add a colon (:) after the drive letter. The drive then appears along with other system drives in *My Computer*.

Briefcase

If you use more than one computer to work on a set of files, Windows 95's Briefcase helps you maintain a single up-to-date version of each file. If Briefcase isn't installed, add it in *Control Panel, Add/Remove Programs.*

A common use for the Briefcase is when you use a portable computer and a desktop computer to work on the same files. You can use Briefcase to synchronize, or maintain up-to-date copies, of files that reside on both computers. To use the Briefcase, establish a Direct Cable Connection with the portable computer as guest and the desktop computer as host. At the guest, use *View Host* to see the shared resources. Copy the files you'll want to synchronize to the guest's Briefcase. The Briefcase uses the syntax *hostname\path\filename* for the host's files. Now you can disconnect the DCC link and work with the files on the guest computer.

When you want to synchronize the files, re-establish the DCC link. In the guest's Briefcase, under the Briefcase menu item, select *Update All* or *Update Selection*. If the two versions of a file differ, Briefcase will display the filename and date and time information and ask if you want to update the older file. If you answer yes, both computers will have identical, up-to-date versions of the file. If both versions have changed, Briefcase allows you to select which version to use, or skip the update entirely. If you no longer want to update a file, select *Split From Original*, and the Briefcase will no longer attempt to synchronize it.

(You can also use the Briefcase without DCC, to synchronize files on a hard disk and a floppy.)

DOS Interlnk and Intersvr

For DOS users, MS-DOS version 6 added the ability to redirect disk and parallel-port operations from one computer (the *client*) to another (the *server*), using a simple serial or parallel connection between the computers. The client can read and write to disks and LPT devices on the server.

DOS provides two programs for this purpose: *Interlnk.exe* and *Intersvr.exe*. You also need either a null-modem serial cable, or a nibble-mode parallel cable. If only one of the computers has the *Interlnk* and *Intersvr* files, you can use *Interlnk* to copy files over a serial link, but not a parallel link.

Using *Interlnk*, the client can read, write to, copy, move, and delete files on the server. MS-DOS's online help has details on how to use these programs.

9

Links and Networks with RS-485

Chapter 8 showed how to use an RS-232 interface to link two computers. When you need to transmit over longer distances or at higher speeds than RS-232 can handle, RS-485 is a solution. Plus, RS-485 links aren't limited to just two devices. Depending on the distance, bit rate, and interface chips, you can connect as many as 256 nodes along a single pair of wires.

This chapter introduces RS-485 signals and interfacing.

About RS-485

What most people call RS-485 is the interface described by a document titled *TIA/EIA-485*. A similar standard is ISO/IEC 8482.1993. In this book, I bow to convention and conciseness and call it RS-485.

RS-485 has several advantages over RS-232:

Low cost. The drivers and receivers are inexpensive and require just a single +5V (or lower) supply to generate the required minimum 1.5V difference at the differential outputs. In contrast, RS-232's minimum output of ±5V requires dual supplies or an expensive interface chip that can generate the supplies.

Networking ability. Instead of being limited to two devices, RS-485 is a *multi-drop* interface that can have multiple drivers and receivers. With high-impedance receivers, an RS-485 link can have as many as 256 nodes.

Long links. An RS-485 link can be as long as 4000 feet, compared to RS-232's typical limit of 50 to 100 feet.

Fast. The bit rate can be as high as 10 Megabits/second.

The cable length and bit rate are related. Lower bit rates allow longer cables.

Table 9-1 shows specifications for RS-485 and a related interface, RS-422, which is limited to one driver and ten receivers, but allows a greater differential input voltage.

In addition to its use in serial interfaces, RS-485 is also used in fast parallel interfaces such as differential SCSI.

Balanced and Unbalanced Lines

The main reason why RS-485 can transmit over long distances is its use of balanced lines. Each signal has a dedicated pair of wires, with the voltage on one wire equal to the negative, or complement, of the voltage on the other. The receiver responds to the difference between the voltages. Figure 9-1 illustrates. A

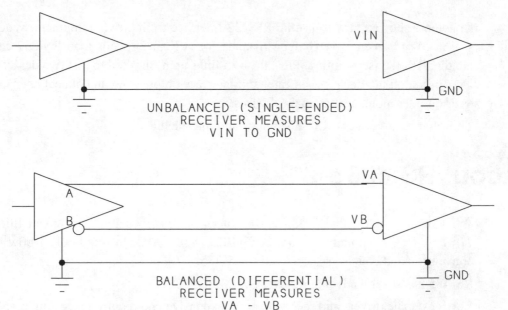

Figure 9-1: An unbalanced line uses one signal wire, while a balanced line uses two.

Table 9-1: Comparison of balanced interfaces

Specification	TIA/EIA-422-B	TIA/EIA-485
Transmission mode	balanced	balanced
Cable length @90 kbps, max. (feet), approximate	4000	4000
Cable length @10 Mbps, max. (feet), approximate	50	50
Data rate, max. (bits/sec)	10M	10M
Differential output (minimum, volts)	± 2	± 1.5
Differential output (maximum, volts)	± 10	± 6
Receiver sensitivity (volts)	± 0.2	± 0.2
Driver load, minimum (ohms)	100	60
Maximum number of drivers	1	32 unit loads
Maximum number of receivers	10	32 unit loads

big advantage to balanced lines is their immunity to noise. Another term for this type of transmission is differential signaling.

In contrast, RS-232 uses unbalanced, or single-ended lines, where the receiver responds to the difference between a signal voltage and a common ground used by all. An unbalanced interface may have multiple ground wires, but all of the signal grounds connect together.

TIA/EIA-485 designates the two lines in a differential pair as *A* and *B*. At the driver, a TTL logic-high input causes line A to be more positive than line B, while a TTL logic-low input causes line B to be more positive than line A. At the receiver, if input A is more positive than input B, the TTL output is logic high, and if input B is more positive than input A, the TTL output is logic low.

Referenced to the receiver's ground, each input must be within the range -7V to +12V. This allows for differences in ground potential between the driver and receiver. The maximum differential input (VA-VB) must be no greater than ±6V.

Why Balanced Lines Are Quiet

Balanced lines are quiet because the two signal wires carry nearly equal, opposite currents. This reduces received noise because most noise voltages are present more or less equally on both wires. Any noise voltage that shows up on one line is cancelled by an opposite voltage on the other. The source of noise may be signals on other wires in the cable or signals that couple into the wires from outside the cable. A balanced receiver sees only the transmitted signal, with noise eliminated or very much reduced.

In contrast, in an unbalanced interface, the receiver detects the voltage difference between the signal and ground wire. When multiple signals share a ground wire, each of the return currents induces voltages on the ground shared by all. Parallel interfaces may have eight or more lines switching constantly, and even serial links often use two data lines and several handshaking signals. If the ground connects to an earth ground, noise from other sources can affect the circuits as well.

Another advantage to balanced lines is that they are immune, within limits, to differences in ground potential between the driver and receiver. In a long link, the grounds at the driver and receiver may vary by many volts. On an unbalanced line, ground differences can cause a receiver to misread an input. A balanced line doesn't care about mismatched grounds, because the receiver detects only the difference between the two transmitted signals.

In reality, RS-485 components withstand ground differences only up to the limit specified in their data sheets. A way to eliminate or reduce ground-voltage problems is to isolate the link so that the driver's and receiver's ground potentials have no effect on the link. Chapter 10 shows ways to ensure that a link's ground potentials are within acceptable limits.

The Circuits Inside

Figure 9-2 shows internal circuits of an RS-485 driver and receiver. You don't have to understand how the circuits work in order to use them, but I've found that taking a look inside a circuit helps to convert it from a mysterious black box to a set of components with predictable behaviors. This in turn can prevent mistakes or at least make it easier to know what to do when it's time to debug.

The components shown are the same as the equivalent circuits in the data sheet for Texas Instruments' 75179B. Other RS-485 chips may differ in the details, but the overall operation is the same.

The schematic shows the drivers' outputs and the receivers' input and output circuits, along with the path current takes when the link transmits a TTL logic 1. Not shown are the circuits between the driver's TTL inputs and the output transistors, and between the RS-485 receiver circuits and the TTL outputs.

A logic high at the driver's TTL input causes transistors *Q1* and *Q4* to switch on, and *Q2* and *Q3* to switch off. The voltage on line A causes *Q6* to switch on. Current flows into *Q6* and returns to the driver via the ground wire. In a similar way, the low voltage on line B causes *Q7* to switch on, and current flows from *Q7* into *Q4*, returning to the receiver via the ground wire. Line A is more positive than line B, and the result is a logic high at the receiver's TTL output.

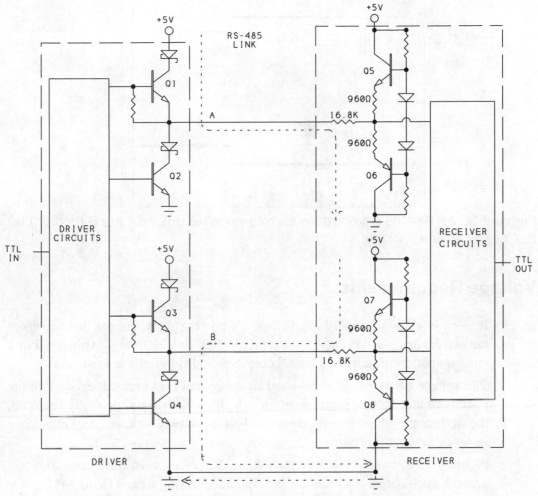

Figure 9-2: The circuits inside an RS-485 driver and receiver.

Each driver's current forms a complete loop from driver to receiver, then back to the driver. A ground wire or other ground connection provides a return path for both signals. But because the two ground currents are equal and opposite, they cancel each other and the actual current in the ground wire is near zero.

If the link has multiple receivers, each behaves like the one shown. If the link has termination resistors, current flows in these as well.

For a logic 0, the situation is the reverse. *Q2, Q3, Q5,* and *Q8* switch on, the others switch off, and the current in the wires flows in the reverse direction.

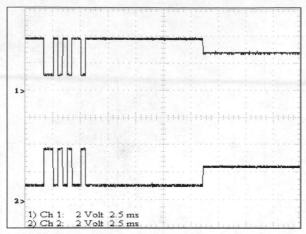

Figure 9-3: An RS-485 driver's outputs, referenced to ground. Line B (bottom) is the inverse of line A (top).

Voltage Requirements

RS-485 interfaces typically use a single 5V power supply, but the logic levels at the drivers and receivers aren't standard 5V TTL or CMOS logic voltages. For a valid output, the difference between outputs A and B must be at least 1.5V.

The voltage between each output and signal ground isn't defined, except that the common-mode voltage must be within ±7V. If the interface is perfectly balanced, the outputs are offset equally from one-half the supply voltage. Any imbalance raises or lowers the offset.

Figure 9-3 shows an RS-485 driver's A and B outputs, each referenced to signal ground. Each output is around 3V in amplitude, varying from +1V to +4V or -1V to -4V referenced to ground. The driver's power supply is +5V. Figure 9-4 shows the same byte as the difference between line A and B. The peak-to-peak amplitude of this differential signal is nearly 6V, or twice the peak-to-peak amplitude of the individual signals.

If one output switches before the other, the combined differential output switches more slowly, and this limits the maximum bit rate of the link. Skew is the time difference between the two outputs' switching. RS-485 drivers are designed for minimum skew. For example, Linear Technology's LTC1685 guarantees a maximum skew of ±3.5 ns.

At the RS-485 receiver, the difference between the A and B inputs needs to be just 0.2V. If A is at least 0.2V more positive than B, the receiver sees a logic 1, and if B is at least 0.2V more positive than A, the receiver sees a logic 0. If the difference between A and B is less than 0.2V, the logic level is undefined.

The difference between the requirements at the driver and receiver results in a noise margin of 1.3V. The differential signal can attenuate or have noise spikes as large as 1.3V, and the receiver will still see the correct logic level. The noise margin is less than on an RS-232 link, but don't forget that RS-485's differential signals cancel most noise to begin with.

Also, in most links, the difference between the drivers' outputs is larger than the minimum 1.5V, so the noise margin is larger. A driver powered at just 3V can also easily provide 1.5V between the outputs.

TIA/EIA-485 defines logic 1 as the state where B > A, and logic 0 as A > B. Using these definitions, RS-485 interface chips are inverters, because B > A on the RS-485 side of the chip corresponds to a logic low on the TTL side, and A > B on the RS-485 side corresponds to a logic high on the TTL side. In reality, the polarities don't matter as long as all nodes agree on a convention.

Current Requirements

The total current used by an RS-485 link varies with the impedances of the components in the link, including the drivers, cable, receivers, and termination components. A low output impedance at the driver and a low-impedance cable enables fast switching and ensures that the receiver sees the largest signal possible. A high impedance at the receiver decreases the current in the link and increases battery life in battery-powered links.

The termination components, when used, have the greatest effect on the amount of current used by the link. Many RS-485 links have a 120-ohm resistor across the

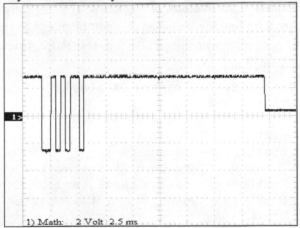

Figure 9-4: An RS-485 driver's differential output (LIne A-Line B). The peak-to-peak amplitude of this signal is nearly 6V.

differential lines at each of the link's two ends. The parallel combination of these is 60 ohms. The terminations create a low-resistance path from the driver with a logic-high output, through the terminations, and into the driver with a logic-low output. On short, slow links, you may be able to eliminate the termination entirely and greatly reduce power consumption. Chapter 10 shows how to select a termination.

When there is no termination, the receivers' input impedance has the greatest effect on the total series resistance. The total input impedance varies with the number of enabled receivers and their input impedance.

An RS-485 driver can drive 32 unit loads. TIA/EIA-485 defines a unit load in terms of required current. A receiver equal to one unit load draws no more than a specified amount of current at the input-voltage extremes specified by the standard. When the received voltage is as much as +12V greater than the receiver's signal ground, a unit-load receiver draws no more than 1 milliampere. When the received voltage is as much as 7V less than the receiver's ground, a unit-load receiver draws no more than -0.8 milliampere. To meet this requirement, a receiver must have an input resistance of at least 12,000 ohms between each differential input and the supply voltage or ground, depending on the direction of current flow.

With one receiver equivalent to a unit load enabled, the resistance of each of the two differential inputs is 12,000 ohms. (Again, this is the resistance from an input to ground or the supply voltage, not the resistance between the two inputs.) Add a second receiver, and the parallel resistance of the combination drops to 6000 ohms. With receivers equivalent to 32 unit loads, the parallel resistance of the combined inputs is just 375 ohms, or slightly less due to leakage currents. Adding two 120-ohm terminations reduces the combination to just 60 ohms. This Visual-Basic code displays the total input resistance for links with receivers equivalent to 2 to 32 unit loads:

```
Dim TotalInputResistance As Single
Dim UnitLoads as Integer
TotalInputResistance = 12000
For UnitLoads= 2 To 32
    TotalInputResistance = _
       (12000 * TotalInputResistance) / _
       (12000 + TotalInputResistance)
    Debug.Print UnitLoads, TotalInputResistance
Next UnitLoads
```

You can increase the receivers' input resistance by using receivers that are a fraction of a unit load. For example, the input resistance of a 1/8-unit-load receiver is 96,000 ohms, and the total parallel resistance of 32 of these is 3000 ohms. The

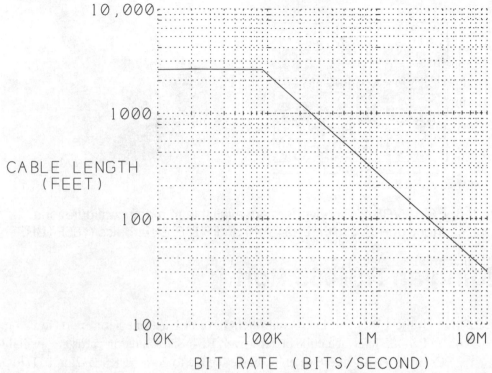

Figure 9-5: RS-485 supports transmissions up to 10 Mbps, but the higher bit rates require shorter cables.

receivers that are a fraction of a unit load may be slower than other receivers, though some, such as the 1/8-unit-load MAX3088, support rates up to 10Mbps.

Speed

An RS-485 link can be as fast as 10 Mbps or 4000 feet, but not both at the same time. Longer cables require slower bit rates. Over long distances, the cable's capacitance slows the signal transitions. Figure 9-5 is a general guideline for determining allowed bit rate for a cable length, as recommended by TIA/EIA/422.

At rates of up to 90 kbps, RS-485 and RS-422 support cable lengths of up to 4000 ft. At faster rates, the maximum allowed cable length drops, to around 400 feet at 1Mbps, and 50 feet at 10Mbps. The graph assumes an AWG #24, unshielded, terminated twisted pair.

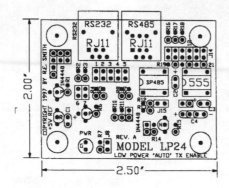 

Figure 9-6: RS-485/RS-232 converters are available in many configurations. (Images courtesy of R.E. Smith (LP24, left) and B & B Electronics (485PTBR, right).

Adding an RS-485 Port

Although most PCs and microcontrollers have at least one serial port, few come with an RS-485 interface built-in. However, RS-485 expansion cards are available for PCs, a variety of interface chips make it easy to convert RS-232 or TTL logic to RS-485 levels, and a few microcontroller boards have an RS-485 interface.

PC Expansion Cards

As with RS-232, you can add an RS-485 port on an expansion card. The port uses one of the PC's COM ports. Chapter 3's tips and cautions about adding and configuring RS-232 ports also apply to RS-485 cards.

The ports themselves can vary in many details. Some have one just pair of data lines for half-duplex communications, while others have two pair for full duplex. Some half-duplex cards include hardware support for automatically enabling the driver at the appropriate time. This greatly simplifies the software required to control the port, as explained later in this chapter.

Converter Chips

It's also possible to convert an existing RS-232 or 5V TTL port to RS-485. You can buy converter modules (Figure 9-6) or make your own.

Converter chips are available for a variety of configuration options. Sources include Linear Technology, Maxim Semiconductor, Motorola, National Semicon-

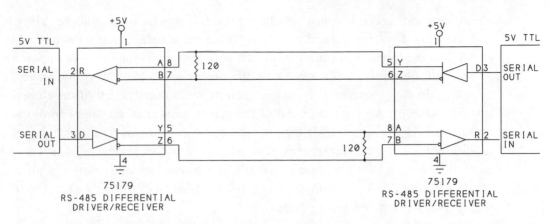

Figure 9-7: A full-duplex RS-485 link.

ductor, and Texas Instruments. Catalogs may list RS-485 chips under Linear, Interface, or Special Purpose categories.

Converting TTL

As Chapter 5 explained, many microcontrollers have an asynchronous serial port that uses 5V TTL or CMOS logic levels. There are many ways to convert 5V logic to RS-485.

Full Duplex

The RS-485 interface is designed for use in multi-point systems, with one or more generators and receivers. Most RS-485 links are half-duplex, where multiple drivers and receivers share a signal path. But you can also use RS-485 in a full-duplex link, where each direction has its own signal path. Swapping an RS-232 link for a full-duplex RS-485 link is completely transparent to the software or firmware that uses the link. You can use the exact same programming for both, though RS-485 supports higher bit rates and the hardware allows longer links.

For this type of link, you can use Texas Instruments' SN75179B differential driver and receiver. The package contains a driver that translates 5V TTL signals to RS-485 and a receiver that translates RS-485 back to 5V TTL. Figure 9-7 illustrates.

This is a simple solution when you want to create a long-distance, full-duplex link between microcontrollers. The RS-485 interface chips are also smaller, simpler, and cheaper than converting to RS-232. You can also use RS-422 interface chips for this type of link.

Figure 9-8 shows that it's also possible to use full duplex with multiple drivers and receivers. One arrangement is in a master/slave network, where a master node (Node 0 in the figure) has control of the network and grants the others permission to transmit. One pair of wires connects the master's driver to all of the slaves' receivers. In the other direction, another pair of wires connects all of the slaves' drivers to the master's receiver. All of the slaves must read messages from the master to find out which node they're intended for. The slave being addressed replies on the opposite pair of wires. The advantage to this arrangement is that it saves time for the slaves because they don't have to read the other slaves' replies. If all nodes share one data path, the slaves have to read all of the network traffic to watch for a message from the master.

Half Duplex

Many RS-485 links are half-duplex, with multiple drivers and receivers sharing a signal path.

When a link has three or more nodes, it usually makes sense to have just one signal path and allow one node at a time to transmit. Having two data paths is convenient when there are just two devices, because each can transmit at any time without worrying about whose turn it is. But with more than one driver on the same pair of wires, there's no guarantee that the signal path will be free when a driver wants to transmit, and figuring out when it's OK to use each of two signal paths just adds more complications (except in master/slave networks like the one just described).

Even a link with just two devices may be half-duplex. On microcontrollers that allow configuring a port bit as input or output, you can send and receive on a single bit, reconfiguring the bit as needed. You might do this if you need to use the fewest number of port bits possible. Or you might use half-duplex to save on cabling. Over short distances, a couple of extra wires is no big deal, but if you're

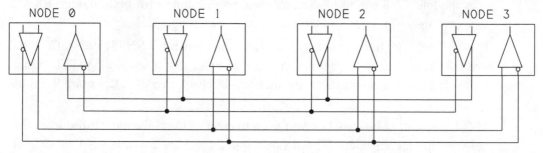

Figure 9-8: In this full-duplex, multi-node link, Node 0 transmits to all other nodes on one path, and receives from all other nodes on the other path.

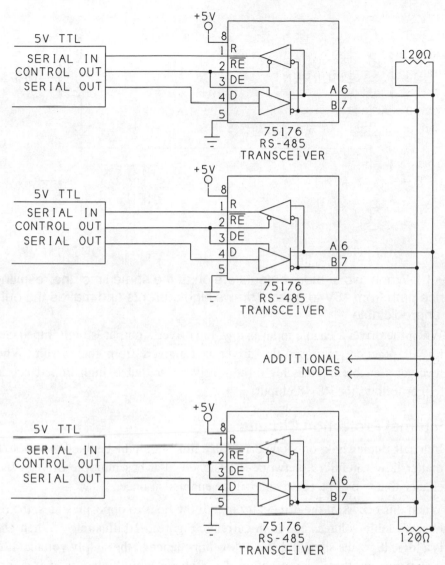

Figure 9-9: A half-duplex RS-485 link.

going half a mile, the cost of the wiring adds up. If you need to transmit in just one direction (simplex), you of course need only one path.

Figure 9-9 shows a half-duplex interface that uses Texas Instruments' SN75176B differential bus transceiver.

The chip includes one driver that translates TTL logic to RS-485, one receiver that translates RS-485 to TTL, and an enable input for each. Unlike the '179B, this chip has just one pair of RS-485 pins, with the enable inputs determining whether the driver or receiver is active.

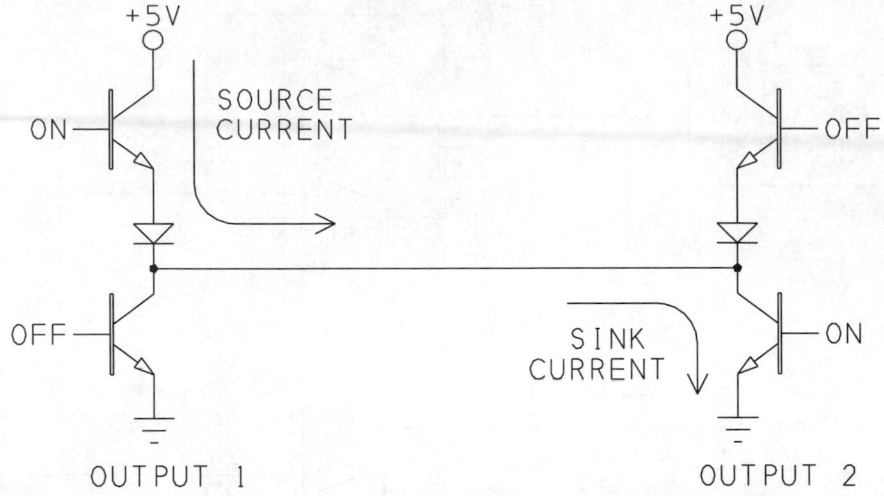

Figure 9-10: When two or more outputs are on at the same time, the resulting low impedance path from +5V to ground draws high currents and makes the output voltage unpredictable.

When the driver's enable input is low, the driver's output is high impedance, and for all practical purposes the driver is removed from the circuit. When the receiver's enable input is high, the receiver's output is high impedance and no longer follows the RS-485 input.

Internal Protection Circuits

In a half-duplex link, only one driver in a link should be enabled at a time. But no matter how carefully a network is designed, if it has multiple drivers, there's a chance that two or more drivers will be enabled at once.

When this occurs, if the drivers try to pull the lines to opposite states, the result is unpredictable voltages and high currents. Figure 9-10 illustrates. When *Output 1* is a logic high, the signal line has a low impedance to the supply voltage. If *Output 2* switches on, there's no problem if it's also a logic high. But if it switches to logic low, it has low impedance to ground. The result is a low-impedance path from the power supply to ground. The components draw high currents, and the voltage is likely to be an undefined logic level. This situation is called line contention.

All RS-485 interface chips include current limiting and thermal shutdown to protect the chips if more than one driver is enabled at once. The current-limiting restricts the output current of the drivers. TIA/EIA-485 says that current must be limited to 250 milliamperes. If an output continues to source or sink high currents, the chip will heat up, and eventually the thermal shutdown circuits in the chip will

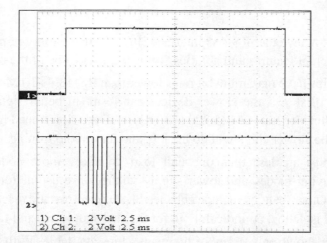

1) Ch 1:   2 Volt 2.5 ms
2) Ch 2:   2 Volt 2.5 ms

Figure 9-11: Trace #1 is the active-high driver-enable signal. Trace #2 is a transmitted byte. The driver-enable must go high before the byte transmits, and may return low any time after the transmission has completed.

switch the output to a high-impedance state. Of course, this makes the output unusable until it cools down, but at least the components survive.

Enabling the Driver

The tricky part of using a half-duplex link is controlling when each driver is enabled, or active. When a driver is transmitting, it must remain enabled until it has finished transmitting, then switch to disabled before an answering node begins its response. Figure 9-11 shows a transmitted byte and its driver-enable signal.

There are three ways to control the enable lines:

- In Figure 9-9, one bit controls both the driver and receiver on each chip. Because the driver's enable is active-high and the receiver's is active-low, only one will be enabled at a time. This setup is useful if a node doesn't want or need to receive its own transmissions.

- In many links, the receiver's output can remain enabled at all times, so the receiver's enable can be tied to ground. The control bit connects only to the driver-enable. Leaving the receiver enabled provides a simple way for a node to detect when a transmission has completed by reading back the data sent.

- For the most flexible control, you can use a separate bit to control the driver's and receiver's enables.

Chips

There are many other RS-485 interface chips, from a variety of manufacturers and with different features and abilities. Table 9-2 lists some of the options.

Some chips have maximum bit rates lower than RS-485's 10 Mbps maximum. As Chapter 10 shows, the slower devices can result in better signal quality. Many RS-485 links operate at 115,200 bps or less. If you don't need high-speed performance, the slower chips will do the job, and may avoid trouble.

Other chips are less than one unit load, to allow more nodes in a network. Power-saving modes and lower supply voltages are useful for battery-operated devices. Other features include enhanced ESD (electrostatic discharge) protection, electrical isolation, an indicator pin for thermal shutdown, and failsafe circuits.

The table shows only a few of the many chips available. With a little searching, chances are that you can find a chip that has whatever combination of features you need for a particular link.

Converting RS-232

Because RS-232 is so popular, many RS-485 interfaces are created by converting RS-232 signals to RS-485. If a PC has a free RS-232 port, adding an external converter is cheaper and easier than buying and installing an RS-485 card. Some microcontroller boards also have RS-232 interfaces built-in, though in these cases it's usually simpler to bypass RS-232 (by removing the interface chip) and wire the RS-485 interface directly to the microcontroller's port pins.

Converter modules are available from many sources, and it's also fairly simple to make your own.

Figure 9-12 shows one way to convert RS-232 to RS-485. The interface uses three RS-232 lines: *TD* transmits data, *RD* receives data, and *RTS* controls direction. A MAX233 converts the RS-232 signals to TTL levels, and the TTL signals connect to a 75176B that provides the RS-485 interface.

When *RTS* is low, the enable inputs of the '176 are high and *TD* can transmit to the RS-485 link. When *RTS* is high, the enable inputs are low and *RD* can receive data from the RS-485 link.

It's likely that the cable from the RS-232 port to the converter will be no more than a few feet long. In this case, you can use Chapter 6's short-range transistor circuit in place of the MAX233 or other converter chip.

In similar ways, you can create full-duplex RS-232-to-RS-485 interfaces using a '179B or other 4-wire RS-485 chip.

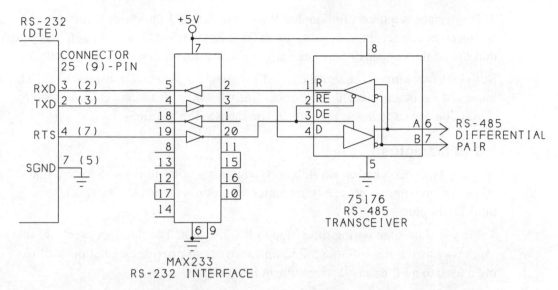

Figure 9-12: This circuit converts between RS-232 and TTL, and between TTL and RS-485.

Short Links between Different Interfaces

Sometimes when you have two devices with different interfaces, all you want is to link them as cheaply and simply as possible. Over short distances, you can use a simple direct link to connect a full-duplex RS-485 or RS-422 interface with RS-232.

RS-232 to RS-485

Figure 9-13 shows a simple RS-232 to RS-485 link. The RS-485's *B* (inverted) output connects to RS-232's *RD* input. Referenced to signal ground, the *B* output is near 0V for a logic 1 and near +5V for a logic 0. As explained in Chapter 6, these voltages don't meet RS-232's minimum specification, just about all RS-232 receivers will interpret them correctly. The A output is unused and left open.

In the other direction, a voltage divider ensures that the differential input voltage doesn't exceed RS-485's maximum of ±6V. The receiver's *A* input is tied to ground. The B input sees about 1/3 of the transmitted RS-232 voltage. If the RS-232's *TD* is ±15V, the RS-485 receiver's input sees a voltage of about ±5V. If the RS-232's *TD* is just ±5V, the RS-485 receiver's input sees a voltage of about ±1.6V, which is well above the minimum requirement of ±0.2V.

This interface requires a full-duplex RS-485 or RS-422 interface. If the differential receiver can accept input voltages as large as the RS-232 driver's outputs, you don't need the voltage divider and can connect the driver and receiver directly.

Both interfaces invert the signals, so a TTL logic 1 at one end translates to a TTL logic 1 at the other end. This link works fine over short distances, at lower speeds. If you don't want to invert the signals, use the RS-485's *A* lines.

PC to Macintosh

Apple's Macintosh has an RS-422 port, which is similar to RS-485 except that it allows a maximum of one transmitter and ten receivers. The port uses a mini-DIN8 plug.

Table 9-3 shows the wiring for a Mac to RS-232 link. The interface works in the same way as the RS-485-to-RS-232 link above, and provides a solution for linking a Mac to a PC or any device with an RS-232 port.

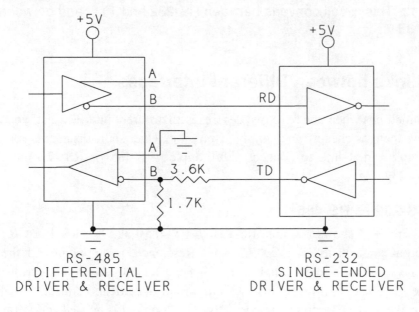

Figure 9-13: Use this wiring for a short link between a device with an RS-485 interface and one with an RS-232 interface.

Serial Port Complete

Table 9-2: Selected RS-485 interface chips.

Source	Part Number	Features
Linear Technology	LTC485	general-purpose half-duplex transceiver
Maxim Semiconductor	MAX485	
National Semiconductor	DS3695	
Texas Instruments	SN75176B	
Linear Technology	LTC490	general-purpose full-duplex driver/receiver pair
Maxim Semiconductor	MAX490	
Texas Instruments	SN75179B	
Linear Technology	LTC491	full-duplex driver/receiver pair with enables
Texas Instruments	SN75ALS180	
Linear Technology	LTC1685	controlled propagation delay; 10 Mbps @400 ft.
Maxim Semiconductor	MAX3088	Maximum speed 10 Mbps
National Semiconductor	DS16F95	Maximum speed 5 Mbps
Maxim Semiconductor	MAX481	Maximum speed 2.5 Mbps
Maxim Semiconductor	MAX483	Maximum speed 250 kbps
Maxim Semiconductor	MAX3082	Maximum speed 115,200 bps
National Semiconductor	DS36C278T	1/2 unit load
Maxim Semiconductor	MAX487	1/4 unit load
National Semiconductor	DS36C278	
Maxim Semiconductor	MAX1483	1/8 unit load
Linear Technology	LTC1481	low-power shutdown mode
Maxim Semiconductor	MAX481	
National Semiconductor	DS36C279	
Maxim Semiconductor	MAX485E	high ESD protection
Linear Technology	LTC1480	3V supply
Maxim Semiconductor	MAX3485	
Maxim Semiconductor	MAX1480A	complete isolated interface
Maxim Semiconductor	MAX3085	short-circuit failsafe
National Semiconductor	DS36276	
National Semiconductor	DS3696	thermal shutdown indicator

Table 9-3:   Wiring for a short Macintosh-to-RS-232 link.

Macintosh RS-422 Mini8 DIN			Connection	RS-232 (DTE)		
Description	Signal	Pin		Pin (DB-25)	Pin (DE-9)	Signal
Handshake Out	HSKo	1	Optional	6 or 5	6 or 8	DSR or CTS
Handshake In	HSKi	2	Optional	20 or 4	4 or 7	DTR or RTS
Transmit -	TD-	3	Required	3	2	RD
Signal Ground	SG	4	Required	7	5	SG
Receive -	RD-	5	Required	2	3	TD
Transmit +	TD+	6	No connection	-	-	-
Unused	-	7	No connection	-	-	-
Receive +	RD+	8	No connection	-	-	-

10

RS-485 Cables & Interfacing

With RS-485, the choice of cable and related components can mean the difference between a link that performs flawlessly or one that fails, either completely and right away, or intermittently and unpredictably. This chapter shows how to select and connect a cable for an RS-485 link, and how to select drivers, receivers, terminations, and other components for the cable and bit rate.

Figure 10-1 has the essence of this chapter: six rules for wiring RS-485 links. To get a link up and running quickly and without problems, follow these guidelines. The rest of the chapter explains the reasons behind the rules. The details are optional, and you may skim or skip them, or save them for later.

Long and Short Lines

RS-485 links come in many varieties. They may have 2, 32, or a couple of hundred nodes. Bit rates may vary from 300 bps or less to 10 Mbps. The link may extend a few feet or thousands of feet.

Over short distances at low bit rates, component and cable choices are less critical, though even here the right choices can save power and reduce noise. Over long

Six Rules for Wiring RS-485 links

1. Use the slowest drivers possible for the bit rate.

2. Terminate long lines with their characteristic impedance.

3. Wire the nodes in a bus topology.

4. Bias inactive links.

5. Use twisted-pair cable.

6. Limit common-mode voltages.

Figure 10-1: Follow these guidelines for trouble-free RS-485 links.

distances and at high bit rates, selecting the proper cables, drivers, receivers, and related components is essential.

The theory and math behind how digital signals behave in long-distance links is complicated, and involves thinking about the signals differently than as simple voltages that transfer instantly and perfectly from driver to receiver. The solutions, fortunately, are usually simple and straightforward, and only require selecting components appropriate for the bit rate and distance.

When Is a Line Long?

An RS-485 link may be a long or short line. In this use, the terms long and short refer not to physical length, but to the amount of time required for a signal to propagate down the line to the receiver. The time varies with the physical length of the wires, and also with the frequencies carried and how fast the signals travel.

When the wires are physically short and the frequencies low, the time required for signals to propagate down the wires has little effect on signal quality. The circuit is considered a *lumped system*, and the wires form a *short line*. In many cases, you can think of short lines as perfect, zero-impedance conductors. When an output switches state, you can assume that the input at the other end of the link instantly sees an identical signal.

When the wires are physically long and the frequencies high, the time required for a signal to propagate down the wires is significant. This type of circuit is considered a *distributed system*, and the wires form a *long line*. Another name for a long line is *transmission line*. On a long line, the proper terminating components ensure that the receiver sees a clean signal by reducing reflected voltages on the line.

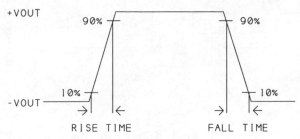

Figure 10-2: Rise and fall times of a digital signal.

Understanding how long and short lines behave requires understanding the effects of two parameters: *rise time* and *cable delay*.

Rise Time

Rise time is the time required for an output to switch from 10% to 90% of full range (Figure 10-2). Its companion, fall time, is often the same, or nearly so, and some sources use rise time to refer to transition time in general. Slew rate, which indicates the rate of change of a signal, is a related parameter.

The rise time of a digital signal is an indication of the frequencies that make up the signal. Faster rise times indicate higher frequencies. Rise time is distinct from the bit rate, or number of bits transmitted per second, though the rise time limits the maximum bit rate.

The data sheets for RS-485 drivers specify typical and maximum rise and fall times. The values range from a few nanoseconds to nearly a microsecond. The specifications assume a specific load, often 54 ohms and 50 or 100pF, with higher capacitance requiring a longer switching time.

Rise time and bit rate are related because low bit rates can tolerate slower rise times. In general, the bit width should be 5 to 10 times longer than the rise time to ensure that the voltage has reached a valid logic level by the time the receiver reads it. For example, an RS-485 driver rated for use at 2.5 Mhz may have a maximum rise time of 0.06 microsecond, which is 15% of the bit width at 2.5 Mhz.

The bit rate is also important because transmission-line effects such as ringing and reflected voltages occur during and immediately after voltage transitions, while receivers read logic levels near the middle of the bits. At a slower bit rate, the bits are wider, and the voltages are likely to have settled by the time the receiver reads them.

Why are rise and fall times a measure of frequency? To understand why, think of the simplest digital signal, a square wave, which has alternating, equal-width high and low voltages. Mathematically, a square wave is the sum of a sine wave of a

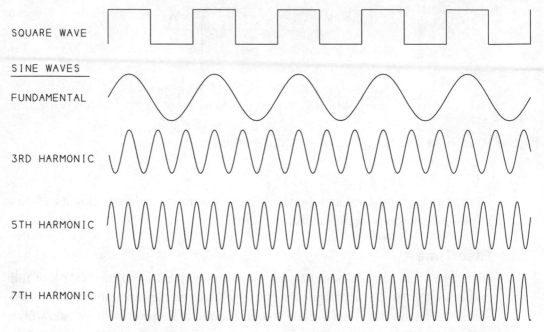

Figure 10-3: A square wave is the sum of a sine wave and its odd harmonics.

fundamental frequency and its odd harmonics. For example, a 100-Hz square wave is the sum of a 100-Hz fundamental plus harmonics of 300, 500, 700 Hz and so on up. Figure 10-3 illustrates.

A square wave containing an infinite number of harmonics has instant transitions and rise and fall times of zero. In real-life components, the laws of physics limit the high frequencies and result in measurable rise and fall times. A signal with a low cutoff frequency and few harmonics will have more gradual transitions and longer rise and fall times. As the number of harmonics increases, the edges sharpen and the rise and fall times shorten.

Serial data is more complex than a simple square wave, but the basic principle is the same: the higher the frequencies that make up the signal, the sharper the transitions.

Cable Delay

Another concept required for understanding long and short lines is cable delay. One-way delay is the time required for a signal to travel the length of the cable. It equals the cable's physical length divided by the propagation rate, or speed, of signals in the cable.

Serial Port Complete

As you might guess, the propagation rates are extremely fast. Light in a vacuum travels 300 million meters per second (186,000 miles per second, or 12 inches per nanosecond). An electrical signal in copper wire travels at around 2/3 to 3/4 this speed: between 200 million meters/sec (124,000 miles/second or 8 inches/nanosecond) and 225 million meters/sec (140,000 miles/sec. or 9 in./nsec.). Other terms for propagation rate are propagation velocity and transmission velocity.

These are one-way delays for cables of different lengths:

Length (ft)	2	10	100	1000	4000
One-way delay (μsecs, @8in./ns)	0.003	0.015	0.15	1.5	15

Because the delays are small, they're of no consequence at all when the cable is short and the rise time slow. But as explained below, with long cables carrying signals with fast transitions, the delays can be long enough to result in reflections that affect the logic levels read by a receiver.

A final related term is *propagation delay*, or *electrical length*. This equals *1/PropagationRate* and is expressed as time per unit length. The propagation delay of light in a vacuum is 85 picoseconds per inch. At 2/3 this speed, the propagation delay of a signal in copper wire is about 125 picoseconds/inch. Another way to find the one-way delay is to multiply propagation delay by cable length.

Calculating Line Length

As a general rule, a link is a long line if its signals' rise time is less than four times the one-way cable delay. Or to put it another way, it's a long line if the cable's one-way delay is greater than 1/4 of the rise time. The dividing line is somewhat arbitrary. Other sources use values from 1/2 to 1/6. RS-232 links are always short lines, because of their limited cable length and slew rate.

Listing 10-1 has two Visual Basic functions for cable calculations. One determines whether a line is long from the propagation rate, the wires' physical length, and the rise time. The other uses a propagation rate and rise time to calculate the maximum length of a short line.

If the rise time is unknown, another way of deciding whether a line is long or short is to compare the shortest expected bit width and the one-way cable delay. This method must consider two factors: the reflections may bounce back and forth several times before settling, and the bit rates of the transmitter and receiver may vary slightly. As a general rule, if the bit width is 40 or more times greater than the delay, any reflections will have settled by the time the receiver reads the bits.

```
Function fncIsTransmissionLine _
  (PropagationRate_PicosecsPerIn As Single, _
  CableLength_Feet As Single, _
  DriversRiseTime_Nanosecs As Single) _
  As Boolean
'Calculates whether a line will behave
'as a transmission line.
If (PropagationRate_PicosecsPerIn * CableLength_Feet * 12) > _
    (DriversRiseTime_Nanosecs * 1000 / 4) Then
    fncIsTransmissionLine = True
Else
  fncIsTransmissionLine = False
End If
End Function
```

```
Function fncMaximumLengthOfShortLineInFeet _
  (PropagationRate_PicosecsPerIn As Single, _
  DriversRiseTime_Nanosecs As Single) _
  As Single
'Returns the maximum cable length
'that will behave as a short line.
fncMaximumLengthOfShortLineInFeet = _
  DriversRiseTime_Nanosecs * 1000 / _
  (PropagationRate_PicosecsPerIn * 48)
End Function
```

Listing 10-1: Visual Basic functions for transmission-line calculations.

Line Terminations

If the calculations show that your link is a long line, the proper termination will help to ensure that the receiver sees the intended logic level. Some short lines also can make use of terminations.

Characteristic Impedance

Terminating a long line requires knowing one more piece of information: the line's characteristic impedance, which is the input impedance of an infinite, open line. Every transmission line has a characteristic impedance. The value varies with the wires' diameter, their spacing in relation to other wires in the cable, and the type of insulation on the wires. It doesn't vary with the wires' physical length, but is constant for any length.

Characteristic impedance is important because a driver initially sees a transmission line as a load equal to the line's characteristic impedance. The value determines how much current flows in a line when a voltage is first applied, as when an output switches. When the receiver's load matches the cable's characteristic impedance, the entire transmitted signal drops across the termination, with minimal distortion due to reflections as the voltage and current settle to final, steady-state values.

And this brings us to rule #1 for RS-485 links:

Terminate long lines with the line's characteristic impedance.

Finding the Value

The simplest, and probably the most accurate, way to find a cable's characteristic impedance is to obtain the value from the cable's manufacturer. Manufacturers specify characteristic impedance for products that are likely to be used as transmission lines. Many links use AWG #24 stranded, twisted pair cable, which has a characteristic impedance of 100 to 150 ohms. But how do the manufacturers find the values? There are several ways to determine it:

- Calculate it mathematically from the properties of the cable. This requires knowing the wire's diameter, length, the distance between the wires, and the effective relative permittivity, which varies with insulation type.

- Calculate it from measured inductance and capacitance. Using an impedance bridge, measure the line's capacitance (C) with the far end of the cable open, and measure the line's inductance (L) with the far end shorted. The characteristic impedance is $\sqrt{(L/C)}$. This calculation ignores the line's series and parallel resistance, which have little effect at high frequencies.

- Find the value empirically by applying a step function to the line and varying the termination resistor until there are no reflections. A step function is a digital pulse with a very short rise time, which ensures that the pulse contains high frequencies. Viewing the signal requires an oscilloscope with very high bandwidth. When the waveform across the termination is identical to the transmitted signal, the termination equals the characteristic impedance.

Adding a Termination

Once you've decided you need a termination, how do you add it? There are several ways to terminate digital lines. Table 10-1 summarizes the options.

Table 10-1: Termination Options for RS-485 Links.

Termination	Advantages	Disadvantages
none	simple, low power	suitable only for short links with slow drivers
parallel end	simple	high power
series	low power	suitable only for 2-node links
AC	low power	suitable only for low bit rates, short links
parallel open-circuit biased	ensures valid logic level when open	high power, requires 2 additional resistors/link
parallel open- and short-circuit biased	ensures valid logic level when open or shorted	requires 4 additional resistors/node

Parallel End Termination

Most RS-485 links use an end termination consisting of a resistor equal to the characteristic impedance connected across the differential lines at or just beyond the farthest receiver. Figure 10-4 illustrates.

For a cable with a characteristic impedance of 120 ohms, the proper termination is 120 ohms across lines A and B, just beyond the *A* and *B* pins at the farthest receiver.

When two or more drivers share a pair of wires, each end of the link has a termination resistor equal to the characteristic impedance. No matter how many nodes are in the network, there should be no more than two termination resistors.

TIA/EIA-485 specifies that RS-485 drivers must be able to drive 32 unit loads plus a parallel termination of 60 ohms. The total load, including the driver, receivers, and terminations, must be no less than 54 ohms. In a full-duplex link, each termination resistor has its own pair of wires, so each driver sees a resistance of 120 ohms. In a link with two termination resistors, the parallel combination of two 120-ohm resistors is 60 ohms. The input impedances of 32 unit-load receivers decrease the total resistance of the link slightly, while the output resistance of the driver and the series resistance of the lines increase it.

Effects of Terminations

You don't have to understand why transmission lines behave as they do in order to design a link that works. But for the curious, the following is an introduction to transmission-line theory, without attempting mathematical proofs.

A transmission line has two wires: one to carry the current from the driver to receiver, and another to provide a return path back to the driver. An RS-485 link is a little more complicated because it has two signal wires that share a termination, plus a ground return, but the basic principles are the same.

In one sense, there's nothing different about how long and short lines behave. The same laws of physics apply whether the driver is slow or fast and whether the signals travel a short or long distance. Both long and short lines may have voltage and current reflections due to an impedance mismatch.

In all cases, the reflections happen very quickly, during and just after an output switches. The difference is that on a long line, the reflections are more likely to continue long enough to cause the receiver to misread logic levels. On short lines, the reflections occur much sooner, and have no effect on the received logic levels.

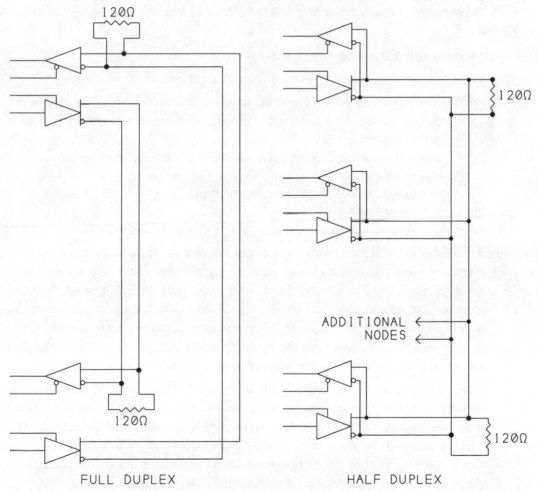

FULL DUPLEX   HALF DUPLEX

Figure 10-4: A parallel end termination requires a resistor across the differential lines at or just beyond the last receiver. A two-way interface uses two resistors.

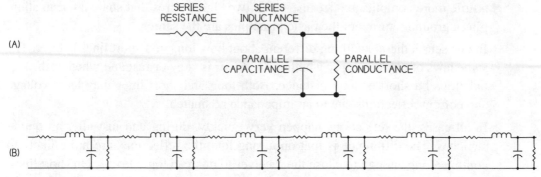

Figure 10-5: (A) A pair of wires has several impedance sources. (B) One way to find the characteristic impedance of a line is to think of the line as a series of short segments.

Impedance Sources of a Line

A pair of wires has several sources of impedance (Figure 10-5A):

> Series resistance varies with the wire's diameter, length, and temperature.
>
> Series inductance varies with diameter and the wire's distance from a ground plane.
>
> Parallel capacitance is a measure of the electric field between the wires.
>
> Parallel leakage resistance is a measure of the effectiveness of the wires' insulation. The leakage resistance is typically a very high value, and is often expressed as conductance (*1/R*).

All of these sources together determine a line's characteristic impedance.

One way to calculate the characteristic impedance is to think of a pair of wires as a series of identical short segments, each having the impedance sources described above (Figure 10-5B). To find the overall impedance of a long line, find the impedance of a short segment and use this value to calculate the impedance of an infinite series of identical segments strung together. For each added segment, the existing line is in parallel with the new segment's parallel impedance, and this combined impedance is in series with the new segment's series impedance.

As you increase the line's length, each segment added has less and less effect on the total impedance, which approaches a fixed value. This value is the impedance of an infinite, open line, and is equal to the line's characteristic impedance. The value is constant for any length of wire. At frequencies greater than 100 kHz, which make up most of the energy in digital pulses, the characteristic impedance is mainly resistive, which means it varies little with frequency.

Initial and Final Currents

Characteristic impedance is important because when a voltage is first applied to a pair of wires, the voltage source has no way of knowing what lies at the end of the pair. It sees the load as an infinite, open line. The driver's initial current is a function of its output impedance and the line's characteristic impedance. The initial current flows even in a pair of open wires, where you might naturally assume that no current flows because the circuit is incomplete.

Shortly after the current reaches the end of the line, it settles to a final current, which is the familiar value determined by the termination and other series resistances in the link. If the initial and final currents vary, the line will see reflected voltages as the current settles.

Each time a driver switches state, it goes through this transition from initial to final currents.

Reflections

Figure 10-6 shows simplified examples of received voltages on lines with different terminations. In each case, what happens when the initial current reaches the end of the wires depends on what it finds there. An RS-485 driver has a low output impedance, so in all cases, the impedance at the source, or driver, is less than the line's characteristic impedance. But the termination at the receiver may vary.

If the termination is greater than the characteristic impedance, the signal oscillates, or rings, before settling to its final level. The same result occurs if a line has no termination except the receiver.

The extreme case of a termination greater than the characteristic impedance is when the wires are open at the far end. The open ends present a *discontinuity* to the current, which can't continue at all. The current has to go somewhere, so it reflects, or turns around and goes back the way it came. As the current reverses, its magnetic field collapses. This increases the electrical charge and induces a voltage that results in the receiver's seeing a higher voltage than what was transmitted.

If the line has a termination, but its value is greater than the characteristic impedance, the effect is similar, but less extreme. Some of the initial current flows in the termination and the rest reflects.

The reflected current eventually returns to the driver. The driver absorbs part of the reflection and bounces the rest back, resulting in a reduced voltage at the receiver. The reflections may continue to bounce back and forth for a few rounds, with each of lower amplitude than the previous one. Eventually, the current settles

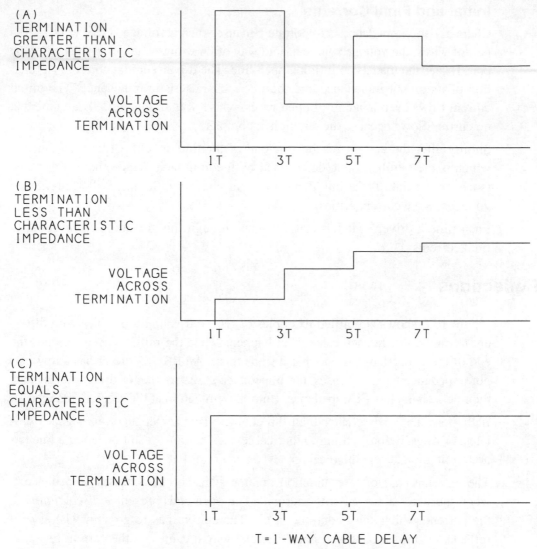

Figure 10-6: Initial voltages on lines with various terminations.

to a final value determined mainly by the termination, the driver's output resistance, and other series resistances.

If the termination is less than the characteristic impedance (and the source impedance is less), the signal gradually rises to its final level.

The extreme case of a termination less than the characteristic impedance is when the wires are shorted together at the far end. When the current reaches the end, there is no load, so there can be no voltage drop at all. The entire transmitted voltage has to reflect back to the driver. The electric field collapses and the magnetic field increases, inducing a current.

If the line has a termination, but its value is less than the characteristic impedance, the effect is similar, but less extreme. Some of the initial voltage drops across the termination and the rest reflects. Each time the driver re-reflects a portion of the voltage, the voltage at the receiver rises, until it reaches its final value.

If the wires terminate in a resistance exactly equal to the characteristic impedance, the current sees no discontinuity. Instead, it sees something that looks exactly like the infinite line it had assumed when it started out. The initial and final currents are equal, and after a single 1-way cable delay, the entire transmitted voltage drops across the resistor, with no reflections at all.

Effects of Cable Length

The reflections happen very fast. The longer the physical length of the line, the more time it takes for the reflections to travel back and forth, and the longer the reflections last. Each reflection bounces from the receiver to the driver and back, so each new reflected voltage arrives at the receiver after two one-way cable delays. For example, a 10-ft cable might have a cable delay of 15 nanoseconds. A series of four reflections would last 0.12 microsecond, plus the initial 15 nsec. Increase the cable length to 1000 ft, and the same reflections last 12 µsecs.

Effects of a Mismatch

If the reflected voltages are large enough and last long enough, they may have any of several effects on a link. If the receiver sees a reduced voltage, its input may drop below the threshold for the intended logic level, causing an error in the received data. If the receiver sees a greater voltage, its input transistors may saturate, slowing its response. A termination of up to 10% larger than the characteristic impedance may improve the signal quality by increasing the initial received voltage. In extreme cases, a mismatch can cause reflections so large that they damage components in the link.

Of course, it's impossible for the termination to match exactly at all times, for all drivers and receivers in a link. But a value that's reasonably close will reduce the amplitude of the reflections and improve signal quality overall.

Effects of a Line's Series Resistance

A line's series resistance has little effect on the characteristic impedance at high frequencies, but the series resistance can become significant for other reasons when the wires are very long. The resistance of stranded AWG #24 wire is about 25 ohms/1000 feet. In a 4000-foot link, each wire has 100 ohms series resistance.

If the link has two 120-ohm termination resistors, a large part of the signal will drop across the wires, and the receiver will see a much smaller differential voltage. But if the signals have the minimum 1.5V difference at the driver, only a fraction of the signal needs to make it to the receiver for it to detect the minimum required 0.2V difference. To decrease the series resistance, use wire with a lower AWG value, which indicates a larger diameter.

Negative Effects of Parallel Terminations

Adding a termination is a tradeoff. Besides reducing reflections, terminating an RS-485 link has negative effects, including increased power consumption, lower noise margin, and overriding the receiver's internal fail-safe circuits.

The higher power consumption is a result of the link's lower series resistance. Figure 10-7A and B show how adding a 120-ohm terminating resistor decreases the parallel input impedance from 12,000 to 119 ohms. Assuming 30 ohms output impedance for each driver, the current in the link increases from 0.4 to 28 milliamps.

The higher current also reduces the noise margin. The driver's output impedance absorbs a larger proportion of the output voltage, reducing the differential voltage at the receivers. If the output impedance of each driver is 30 ohms, 1/3 of the voltage drops across the drivers' output impedances, leaving only 3.3V across the termination. The received differential signal is still 3.1V greater than the receiver's input threshold, however.

Adding a second termination resistor exaggerates both of these effects.

One way to conserve power is to disable all drivers except when they are transmitting. If the link is often idle, disabling the drivers will cut power consumption dramatically. If you want to use spare RS-232 signals as a power source for an RS-232-to-RS-485 converter, the link can't use a resistive parallel termination, because it requires too much current.

Figure 10-7C and D show how adding a termination defeats the fail-safe circuits included in RS-485 receivers. The failsafe circuits ensure that the receiver sees a defined logic level when the inputs are open. Without a termination, the internal pullup and pulldown in many RS-485 receivers holds input A more positive than input B. But adding a termination lowers the open-circuit differential voltage to just a few millivolts. This chapter shows how to add circuits that replace the fail-safe.

Series Terminations

Another type of termination used in some links is the series, or back, termination. Instead of a parallel resistor across the lines at the end of the link, the resistor is at the driver, in series with the line (Figure 10-8). The termination plus the driver's output impedance equal the line's characteristic impedance.

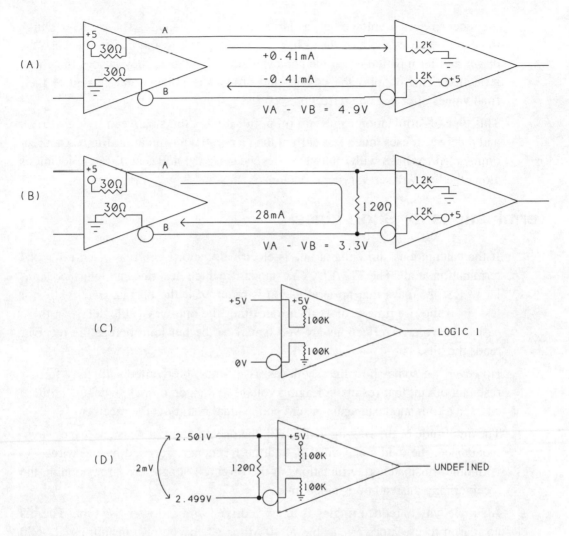

Figure 10-7: (A) and (B) show that a parallel termination increases power consumption and decreases the noise margin. (C) and (D) show how the termination defeats a receiver's internal open-circuit failsafe circuits.

When the output switches, half of the voltage drops across the output impedance and termination, so the initial current is only half as large as the final current, and

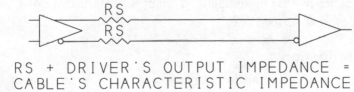

RS + DRIVER'S OUTPUT IMPEDANCE =
CABLE'S CHARACTERISTIC IMPEDANCE

Figure 10-8: Series termination on a differential line.

the receiver sees a voltage half as large as the final voltage. The receiver's high impedance causes most of the voltage to reflect back to the driver. Because the driver and termination equal the characteristic impedance, they absorb the entire reflection. This doubles the voltage and brings the voltage and current to their final values after just one reflection.

This type of termination can be useful in full-duplex links between a single driver and receiver. It uses much less current than a parallel termination. But it's not recommended for links with multiple nodes, because the nodes at different locations along the line will see varying reflections.

Terminations for Short Lines

If the calculations show that a line is electrically short, you may need no added termination at all. The TIA/EIA-422 standard, which describes an interface similar to RS-485, says that no termination is required if the bit rate is 200 kbps or less, or if the rise time is more than four times the one-way cable delay. In these cases, the voltage reflections are very small or die out long before the receiver reads the bits.

However, on some short lines with fast rise times, the components may form a resonant circuit that results in ringing voltages when an output switches. In these cases, a termination can again ensure good signal quality at the receiver.

The amplitude of the ringing varies with the driver's output resistance, the wires' inductance, the load's capacitance, and the frequencies carried by the wires. As with other mismatched terminations, if the ringing voltages are large enough, the receiver may misread transmitted bits.

A simple way to reduce ringing is to use a driver with a slower rise time. There's no reason to use a driver capable of 10 Mbps when you're transmitting at 9600 bps. If you can't change the hardware, using a low bit rate with a fast driver at least gives the ringing more time to settle before the receiver reads the input.

You can also reduce ringing by reducing the circuit's Q, which is a measurement of its ability to resonate. To do this, decrease the wires' inductance or increase the load's capacitance. To decrease the inductance, use larger diameter wires, or wires that are twisted more tightly. To increase capacitance, use an AC termination like those described next.

AC Terminations

An AC, or active, termination can reduce power consumption of idle links, and may also reduce ringing voltages. However, it also reduces the maximum cable length and bit rate. Figure 10-9 shows two examples.

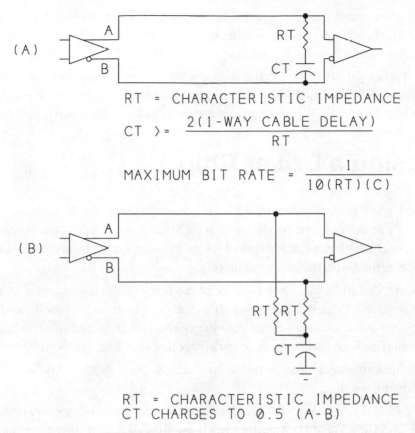

RT = CHARACTERISTIC IMPEDANCE

$$CT \geq \frac{2(1\text{-WAY CABLE DELAY})}{RT}$$

$$\text{MAXIMUM BIT RATE} = \frac{1}{10(RT)(C)}$$

RT = CHARACTERISTIC IMPEDANCE
CT CHARGES TO 0.5 (A-B)

Figure 10-9: An AC termination can conserve power on some links.

In Figure 10-9A, a resistor and capacitor connect in series across the differential lines. The capacitor prevents ringing by absorbing the high frequencies that make up the ringing voltages. It also reduces power consumption, because the current on the lines will be near zero when the capacitor has charged after each transition. The added capacitance also lowers the maximum bit rate and cable length, so this termination is limited to shorter, low-speed links.

TIA/EIA-422 gives this formula to select the capacitor's value:

CT (pF) < 2 * (one-way cable delay (ps)) / (characteristic impedance (ohms))

Assuming a propagation rate of 125 ps/in. and a characteristic impedance of 120 ohms, a 10-ft. cable should use a capacitor of 250 pF or less. A 100-ft. cable can use up to 2500 pF.

In addition, the product of the terminating resistance and capacitance should be no more than 1/10 the width of a bit. For example, with 120 ohms and 2500 pF, the minimum bit width is 3 microseconds, for a maximum bit rate of 330 khz.

Unlike a purely resistive parallel termination, this termination doesn't defeat the receiver's internal biasing circuits. When all drivers are off, the capacitor remains charged and the receiver's internal pull-up and pull-down hold input A > B.

In Figure 10-9B, two termination resistors share a capacitor that connects to ground. When idle, this termination draws half the current of a single parallel resistor termination. The capacitor charges to half the differential voltage.

Choosing a Driver Chip

Two ways to reduce the effect of reflected voltages are to decrease the cable length or increase the rise time. There's usually not much you can do about the physical length of a cable required for a particular application, but you can control the rise time with the choice of drivers.

A link should be designed to work at the driver's minimum and maximum rise times. For 2.5Mhz drivers, typical rise time is 10 to 15 nanoseconds, and the maximum, 60 nanoseconds. Some data sheets also specify a minimum, which may be as short as 3 nanoseconds. Also remember that rise time varies with the load.

The maximum rise time limits the bit rate. Rise time should be no more than 20% of the bit width.

The minimum rise time determines whether or not a line is long and requires a termination. As Table 10-2 shows, with a rise time of 3 nanoseconds and a propagation rate of 125 picoseconds per inch, a cable just 6 inches long behaves like a long line.

In contrast, the MAX3080 is very slow, with a minimum rise time of 667 nanoseconds. This increases the maximum length of a short line in the above example to 111 feet. The chip is rated for use at up to 115,200 bps, which is fast enough for many PC and microcontroller applications. If your link doesn't require fast bit rates, using slower drivers is a simple, no-cost way to improve signal quality.

In addition to reduced transmission-line effects, slower chips reduce the emanated EMI (electromagnetic interference). And as explained above, a slow driver can reduce ringing on short links.

This brings us to rule #2 for RS-485 links, whether long or short:

Use the slowest drivers possible for your bit rate.

Table 10-2: Maximum length of a cable that does not behave as a transmission line. Assumes a propagation rate of 125 ps/in.

Chip	Maximum Bit Rate (kHz)	Rise Time (nanoseconds)	Maximum Length of Short Line (feet)
Max3080	115	667 (min.)	111
Max483	250	250 (min.)	41
Max3083	500	200 (min.)	33
Max485	2,500	15 (typical)	2.5
Max3490	10,000	3 (min.)	0.5

Network Topologies

When there are more than two devices in a link, how the nodes are wired together can also affect signal quality. Figure 10-10 shows several network topologies, or wiring configurations. RS-485 drivers and receivers are designed for use in a bus, or linear, topology. This means that the network cable begins at one node, connects in sequence to each of the others, ending at the last node. This enables the use of terminations at each end of the bus, and brings us to rule #3 for RS-485 links:

Wire the nodes in a bus topology.

A stub is the wires that connect a node to the network cable. Stubs should be as short as possible. Many sources recommend limiting stub length so that its one-way delay is 1/4 to 1/2 of the signals' rise time.

But what if connecting the nodes along a bus isn't convenient? Sometimes, as in wiring throughout a house, it would be simpler to branch cables from one or more central locations, in a star, or hub-and-spoke, topology. An advantage to this arrangement is that if a connection should open at one of the nodes, communications among the others can continue normally.

In this case, there are several options:

- Use slow drivers to increase the rise time and allow longer lines. With the Max3080's minimum rise time of 667ns, a stub of 1/3 the rise time is 150 ft.

- Wire the nodes as a bus, even if this means that each node has a pair of wires running out to it, then doubling back before going on to the next node. The link uses twice as much wire, but without compromising performance. If you use a cable that contains two pairs of wires, you can use a pair for each direction.

- Add a repeater circuit to regenerate the RS-485 signals at a juncture where a stub connects to the main bus. The regenerated signals begin a new RS-485 link. A complication is the need to control the direction of the repeater. This requires either an added wire to act as a direction-control signal, or circuits that

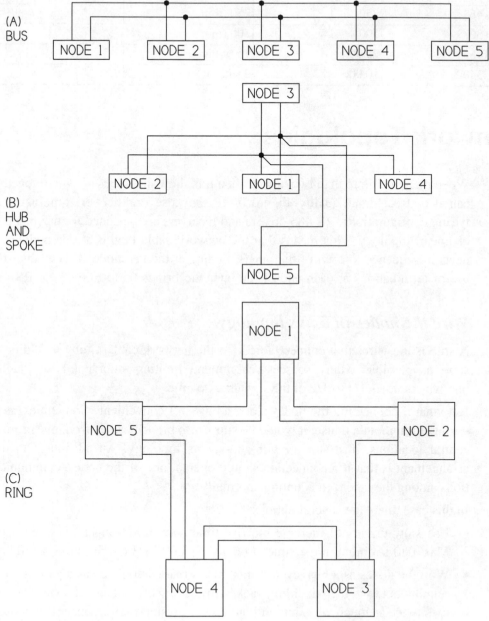

Figure 10-10: Network topologies. RS-485 networks use a bus topology.

control the direction automatically. (This chapter has more on repeater circuits.)

Another topology used by some networks is the ring, which is similar to a bus, except that the last node connects back to the first, and each node transmits only to its neighbor. The distance around a ring is unlimited in theory, but the more nodes you have, the longer it will take to pass a message all the way around. An RS-485 network can use a ring topology if each node has two ports, and each link between two nodes is a separate RS-485 link.

Open and Short-circuit Biasing

In a half-duplex RS-485 link, there are times when no driver is enabled. Even a full-duplex link may disable its drivers to save power whenever possible. In these cases, it's important that all receivers see a valid logic 1, indicating an idle state. It can also be useful to ensure a logic 1 input if the RS-485 lines accidentally short together. This brings us to rule #4:

Bias inactive links.

There are several ways to accomplish this, using additional terminating components or chips with fail-safe circuits built-in.

Open-circuit Protection

An RS-485 network should be designed so that only one driver at a time is enabled. In order to achieve this, each node must wait for the previous driver to finish transmitting before it enables its driver. In between, there will almost certainly be times when no driver is enabled.

If no driver is enabled, the signal level at a receiver's inputs may be undefined. If the receiver detects a logic 0, it will think it's received a Start bit and will try to read a byte. The same situation exists if one or both wires in the link accidentally open.

Most RS-485 chips include a fail-safe feature that holds input A more positive than input B when no signal is applied to the receiver. The fail-safe works fine on links that don't use a terminating resistor.

But as Figure 10-7 showed, the fail-safe is defeated on lines with terminations. Figure 10-11 shows a solution. It adds two 470-ohm resistors: one from input A to +5V and the other from input B to ground. This configuration holds terminal A

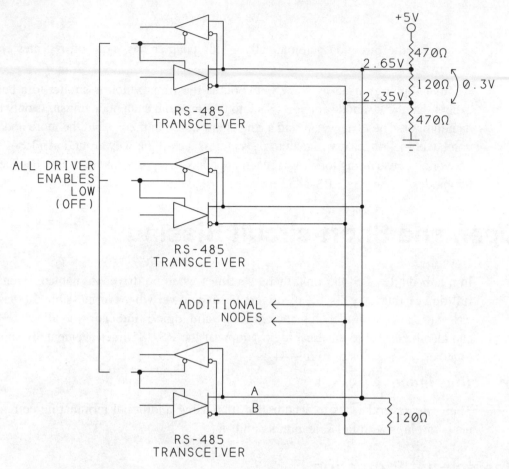

Figure 10-11: Open-circuit biasing for RS-485.

about 0.3 more positive than terminal B when no drivers are enabled. The receiver's TTL outputs are high, while still allowing any driver to pull line A low.

One pair of resistors at one end of the link biases the entire network. In a master/slave network, the biasing resistors are usually at the master. If a node becomes disconnected from the network, or if a network wire opens, its internal fail-safe circuits hold the inputs at logic 1.

The external fail-safe components have a small effect on an active link's current. When a driver is enabled and A is more positive than B, the output current is in the same direction as the bias current, so the two currents add. When the driver brings B more positive than A, the bias current is in the opposite direction, and subtracts from the signal current. But because the drive current is much larger, the opposing bias current doesn't affect the logic level seen by the receiver.

The biasing resistors and the parallel combination of the terminating resistors and the receivers' inputs form a voltage divider. The 470-ohm biasing resistors will work with any 5V link that has two 120-ohm terminations and up to 32 unit loads. Smaller biasing resistors will increase the noise margin but also increase power consumption. With larger terminations, the biasing resistors can be a little larger. For example, a network with 150-ohm terminations can use bias resistors of 560 ohms. A 3V supply requires smaller values.

For an exact match, slightly increase the value of the termination at the node with the biasing resistors. At this node, the terminating resistance equals the terminating resistor in parallel with the series combination of the biasing resistors:

```
TerminationResistance =  _
(TerminatingResistor * 2 * BiasResistor) / _
(TerminatingResistor + (2 * BiasResistor) )
```

This combined resistance is typically 10 to 30 ohms less than the termination. So for a more exact match, use a slightly large terminating resistor at the biasing node. For example, in Figure 10-11, the combined resistance is just 106 ohms, while increasing the termination to 140 ohms results in a better match of 122 ohms.

Listing 10-2 is a Visual Basic function that returns a bias-resistor value for any supply voltage, termination, number of unit loads, and noise margin (the desired difference between A and B on an open line).

Figure 10-11's circuit differs from RS-232's convention that an idle link should be in a marking, or logic 1 state. TIA/EIA-485 defines logic 1 as the state where B > A, but the biasing holds A > B.

One situation where this can cause confusion is when using an RS-485 interface with a Basic Stamp II. The Stamp's host software assumes a direct connection to an RS-232 interface, where *Sin* is low, or negative, when idle. But Figure 10-11's biasing would result in *Sin* being high. A solution is to add a 74HC14 or similar inverter between *Sin* and the interface chip's TTL output and between *Sout* and the interface chip's TTL input. If you're not using the host software, but want to use *Sin* and *Sout* to communicate with other software on a PC, you can invert the signals with the baudmode parameter of the Stamp's `SerIn` and `SerOut` statements.

An emergency way to invert RS-485 signals is to swap the A and B lines. Connecting a transceiver's *A* pin to the cable's B line and the *B* pin to the A line has the effect of inverting the signals in both directions. But this technique is likely to be more trouble than its worth, when you return months or years later to modify or troubleshoot the link and have long forgotten that the miswiring was deliberate.

```
Function fncFindBiasResistor _
    (Termination As Single, _
    NumberOfUnitLoads As Single, _
    SupplyVoltage As Single, _
    BiasVoltage As Single) _
    As Integer
'Calculates the value of fail-safe bias resistors
'for an RS-485 link.
Dim Count As Integer
Dim TotalTermination As Single
Dim Current As Single
'First find the parallel resistance of the termination resistors
'and the receivers.
'Assume two Terminations in parallel.
TotalTermination = Termination ^ 2 / (Termination * 2)
'One unit load is 12,000 ohms.
For Count = 1 To NumberOfUnitLoads
    TotalTermination = _
        TotalTermination * 12000 / (TotalTermination + 12000)
Next Count
'Find the current in the bias network.
Current = BiasVoltage / TotalTermination
'Each bias resistor equals
'input B's open-circuit voltage divided by the current.
fncFindBiasResistor = _
    CInt(((SupplyVoltage / 2) - (BiasVoltage / 2)) / Current)
End Function
```

Listing 10-2: Use this function to find the value of bias resistors.

Also, the chips' internal (and possibly external) biasing brings A high and B low, and swapping the lines conflicts with this.

Short-circuit Protection

Another concern in RS-485 links is ensuring a logic 1 input if the network wires accidentally short together, or if two drivers are enabled at the same time and hold the differential voltage near 0V.

A simple solution is to use Maxim's MAX3080. TIA/EIA-485 says that receivers must recognize valid logic levels when the difference between inputs A and B is at least 200mV. The MAX3080's receivers comply with the standard but expand the definition for logic 1 to include the range where input A is between 50mV less than, and 200mV greater than, input B. In other words, the only undefined range is when one input is 50 to 200 mV less than the other.

With these definitions, the receiver sees a logic 1 if the difference between input A and B is zero, which will occur if the RS-485 wires short together. The shorted lines can have up to 50mV of noise, and the voltage will remain a logic 1.

Another approach shown in Figure 10-12 uses 75ALS180B or MAX491 driver/receivers with a resistor network to provide the fail-safe. These are full-duplex driver/receiver pairs, similar to the '179 introduced in Chapter 9, but with an enable line for each direction. Figure 10-12's circuit is half-duplex, with the 2-wire interface created by tying the driver and receiver pairs together.

Resistors *R1* and *R2* bias the line to a logic 1 if no driver is active, and *R3* and *R4* protect the receiver and ensure that the input remains biased even if the line is shorted. Only the two end nodes have termination resistor *R5*, but each node has its own set of R1-R4.

This termination reduces the noise margin, because *R3* and *R4* each drop a few tenths of a volt. If the network has fewer than 32 unit loads, you can increase the noise margin slightly by reducing the values of *R1–R4*. Multiply each value by half the total number of unit loads in the network. To calculate the resistor values in ohms, use:

```
R1 = NumberOfUnitLoads * 1100
R2 = R1
R3 = NumberOfUnitLoads * 55
R4 = R3
```

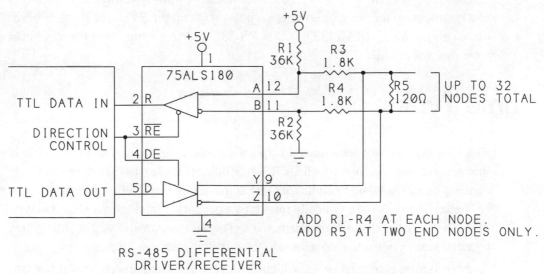

Figure 10-12: RS-485 interface with open- and failsafe biasing.

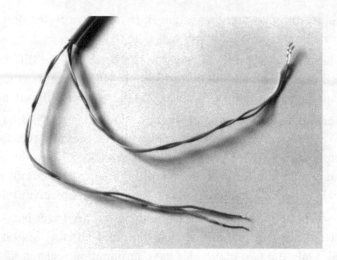

Figure 10-13: A twisted pair cable containing two twisted pairs.

For example, with just two unit-load nodes, *R1* and *R2* would be 2.2K and *R3* and *R4* would be 110 ohms.

Biasing Receiver Outputs

In some half-duplex links, including those with one control signal for the driver and receiver enable, the receiver is disabled at times, causing the receiver's TTL output to be undefined. To ensure that the output remains high, add a 10k pullup resistor from the output to +5V. You don't need the pull-up if the output connects to a microcontroller pin with an internal pull-up (as on the 8051), or if the receiver drives an input to a MAX232 or other RS-232 interface chip, because these also have internal pullups.

Cable Types

TIA/EIA-485 doesn't recommend a specific cable type, but twisted pair cable is inexpensive and performs well in RS-485 links (Figure 10-13). A twisted pair consists of two insulated conductors that spiral around each other forming a double helix. The twists are typically one or two per inch. Catalogs may list this type of cable as network wire or alarm wire. The simple act of twisting the wires together causes noise that couples into the wires to cancel.

Another option is triaxial cable, which is like coaxial cable except that it has two conductors, rather than one, surrounded by a shield. Triaxial cable is expensive, however, compared to twisted pair.

This results in rule #5 for RS-485 links:

Use twisted-pair cable.

How a Wire Picks Up Noise

To understand how a twisted pair cancels noise requires understanding something about how noise couples into a wire. Noise is any signal you don't want in a circuit. The noise can enter a wire in many ways, including by conductive, common-impedance, magnetic, capacitive, or electromagnetic coupling.

Conductive and common-impedance coupling require direct contact between the signal wire and the wire carrying the noise. Conductive coupling occurs when a wire brings noise from another source, such as a noisy power-supply line, into a circuit. Common-impedance coupling occurs when two circuits share a wire, such as a common ground return. In RS-485, the differential signals cancel much of this type of noise.

The other types of coupling result from interactions between the electric and magnetic fields that emanate from the wires themselves, or that couple onto the wires from outside sources.

Capacitive and inductive coupling are a source of crosstalk, where voltages in one wire couple into another. When two wires carry charges at different potentials, an electric field exists between the wires. The strength of the field varies with the distance between the wires. This electric field is the source of capacitive, or electric, coupling. Current in a wire causes the wire to emanate a magnetic field. Inductive, or magnetic, coupling occurs when magnetic fields of two wires overlap, causing the energy in one wire's field to induce a current in the other wire.

When wires are greater than 1/6 wavelength apart (1/4 mile at 10 Mhz), the effects of the capacitive and inductive fields are considered together, as electromagnetic coupling. An example of electromagnetic coupling is when a wire acts as a receiving antenna for radio waves.

Twisted-pair Cable

Twisted pairs are effective at canceling low-frequency noise caused by magnetic coupling. In a twisted pair, each twist of the cable swaps the physical positions of the wires, and any noise that magnetically couples into one wire is canceled in the next twist by an equal, opposite noise in the other wire.

If the twisting isn't perfectly uniform, the canceling will be less than 100 percent, but the noise will be much reduced. The twisting is most effective in reducing magnetic coupling of low-frequency signals, such as 60-Hz power-line noise. For a similar reason, twisted pairs also reduce the electromagnetic radiation emitted by a pair.

The magnetic field emanating from a circuit is proportional to the area between the conductors. Twisting the wires tightly reduces this area, and thus the size of the magnetic field and the amount of noise that couples into it.

With cable containing two twisted pairs, you can use one pair for the RS-485 signals and the other for a ground connection. (Connect both wires in the pair to ground.)

Selecting Cable

Both IBM and the EIA have published specifications for cable types. This makes it easy to buy cables of known quality. Each type has a defined characteristic impedance and maximum bit rate. The propagation velocity may be specified as well. Manufacturers also publish specifications for cables designed for use in data links.

Many RS-485 links use 120-ohm cable, but higher values are also fine. IBM's Type 1 cable contains unshielded twisted pairs, is rated for use at up to 100 Mbits/sec., and has a characteristic impedance of 150 ohms.

Some cable intended for data links, including EIA/TIA-568's Category 3, 4, and 5 cable, uses 100-ohm, unshielded twisted pairs. This is fine for 1-way or full-duplex RS-485 or RS-422 links. RS-422 allows just one driver and often uses 100-ohm cable with a single 100-ohm termination. But a 2-way, half-duplex RS-485 link would need two 100-ohm resistors in parallel, which brings the parallel combination to just 50 ohms. This is less than TIA/EIA-485's specified minimum. Most RS-485 drivers can source and sink 60 milliamperes, however, so they will work with 100 ohm cable and terminations. But a cable with 120-ohm or greater characteristic impedance is a better choice for most RS-485 links.

Shielding

Metal shielding is effective at blocking noise due to capacitive, electromagnetic, and high-frequency magnetic coupling. The shielding is typically grounded at one end only. If the link has a single power source, the shield ground is at this node. Many RS-485 links successfully use unshielded cable, however.

Connectors

Unlike RS-232, the RS-485 standard doesn't specify a connector, signal functions, or pin assignments, so these are left for you to designate. Many links use

RJ-type modular connectors (described in Chapter 7). On any connector, keep the two signal wires (A and B) next to each other.

The two differential lines for each signal should of course be in the same twisted pair. Also be careful not to transpose the wires: all of the drivers' and receivers' *A* pins should connect to one wire, and all of the *B* pins, to the other.

Grounds in a Differential Link

An RS-485 link forms a single circuit, though it may extend over thousands of feet. Because the differential drivers cause equal and opposite return currents that essentially cancel each other out, it may seem that RS-485 has no need for a ground connection at all. With few exceptions, however, the entire link should share a ground connection, though the link itself may be isolated from the circuits it connects to. Chapter 7 introduced the topics of power supplies, grounding, and isolation. This section looks at grounding and isolation as it relates to RS-485 links, which may extend much farther than RS-232.

Ensuring a Common Ground

The currents in RS-485 balanced lines are nearly, but not exactly, equal. They will differ slightly due to imbalances between the components and noise that isn't exactly equal in both wires. The current in the ground wire may be very small, but it's not zero. If there is no ground connection, the energy in the return current has to dissipate somehow, possibly as radiated energy that shows up as EMI.

In some RS-485 links, all of the nodes and the link itself share a common ground. In others, the link is isolated from the nodes it connects to. In either case, all of the link's drivers and receivers should share a ground connection, which may have any of several sources. Most obviously, the RS-485 cable may include a wire that connects to signal ground at each node. Or the nodes' power supplies may share a common ground, either through electrical wiring or via an earth ground. In a very short link, multiple nodes may share a power supply.

The specifications for RS-485 chips limit the permitted difference in ground potentials. Isolating the link is sometimes easier than ensuring that earth grounds at distant nodes are within the required limits.

Common-mode Voltages

Common-mode voltage is a measure of the difference between a ground voltage and signal voltages at one location in a circuit. The common-mode voltage at a receiver is the mean, or average, of the voltages on the two differential lines, referenced to the receiver's signal ground. To comply with TIA/EIA-485, components must work properly with common-mode voltages from -7V to +12V. In addition, each of the receiver's inputs must also be in the range of -7V to +12V, referenced to the receiver's ground.

To remain within the standard's common-mode limit, the ground potentials at the driver and receiver may vary as much as ±7V with differential signals as large as ±5V. The data sheets for interface chips specify a common-mode limit, which is often larger than the minimum requirement. A link should be designed so that it doesn't exceed the limit of its components.

This brings us to the rule #6 for RS-485 links:

Limit common-mode voltages.

If the ground potentials of the driver and receiver are equal, the common-mode voltage at the receiver is the mean of the two inputs, or +2.5V with a 5V supply.

The common-mode voltages also remain within the limits when the ground potentials of two nodes vary by ±7V. For example, if the driver's outputs are +5V and 0V relative to the driver's ground, and the driver's ground is 7V higher than the receiver's, the receiver's inputs, relative to the receiver's ground, will be +12V and +7V (assuming no losses in the differential lines). The common-mode voltage at the receiver's inputs is:

```
((DriverOutputA - DriverOutputB) / 2 ) + _
DriverGroundVoltage - ReceiverGroundVoltage
```

or

```
((+5 - 0) / 2) + 7 = +9.5
```

which is within the +12V limit.

In the other direction, if the driver's outputs are +5V and 0V and the driver's ground is 7V lower than the receiver's, the receiver's inputs relative to the receiver's ground will be +2V and -7V. The common-mode voltage is:

```
((+5 - 0) / 2) - 7 = -4.5
```

which is also within the -7V limit.

If the receiver's inputs are within their specified limit, the only time the common-mode voltage approaches its limit is when the received signal is very small and has a large offset. For example, if the receiver sees inputs of +11.8V and +12V, the common-mode voltage is +11.9V.

The difference in grounds is a result both of any DC differences in the ground potentials plus any AC oscillations or spikes in the ground connection. Some

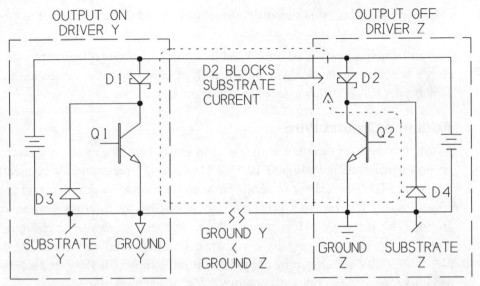

Figure 10-14: Schottky diodes in RS-485 drivers block large substrate currents between an active driver and disabled drivers.

chips, such as National's DS26LS32A, allow common-mode voltages as high as ±25V.

Why a Common-mode Voltage Limit?

Why do the chips have the common-mode limit? To understand what's happening requires looking inside the chips. Figure 10-14 shows the internal circuits for a portion of a two-way, half-duplex link. The components are as presented in National Semiconductor's application note AN-409. A signal wire connects the two drivers' outputs. The receivers, termination, and the rest of the drivers' circuits aren't shown, and a complete link would include a similar circuit for the other differential signal.

A wire connects the grounds of the two nodes. Each driver also has a parasitic diode connection between the chip's grounded substrate (base material) and the collector of the output transistor. The parasitic diode is a result of the physics of the semiconductor material that makes up the chip. The chip's ground pin also connects to the substrate.

Schottky diodes *D1* and *D2* prevent damaging substrate currents from flowing when one of the drivers is on and the other is off.

For example, if Node Y's ground potential is 5V less than Node Z's, if *D1* and *D2* were replaced by a direct connection, current could flow in a loop through *D4*, *Q1*, and back to *D4*. Series resistors in the ground wire would limit the current, but driver Y's output voltage would clamp at -0.7V due to the voltage drop across

D4. Diode *D2* blocks this substrate current and allows the active driver to co-exist with disabled drivers.

The protection is guaranteed only when the common-mode voltages are within the chip's specified limits. RS-422 interface chips don't have the protection diodes. This is why RS-422 allows only one driver per link.

Adding a Ground Wire

A simple way to ensure that a ground path exists between nodes is to include a ground wire in the link (Figure 10-15). TIA/EIA-485 recommends connecting a 1/2-Watt, 100-ohm resistor in series between each node's signal ground and the ground wire. The resistors protect the components by limiting current in the ground wire if the ground voltages do vary. It doesn't hurt to use resistors with higher power ratings, especially if you expect large ground variations. For example, with a 20V difference in grounds, 100 milliamps will flow in each of two resistors (one at each node), dissipating 1 Watt in each resistor.

Don't assume that adding a ground wire brings the ground voltages closer together. An added wire may lower the impedance between the grounds, but if the ground potentials vary, the voltage difference drops across the resistors.

Isolated Links

RS-485 links can be much longer than RS-232, and over long links, the nodes' grounds may vary by many volts. Chapter 7 introduced galvanic isolation as a way of making a circuit immune to ground noise in other circuits.

As with RS-232, if the nodes in an RS-485 link have a common earth ground and a ground wire, ground currents from all sources will choose the path of least resistance. If the power supplies of all nodes use the same electrical system and their ground wires connect at an earth ground, the ground connection may be quiet. Even here, though, motors, switches, and other electrically noisy equipment can induce ground noise. If the nodes are in different buildings, using different power systems, the earth ground is likely to have higher impedance, and ground currents from other sources may find their way into the link's ground wire. Isolating the link can reduce or eliminate these problems.

TIA/EIA-485 specifies that RS-485 links must have a common ground, either via a wire or an earth ground. If you can't guarantee that the earth grounds of the nodes will be within the components' common-mode limits, or if you just don't want to worry about earth-ground noise, galvanic isolation is a solution.

Figure 10-16 shows four ways to isolate an RS-485 link.

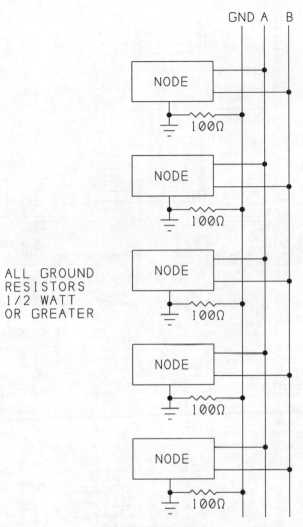

Figure 10-15: A 100-ohm resistor between each node and the link's ground wire limits the current in the ground wire when two nodes' grounds vary.

Figure 10-16A has full isolation. Each node's interface has an isolated power supply and an optoisolated data link. The link's ground wire has no connection to any node's signal ground or earth ground. This arrangement protects the link from noisy earth grounds and from variations in ground voltage at different nodes. It also protects the nodes from noise picked up by the link's ground wire. The nodes themselves may or may not share an earth ground.

To isolate a link, you can use discrete components or a chip designed for this purpose. Maxim's MAX1480 is a complete, isolated RS-485 interface that contains a

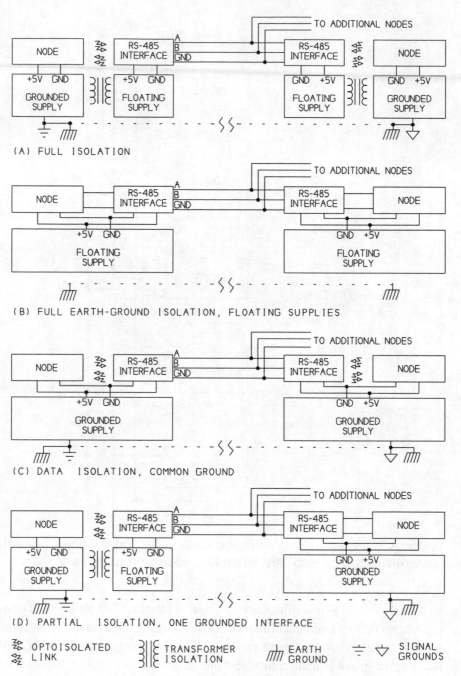

Figure 10-16: Four ways to isolate an RS-485 link.

tiny transformer that isolates the link's power supply, plus optical isolators for the signal lines.

Partial isolation can be cheaper or more convenient than full isolation, and in some cases is enough.

In Figure 10-16B, the nodes and the link are isolated from earth ground, but the RS-485 link isn't isolated from the nodes it connects to. The power supplies may be batteries or floating AC supplies. This arrangement is useful if the nodes' circuits are relatively quiet but you want to isolate the nodes and link from variations in earth ground. A system where each node is battery-powered has this type of isolation.

In Figure 10-16C, the signals wires are isolated, but the grounds aren't. This partial isolation offers some protection to the nodes if a voltage surge hits the link. Because the link shares its ground with the nodes, the grounds must be within the common-mode limit of the components. If for some reason the link can have only two wires, the link may use a common earth ground instead of a ground wire as the return path.

Figure 10-16D shows another partially isolated link. The link shares its ground with just one node, while all of the other nodes are isolated from the link. Because the link has a single ground connection, the common-mode voltage is small.

Extending a Link with Repeaters

TIA/EIA-485 specifies that a link may have up to 32 unit loads, or driver/receiver pairs, but what can you do if you need more than this? Often, the simplest solution is to use interface chips that are less than a unit load. The downsides are that each node adds a small amount of capacitance to the line, and some fraction-of-a-unit-load chips don't support fast bit rates.

Another option is a repeater circuit, which regenerates the RS-485 signals and allows you to add up to 32 more nodes. You can also use a repeater to extend the length of a network or to add a spoke to a bus.

Figure 10-17 shows a network with a repeater circuit containing one 75177 and one 75178 repeater chip. As with transceivers, the repeaters each have a control input that determines the direction of signal flow through the chip. The '177's input is active-high, and the '178's is active-low.

In a half-duplex link, the link must control the repeater's direction. For example, the repeater might match the direction of a master node. To do so, you can use the same signal to control both the master node and the repeater. If the repeater is far

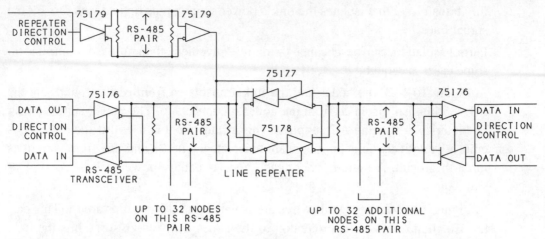

Figure 10-17: Repeater circuit for RS-485.

from the master node, however, you may have to wire the direction-control signal as another RS-485 signal, as Figure 10-17 shows.

A microcontroller-based repeater may require no control signal at all. Some designs are similar to the automatic enable control described in Chapter 11. When the repeater detects a Start bit from either side, it enables the appropriate driver and uses timing circuits to calculate the width of a byte. After allowing enough time for the byte to transmit, plus a margin of error, the repeater disables the driver, unless another Start bit has been detected. A more sophisticated automatic repeater detects the Start bit as well as the data bits that follow, and disables the driver precisely on the Stop bit.

11

Network Programming

Programming serial links becomes more complicated when three or more devices share a communications path. Each node needs to know when it's OK to transmit and which received messages are intended for it. Chapter 2 described techniques to help ensure that each receiver sees all of the data intended for it, and that the data contains no errors. This chapter introduces issues and options related to ensuring reliable, efficient communications in a network.

Managing Traffic

One of the first things to decide is how the network will manage its traffic. There are many types of networks, and many ways of programming them, but most have all of the following features:

- Each node can both send and receive.
- Only one node transmits at a time.
- Each node recognizes and responds to the messages intended for it, and ignores all others.
- The transmitting node detects when a node doesn't receive a transmission or doesn't understand what it has received, and takes appropriate action.

In a full-duplex link, you usually don't have to worry about whose turn it is to transmit. Each driver has its own pair of wires and can transmit whenever it wants. In a network, you have multiple nodes sharing a single path, and the nodes need a way to decide when it's OK to transmit.

Steps in Exchanging a Message

Even in the simplest network, it's important to ensure that all messages get to their intended destinations without errors, and that each node responds only to those messages intended for it.

For example, assume that Node 1 wants to send a message to Node 2, telling it to set an output port to a value and send back the value of another port. All of the following must take place:

Node 1 must:

> Enable its network driver.
>
> Send the address of the node it wants to talk to.
>
> Send the message.
>
> Disable its network driver and wait for a response.

Then Node 2 must:

> Read incoming data.
>
> Recognize its address.
>
> Read the message that follows.
>
> Recognize when the message has ended.
>
> Take the requested actions.
>
> Prepare its response.
>
> Enable its network driver.
>
> Send the response.
>
> Disable its driver.

Node 1 then must:

> Read the incoming response.
>
> Take any required action.
>
> Enable its driver in preparation for polling the next node.

And at the same time, all of the other nodes must:

> Read all incoming data.
>
> Recognize that the messages are not for them.

Protocols

There are several options in the form of protocols, or sets of rules, for handling the task. Three of these are master/slave, token passing, and collision detecting.

Master/Slave

Master/slave is the simplest protocol to implement, and it's what I use in Chapter 12's example network. One node is designated the master and is in charge of controlling all network traffic. To ensure that each node has a chance to speak, the master typically polls, or sends a message to, each of the slaves in sequence. Each poll requests a response, which may be a simple acknowledgment, or it may include requested data, an error message, or other information. A slave may transmit only after the master requests a response. Any message from one slave to another has to pass through the master.

The main disadvantage is the delays that occur because each node has to wait to be polled before it can transmit. Depending on the network's purpose and speed, the delays may be no problem at all, or much too long to be practical.

For example, imagine a network with a master (Node 1) and nine slaves (Nodes 2-10). The master polls each node in sequence, and each poll takes 10 seconds. If Node 2 detects an emergency condition and needs to tell the master to take action, it may have to wait as long as 90 seconds before the master gets around to polling it.

Token-passing

A token-passing protocol gets rid of the single master and allows any node to have control of the network. The node in control is said to have the token. Only one node at a time can have the token.

The network protocol must define how a node knows if it has the token as well as how to pass it to another node. The token may be just a designated bit or variable in each node that is set or cleared to indicate whether or not the node has the token.

When a node wants to pass the token to another node, it gives up the token it has (by clearing its token bit, for example), and sends a message telling another node that it now has the token. This node then takes whatever action it wants and passes the token on.

This protocol enables any node that has the token to talk directly to another. But it still doesn't allow a node to interrupt with an emergency message, unless the node happens to have the token when the emergency occurs.

Collision Detecting

A collision-detecting protocol allows any node to transmit whenever the transmission path is free. If two or more nodes try to transmit at the same time, the nodes, or all nodes but one, must detect the collision, stop transmitting, and try again after a delay. This protocol is useful when any node has to be able to transmit when it wants, with minimal delay, and when the overall traffic on the network is light, so collisions will be few.

But the programming required to detect collisions isn't always feasible. And the network's hardware has to withstand multiple drivers being enabled at once, if only briefly.

One way to detect a collision is for the sending node to attempt to read back what it sends. As long as the reads match the writes, it assumes there is no collision and the transmission can continue. If the read doesn't match what was written, the node assumes that another node is trying to transmit. The node waits a bit, then tries again.

How well the protocol works depends on the setting of the delay times after a collision. Different nodes should use different delay times, either by assigning each a different, fixed delay or by using random values. Otherwise, the nodes will all retry at the same time and no one will ever get through.

The receiving nodes also have to be able to recognize and ignore failed attempts at transmitting. These attempts should be brief, however, just long enough for the node to detect the collision.

There are a couple of reasons why RS-485 isn't suited for collision-detecting protocols. RS-485 drivers are intended for use in links where only one driver is enabled at a time. If two or more drivers are enabled, the chips have protection circuits that limit the current and eventually disable the outputs, but the currents can be as high as 250 milliamperes. The safety features are intended only for use during occasional malfunctions. High currents stress the circuits, and a network protocol shouldn't cause this, if only briefly.

Plus, with the asynchronous transmissions used by most RS-485 links, the software or firmware usually has no way of examining each bit as it's received, so bit-by-bit collision detecting isn't possible.

In contrast, open-collector and open-drain logic used in synchronous links are capable of use with multiple drivers enabled, and the software or firmware is often capable of bit-by-bit monitoring. Chapter 5 described the Basic Stamp's open baudmode, which uses open-drain outputs.

I²C is an example of a network interface that uses open-drain outputs and has a bit-by-bit collision-detecting protocol. In an I²C link, any low output brings the data line low. When two nodes try to transmit at the same time, the node that wins is the one sending a message with the most consecutive logic lows, beginning with the first bit. Each transmitting node checks the data line after writing a logic-high, to find out if the logic level matches what was sent. If it doesn't match, it means that another node has pulled the line low, and the node with the logic-high output must stop sending data, hold its output high, and delay before retrying the transmission from the beginning.

I²C's clock line is also open-drain, and multiple masters may generate the clock. The hardware handles multiple clocks automatically by going low when any clock goes low, and going high only when all outputs are logic highs.

Addressing

The network programming also has to manage addressing. Each node has an assigned address. Each message should include the address of the recipient, to enable the nodes to detect whether or not a message is intended for it. Here again, there are several options.

Assigning

An obvious way of handling node addresses is to assign each node a numeric address. The address may be a byte, or a portion of a byte. The byte may represent an ASCII character (41h for node A, 42h for node B), or it may be any unique value (0 through FFh).

If there are fewer than 128 nodes, you don't need a complete byte to specify the node, and you can get the most use out of the transmitted byte by assigning extra bits to other uses. For example, in a 32-node network, bits 0 through 4 can specify the node number, with bits 5 through 7 giving a command or other information.

Detecting

One challenge in sending addresses is that the nodes have to distinguish between bytes that are addresses and bytes that contain other information. For example, imagine a network where each transmitted message begins with the address of the node the message is intended for. When a node recognizes its address, it knows that the bytes that follow are intended for it. Only the addressed node has to read and act on the bytes in the message. The others should ignore it.

But how do the nodes know when the message is finished? If the byte following an address has the value 5, how does Node 5 know whether this is part of a message meant for another node, or the beginning of a message meant for it?

There are several solutions:

- The addresses may reserve a set of values that the messages never use.
- The network may use a defined message format that lets all nodes know when a message is finished.
- The transmissions may use a 9th bit to indicate whether a byte holds data or an address.

Reserving Address Values

One way to distinguish between addresses and message data is to reserve a set of values to be used only for addresses. This makes it very easy for receivers to distinguish addresses from data, but with the obvious problem that it limits what the messages can contain. A byte that represents binary data, such as a sensor reading, may consist of any value from 0 to FFh, and a format that prohibits sending of some values would be worthless.

A way to get around this limitation is to send all binary data in ASCII Hex format, as described in Chapter 2. This format can represent any numeric value using only the ASCII codes 30h through 39h (for 0 through 9) and 41h to 46h (A through F).

Because ASCII Hex can represent any binary value using just 16 codes, there are plenty of codes left for addressing, commands, or other uses. For example, a network with 32 nodes may use 80h to 9Fh for addresses, and it may define a set of commands from A0h to AFh.

This method has two drawbacks: it requires more time both to process the data and to send it. Each transmitting node must convert all binary values to ASCII Hex, and the receiving node has to convert back. And a binary byte represented in ASCII Hex uses two bytes, one for each digit, so transmissions take twice as long.

But the simplicity of being able to distinguish so easily between addresses, data, and commands makes this method popular for networks that can afford the extra time to send and convert the data.

Defining the Message Format

Another approach is to use a defined message format, with the address and other information in assigned locations in the message.

For example, an 8-byte message might consist of an address byte followed by seven message bytes. When a node receives a byte, it examines it to see if the address matches its own. If yes, it reads and acts on the seven bytes that follow, then waits for another address byte to examine. If the address doesn't match, the node counts, but otherwise ignores, the seven bytes that follow before watching for the next byte.

The complication with this method is that every node has to detect every byte sent, if only to know when the message is finished. If a node misses a byte for any reason, it will be lost and won't know when its address comes up.

A way around this is to dedicate bytes to indicate *Start of Transmission* and *End of Transmission*. Conventional values for this are 2 (Control+B) for Start of Transmission and 3 (Control+C) for End of Transmission. In Visual Basic, MSComm's comEvEof event detects a received end-of-data code (usually 1Ah, Control+Z)). But using dedicated bytes again results in values being unavailable for other uses.

9-bit Format

The final option for distinguishing between addresses and data is an elegant method that uses a 9-bit format that lets the hardware do much of the work. The ninth bit (data bit 8 if you count from 0) indicates whether the byte contains data (0) or an address (1).

Some microcontrollers have a built-in ability to use the ninth bit to detect an address. Intel's 80C51FX series of microcontrollers supports 9-bit communications. The serial port sends and receives 11-bit words, including Start, 8 data bits, a 9th bit, and Stop. One way to use the 9th bit is to set it to 1 to indicate an address, and 0 to indicate data. Special-function registers can store two addresses. One is intended as a given address specific to the node, and the other is a broadcast address common to all in the network.

The microcontroller monitors all received serial data, ignoring all words whose ninth bit is 0. When the ninth bit equals 1, the microcontroller compares data bits 0 through 7 with the stored addresses. If it detects a match, the microcontroller jumps to a routine that reads and acts on the data that follows.

Once the addressing and configuring are set up, all of this is done automatically. All the firmware has to do is handle the communications addressed to that node.

PCs' UARTs don't have full hardware support for 9-bit networks, but you can use Mark or Space parity in a software-assisted 9-bit protocol. Configure MSComm's Settings property for 8 data bits and Space parity. Set MSComm's Parity-Replace property to " " to disable parity replacing, which overwrites received bytes that have parity errors.

When a byte with the parity bit set to 1 reaches the top of the FIFO (meaning that it's the next to be read), the UART (and MSComm in Visual Basic) triggers a parity error. The routine that executes on comEventRxParity should compare the received byte to the node's address. If it's not a match, the routine should take no action. If it does match, the routine should read the data that follows, until the next parity error indicates a new address. Each time a transmitting node needs to switch between sending an address and data, it must close the port, change the parity, then reopen the port.

Not all UARTs and programming languages allow sending 8 data bits plus a parity bit. A link that sends only ASCII text can use the same technique with seven data bits and a parity bit.

Cimetrics Technology specializes in 9-bit networking and offers software for PCs and many other CPUs.

Other Information in Messages

Besides the node address and data intended for the recipient, a message may contain other types of information:

- If messages don't have a fixed length, each message may include the message length.

- For error-checking, the message may contain a checksum or other value used for error detection.

- The message may include the address of the sending node.

- Other information may describe the type of data in the file (binary or ASCII, for example), time and date information, or anything else the receiver needs to know about the message itself.

This type of information often resides in a header, a block of data at the beginning of the message. The header typically has a defined size, with each piece of information in a defined location.

Using Existing Protocols

One quick way to get network programming up and running is to use an existing protocol. Some data-acquisition devices have an RS-485 interface and respond to a simple ASCII command set. Other, more complex protocols are defined by various standards documents. Some of the standards also describe a hardware interface. A fieldbus is a digital link designed for use by monitoring and control systems. These are some examples of standard fieldbuses used with RS-485 networks:

- BACnet. For building automation and other monitoring and control applications. From the American Society of Heating, Refrigerating, and Air-Conditioning Engineers (ASHRAE).

- DIN 66348 Measurement Bus. For industrial test and measurement. From the Association of Measurement Bus Users.

- IEEE-1118. General-purpose master/slave protocol. Began life as Intel's BIT-Bus.

- Profibus (Process Fieldbus). For use in manufacturing, process control, and building automation. From Profibus International.

- SAE J1708. For vehicle applications. From the Society of Automotive Engineers.

Transmitter Enable Timing

In a half-duplex link, only one driver can be enabled at a time. When two nodes exchange data, to ensure that two drivers aren't enabled at once, the nodes must do two things:

- After sending data, disable the driver as quickly as possible, to enable the receiver to enable its driver for a reply.

- After receiving data, delay before re-enabling the driver, to allow the sender time to disable its driver.

The two are related. How long to wait before enabling a driver depends on how quickly the last node to transmit disables its driver.

The delay is needed because in most cases, a program writes the serial data to a hardware or software buffer. Often, a combination of the system hardware, port drivers, and the operating system handles the details of feeding the bytes from the buffers to the UART. Even if the data goes directly to the UART's buffer, the UART must send the bits out one by one, and the driver must remain enabled until the last Stop bit has gone out.

On microcontrollers, the delays are usually very predictable. On a PC, the transmitting time can vary, due to delays in writing data to the port's transmit buffer or other operating-system delays.

With the Basic Stamp, you don't have to worry about this at all. A Stamp program won't jump to the next line until all of a SerOut statement's bits have transmitted. So a Stamp program can disable the driver immediately after a SerOut statement.

When necessary, there are several ways to control the timings and delays in hardware or software.

Software Methods

Ways to time delays in software include calculating the expected time to transmit and reading back the data after it transmits.

Calculated Delay. Calculating a delay doesn't require any special hardware configuration, so the method is available to any system. The downside is that it isn't the quickest, most efficient method, because of the need to add enough of a safety margin to handle the longest delays expected.

The program calculates how long the system will need to send the data. It enables the driver, sends the data, and waits the calculated time before disabling the driver. For short messages, at minimum, the delay should equal the time required to transmit a byte multiplied by the number of bytes, plus a safety margin of one byte. The time required to transmit a byte is `10/BitRate`, assuming 8 data bits, no parity, and 1 Stop bit. Chapter 4 has a routine for calculating these delays.

When transmitting large files, the safety margin should be larger, and may require some experimenting with the values. If the amount of data is larger than the port's software transmit buffer, the program should wait until the buffer has filled for the last time before timing a delay equal to the buffer's size.

When the transmitter uses a calculated delay to disable the driver, the receiving node needs to allow a generous delay, greater than the transmitter's delay, before enabling its driver to send a reply.

Read-back Delay. Another way to ensure that all data has transmitted is for the transmitting node to read the data back after it transmits. This method requires the receiver to be enabled when transmitting, so it won't work if a transceiver's two enable inputs are tied together.

This method is quicker than using a generous calculated delay. It also detects many problems that prevent the data from transmitting, such as a disconnected transceiver or another driver being enabled at the same time.

To use this method, the program enables the driver, sends the data, and waits to receive the data just transmitted. The transmitting node may just count the bytes received, or it may compare their values with those transmitted. If the data doesn't arrive within a specified time, or if the values don't match, the program should handle the problem, perhaps by retrying or by giving up and displaying an error message.

With this method, the receiving node can enable its driver almost immediately after receiving an expected amount of data. It only needs to ensure that the transmitter has had enough time to read the data and disable its driver. For example, if operating-system delays may make the transmitting node slower to read the data than the receiving node, the receiving node should allow for this.

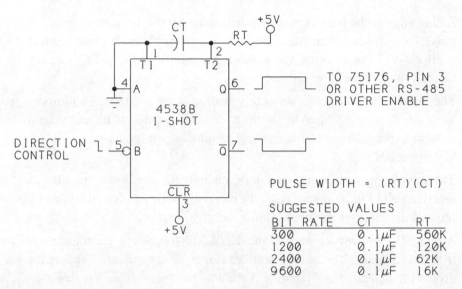

Figure 11-1: This retriggerable 1-shot can automatically enable an RS-485 driver. A Start bit or logic 0 results in a pulse of 1.5 word widths.

Hardware Methods

It's also possible to use hardware to control the driver's enable line. A hardware solution frees the software from having to control the enable line, though it may still have to ensure delays before sending data, to allow other nodes to disable their transmitters. If you don't want to design and build your own hardware, converters and boards with hardware control built-in are available from several sources.

Figure 11-1 shows hardware enable control using a retriggerable 1-shot multivibrator. The 1-shot automatically enables the driver whenever the node is transmitting.

The 1-shot uses the Start bit to detect when a byte begins to transmit. Each byte begins with a falling edge that signifies the Start bit. Capacitor *CT* and resistor *RT* set the width of the 1-shot's output pulse to slightly longer than the time to transmit one byte.

On the falling edge of the Start bit, the one-shot's output goes high for at least one delay time. Because the 1-shot is retriggerable, if another byte begins to transmit before the 1-shot times out, the new byte's Start bit will hold the output high until that byte has finished transmitting. If another byte doesn't arrive, soon after the last byte's transmission is complete, the one-shot's output goes low and the driver is disabled.

Because the 1-shot retriggers on every falling edge, the time that its output remains high will vary depending on the data sent. If bit 6 is 1 and bit 7 is 0, the falling edge at the transition to zero will retrigger the 1-shot and result in a longer pulse. (remember that the data transmits least-significant-bit first.) But if the byte is all 1's (FFh) or all zeros, the 1-shot triggers only on the falling edge of the start bit, and the pulse will be shorter.

The biggest inconvenience about this method is the need to set a jumper or switch to match the delay time to the bit rate. The other option is to set the delay for the slowest expected bit rate, but this will result in much longer than needed delays at higher speeds.

The answering node must wait long enough for the 1-shot to time out. After receiving all of the expected data, the receiving node needs to wait one byte width, plus a safety margin, before enabling its driver to reply.

A more elegant way to generate the delays in hardware is to dedicate a microcontroller to the task. The microcontroller can be programmed to enable the RS-485 driver on detecting a Start bit. A timing routine can then calculate the time required to transmit one byte and disable the driver after the delay. A microcontroller can time the delays precisely, eliminating the need to wait an entire byte width after transmitting any 0.

In fact, because the line is biased to an idle state when all drivers are disabled, the driver can be disabled any time after the Stop bit's rising edge. Because the Stop bit is the same logic level as the idle state (A > B), when the driver is disabled, the line remains in the idle state.

If the microcontroller detects the Stop bit in the middle of the bit and disables the driver, the driver is guaranteed to be disabled when the receiving node replies. The receiving node doesn't have to add any delay at all before enabling its driver. Several sources offer RS-485 adapters with this type of automatic enable control built-in.

12

Two Networks

This chapter presents circuits and programming for two networks for monitoring and control jobs. Both are generic, general-purpose examples that show what's involved in putting together and programming this type of a network.

The first example is an RS-485 network for PCs and Basic Stamps. The second example is a simple, short-distance Stamp-only network using open baudmode.

An RS-485 Network

The RS-485 network uses the master/slave protocol described in Chapter 11. The master node communicates with up to seven slave nodes. Each node connects to the network via an RS-485 interface. The master is a personal computer running Visual Basic, and the slaves may be other PCs or Basic Stamps. Each slave detects, reads, and responds to messages directed to it.

You can use the network as a base for designing your own projects using personal computers or microcontrollers of any type, in any combination, and any programming language.

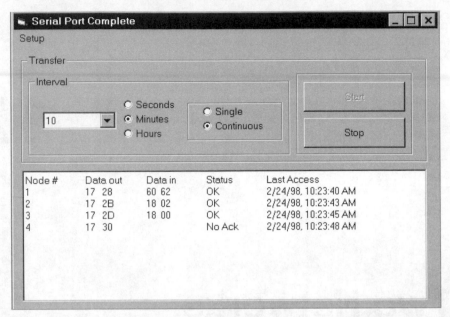

Figure 12-1: The main window for the RS-485 network enables users to select an interval for polling the network, to start and stop polling, and to view the latest results.

The Protocol

The network uses a communications protocol designed for simplicity and reliability in exchanging short messages. A master polls each slave in turn.

Byte Definitions

The network uses the following conventions:

- All data is sent in ASCII Hex format, using the characters *0* through *9* (30h through 39h) and *A* through *F* (41h through 46h). A pair of ASCII Hex bytes represents one binary value.

- Node addresses use ASCII codes for the characters *g* to *n* (67h through 6Eh).

- Messages are a defined length. Each message contains four ASCII Hex data bytes.

Polling the Nodes

Figure 12-1 shows the main window for the program. It uses Chapter 4's template file as a base. The user can do a single poll of the network, or select an interval for continuous polling. A Rich Text box displays the results, including the nodes polled, data sent and received, and time of the last transfer.

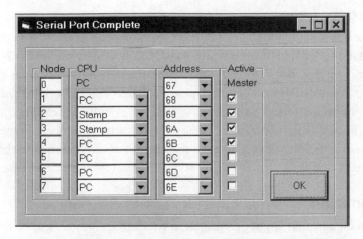

Figure 12-2: The Nodes window enables users to select an address and CPU type for each node, and to indicate whether or not the node is in use.

The Setup menu includes three selections. Two were introduced in Chapter 4. The Port Settings form allows selecting a port and bit rate. The Data File form allows saving of transferred data in a file. A new form is Nodes (Figure 12-2), which displays the eight nodes by number, CPU type, address, and whether or not the node is active (currently in use). All of these are user-selectable, except the master's node type and Active check box.

The master polls each slave in turn, using the following procedure:

• The master sends a slave address, disables its transmitter and waits for a reply.

• All slaves read the address and compare it to their own address.

• The slave that recognizes its address responds by enabling its transmitter, sending its address back to the master as an acknowledgment, then disabling its transmitter and waiting for data.

• When the master receives the acknowledgment, it knows that the slave is waiting for a message. The master sends the message, consisting of four ASCII Hex bytes. It then disables its transmitter and waits for a reply.

• When the slave receives the message, it stores the data, enables its transmitter, and sends five bytes back to the master: its address, plus four ASCII Hex bytes. It then disables its transmitter and takes any action requested by the master's message.

• The master stores the reply from the slave, re-enables its transmitter, and is then free to poll another slave.

The other nodes may read the addresses and messages, but take no action because none of the bytes match their addresses.

Messages

The data bytes in the messages can represent anything at all. The master may send a command to tell the slave to read a sensor, followed by an ASCII Hex value that indicates which sensor to read. Or the master may send a a byte that selects a motor to control, and another that selects a speed and direction for the motor. In reply, a node may send data about switch states, sensor readings, alarm conditions, time and date information, or any digital outputs or logic levels. The slaves also transmit their address with each message to assure the master that the correct node is replying.

Customizing

You can change and adapt this format to fit a particular use. For example, the link may transfer more or fewer data bytes, and it may allow more or fewer nodes.

Table 12-1 shows the defined uses for each of the 256 byte values. Many values are undefined, and you can assign meanings to these and use them as needed. For example, F0h through FFh may each indicate a command.

The Link

Figure 12-3 is shows an example of wiring you can use for this network. This is just one possibility. The network may use any appropriate components for a half-duplex link, including high-speed, low-speed, low-voltage, short-distance, and isolated components. A PC may also use an expansion card with an RS-485 interface, allowing higher speeds and eliminating the need to convert RS-232.

Each node uses a 75176B RS-485 transceiver to interface to the network. At the master, the receiver is always enabled, and *RTS* controls the driver enable. At the slaves, the driver and receiver enables are tied together and controlled with one port bit.

At the master node, a MAX232A converts the PC's RS-232 voltages to TTL voltages. The MAX232A also re-inverts the signals: at its TTL inputs and outputs, a high voltage represents a logic 1 and a low voltage represents a logic 0. The TTL voltages interface to the 75176 transceiver.

At the PC, the *RTS* line determines the direction of the 75176. For the microcontrollers, any output port pin can perform this function.

The first and last nodes on the bus each have a 120-ohm termination resistor. Two 470-ohm biasing resistors at one end hold the inputs high when no drivers are enabled on the network. If your link is short line as defined in Chapter 10, you don't need the 120-ohm terminations or the 470-ohm biasing resistors.

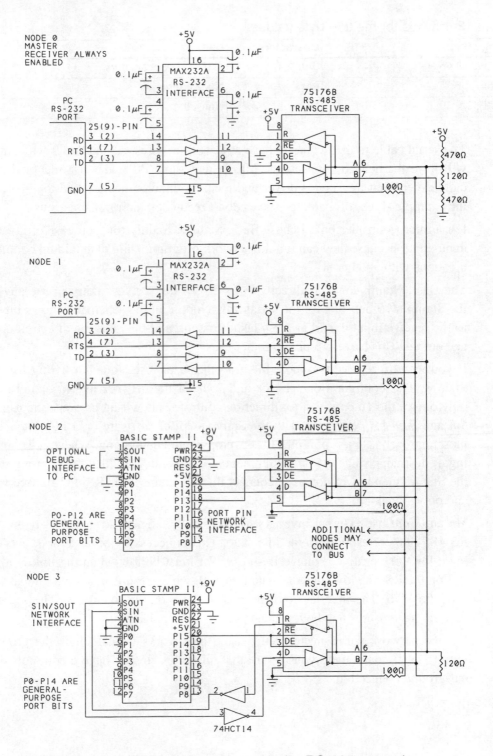

Figure 12-3: Example wiring you can use for the RS-485 network.

Table 12-1: Uses for the 256 byte values

Range (hex)	Characters	Use
30 -39, 41-46	0-9, A-F	ASCII Hex characters
67-6E	g-n	Node addresses
00-2F, 3A-40, 47-60, 6F-FF	Various	Unused

The serial cable to the PC has to have at least four wires. A standard 9-wire cable will have the needed connections. Master and slave PC nodes use identical circuits except that the slave's driver and receiver enable lines are tied together. In the example slave software, the slaves don't read back their transmissions.

For a microcontroller link, I chose Basic Stamps, mainly for their ease of use for debugging, because they can run the network program while maintaining communications with another host PC.

The Basic Stamp connects directly to its 75176 transceiver. You can use any of the Stamp's 16 port bits for the serial link. Node 2 in the schematic shows bit 15 as the receive input, bit 14 as the transmit output, and bit 13 as the direction-control output. This leaves 13 bits for other uses.

If you want to reserve two more bits for other uses, use Node 4's wiring for the Stamps. This configuration uses *Sin* and *Sout* for the network interface, and uses only one of the 16 port bits, for direction control. This wiring prevents the use of *Sin* and *Sout* for debugging with the Stamp's editor software on a PC. The simplest approach is to use port pins for developing and debugging. When all is working, if desired, change the pin assignments for *Sin* and *Sout*, load the program into the Stamp, then power down, disconnect the PC, connect the RS-485 transceiver, and power back up.

Sin and *Sout* use external inverters to reinvert the signals so that A > B on the RS-485 line corresponds to the idle state. This is necessary because *Sout* gets its logic-low (or negative) voltage from *Sin*. *Sin* must be low when the link is idle. But on the RS-485 link, the idle state is A > B, which results in a logic high at pin 1 of the '176. The inverter converts this to the required logic low. The second inverter just ensures that both signals use the same polarity.

For the network wires, unshielded twisted pair works well. Include the ground wire to each node unless you're sure that all nodes already have a common signal-ground connection.

The Master's Programming

Listing 12-1 is Visual-Basic program code for the master node. Many parts of the code are similar or identical to Chapter 8's 2-device link. Both applications exchange data with remote computers, but this time there are multiple nodes to deal with.

The master reads back all data it sends. When the transmitted data has been read back, the master knows that it's safe to disable its transmitter. Reading back the data also provides error-checking. If another node has mistakenly enabled its transmitter, or if Windows' timeout delay expires, the master's data won't transmit and won't be read back. After receiving data, the master delays before re-enabling its transmitter, to give the sending node time to disable its transmitter.

Selecting Nodes

Listing 12-2 is the code for the Nodes window that enables users to select which nodes are active, and what type of CPU the node contains.

Slave Programming

Listing 12-3 is the program stored in each Basic Stamp when using port bits for serial communications. Each node must have a unique address. The program disk also includes Stamp code for using *Sin* and *Sout* for communications and Quick-Basic code for a slave node on a DOS PC.

A Simple Stamp Network

The second network is example is a very simple one. It connects multiple Basic Stamp II's using open-baud mode. Chapter 5 showed the circuits for open-baud mode. The programming uses non-inverted communications, so the data line uses a pull-up resistor to +5V.

The programming is again a master/slave network. Listing 12-4 is the master's program, and Listing 12-5 is the slave's. For use in debugging, the code reads and sets I/O bits on each Stamp.

This network is suitable for as many as eight Stamps, over a total distance of about 15 feet. With more nodes and over longer distances, proceed at your own risk!

The network traffic is half-duplex and uses just one port bit.

```
Option Explicit
'A master node communicates with up to 7 slave nodes
'over a half-duplex RS-485 interface.
'Each node has an address.
'Each message consists of the receiver's address, followed by
'4 ASCII Hex bytes representing 2 binary values.
'Each reply consists of the sender's address,
'followed by 4 ASCII Hex bytes representing 2 binary values.
Option Base 0
'Delay (milliseconds) to ensure RTS has toggled (Windows delay):
Const RTSDelay = 200
'Delay (milliseconds) before enabling transmitter,
'to allow the slave to disable its transmitter.
Const EnableDelay = 500
'Delay (milliseconds) to wait for a reply from a slave.
Const ReplyDelay = 3000
'Node 0 is the master; other nodes are slaves.
Const HighestNodeNumber = 7
'With each message, the master sends and receives
'4 ASCII Hex bytes.
Const NumberOfDataBytesOut = 4
Const NumberOfDataBytesIn = 4

Private Type typNodes
    Address(0 To HighestNodeNumber) As Byte
    DataOut1(0 To HighestNodeNumber) As Byte
    DataOut2(0 To HighestNodeNumber) As Byte
    DataIn1(0 To HighestNodeNumber) As Byte
    DataIn2(0 To HighestNodeNumber) As Byte
    Status(0 To HighestNodeNumber) As String
    Cpu(0 To HighestNodeNumber) As String
    Active(0 To HighestNodeNumber) As Integer
    LastAccess(0 To HighestNodeNumber) As String
End Type
Private Type typDataTransferFormat
    SingleOrContinuous As String
    IntervalUnits As String
    IntervalValue As Single
End Type
```

Listing 12-1: Code for the RS-485 network's main window. (Sheet 1 of 16)

```
Dim SelectedNode As Integer
Dim PollInterval As Integer
Dim DataOut(NumberOfDataBytesOut - 1) As Byte
Dim DataIn(NumberOfDataBytesIn - 1) As Byte
Dim DataTransferFormat As typDataTransferFormat
Dim PreviousTime As Date
Dim TimeOfTransfer As String
Dim TransferInProgress As Boolean

Dim Nodes As typNodes
```

```
Private Function fncConfirmTransmittedData _
    (Buffer As Variant) _
    As Integer
'Ensure that all data has transmitted by reading it back.
'Receiver must be enabled!
'Returned values:
'-1 = Data read back successfully
'0 = Data didn't match
'1 = Timeout
Dim DataReadBack As String
'Estimate the time to transmit the data:
tmrTimeout.Interval = OneByteDelay * LenB(Buffer) + 500
tmrTimeout.Enabled = True
TimedOut = False
Do
    DoEvents
Loop Until MSComm1.InBufferCount >= Len(Buffer) Or TimedOut = True
DataReadBack = MSComm1.Input
If StrComp(DataReadBack, Buffer, vbBinaryCompare) = 0 Then
    fncConfirmTransmittedData = -1
Else
    If TimedOut = False Then
        fncConfirmTransmittedData = 0
    Else
        fncConfirmTransmittedData = 1
    End If
End If
tmrTimeout.Enabled = False
TimedOut = False
End Function
```

Listing 12-1: Code for the RS-485 network's main window. (Sheet 2 of 16)

```
Private Function fncCreateMessage _
    (NodeNumber As Integer) _
    As String
'A message consists of four bytes in ASCII Hex format.
'Each ASCII Hex pair represents the value of a byte.
Dim MessageLength As Integer
Dim MessageToSend As String
    MessageLength = NumberOfDataBytesOut - 1
    Call GetDataToSend(NodeNumber)
    'Create the message, consisting of
    '4 bytes that contain the 2 data bytes in ASCII Hex format.
    'Each byte represents 1 hex digit (4 bits).
    'Convert the 2 data bytes to ASCII Hex
    'and store in the Message string.
    MessageToSend = _
        fncByteToAsciiHex(Nodes.DataOut1(NodeNumber)) & _
        fncByteToAsciiHex(Nodes.DataOut2(NodeNumber))
    fncCreateMessage = MessageToSend
End Function
```

```
Private Function fncDisplayDateAndTime() As String
'Date and time formatting.
fncDisplayDateAndTime = _
    CStr(Format(Date, "General Date")) & ", " & _
        (Format(Time, "Long Time"))
End Function
```

Listing 12-1: Code for the RS-485 network's main window. (Sheet 3 of 16)

```
Private Function fncWaitForAck(NodeNumber As Integer) As Boolean
'End on receiving Acknowledge from the slave or timeout.
Dim Ack As Boolean
Dim NodeAddress As String
Dim ReceivedData As String
'The Acknowledge is the node address.
NodeAddress = Chr(Nodes.Address(NodeNumber))
Ack = False
tmrTimeout.Interval = ReplyDelay
'Disable the transmitter until Ack is received or timeout.
Call DisableTransmitter
'Wait for Acknowledge.
Do
    tmrTimeout.Enabled = True
    TimedOut = False
    Do
        DoEvents
    Loop Until (MSComm1.InBufferCount >= 1) Or (TimedOut = True)
    If TimedOut = False Then
        tmrTimeout.Enabled = False
        'Read the byte & compare to what was sent.
        ReceivedData = MSComm1.Input
        If StrComp _
            (ReceivedData, NodeAddress, vbBinaryCompare) = 0 Then
            Ack = True
            Nodes.DataIn1(NodeNumber) = Asc(ReceivedData)
        Else
            'if the Ack doesn't match the node address:
            Ack = False
            Call SaveResults(NodeNumber, 0, 0, "Ack Error")
         End If
    Else
        Ack = False
        Call SaveResults(NodeNumber, 0, 0, "No Ack")
    End If
Loop Until Ack = True Or TimedOut = True
tmrTimeout.Enabled = False
fncWaitForAck = Ack
TimedOut = False
Call EnableTransmitter(EnableDelay)
End Function
```

Listing 12-1: Code for the RS-485 network's main window. (Sheet 4 of 16)

```
Private Function fncWaitForReply _
    (NodeNumber As Integer) _
    As Boolean
'From the slave, read the node address & 4 ASCII Hex bytes.
Dim Ack As Boolean
Dim Reply As Boolean
Dim ReceivedData As String
Ack = False
Reply = False
TimedOut = False
tmrTimeout.Interval = ReplyDelay
'Disable the transmitter until bytes are received or timeout.
Call DisableTransmitter
tmrTimeout.Enabled = True
Do
    'Wait for reply
    TimedOut = False
    Do
        DoEvents
    Loop Until (MSComm1.InBufferCount > 4) Or (TimedOut = True)
    If TimedOut = False Then
        tmrTimeout.Enabled = False
        ReceivedData = MSComm1.Input
        Reply = True
        If StrComp(Asc(Left(ReceivedData, 1)), _
            Nodes.Address(NodeNumber), vbBinaryCompare) = 0 Then
            'If the first byte equals the slave's address,
            'get the numeric value of each pair of ASCII Hex bytes.
            Call SaveResults _
                (NodeNumber, _
                Val("&h" & Mid(ReceivedData, 2, 2)), _
                Val("&h" & Mid(ReceivedData, 4, 2)), _
                "OK")
        Else
            'If the first byte doesn't equal the node address:
            Call SaveResults(NodeNumber, 0, 0, "Data Error")
        End If
    Else
        'If the wait for a reply times out:
        Call SaveResults(NodeNumber, 0, 0, "Reply Timeout")
    End If
Loop Until Reply = True Or TimedOut = True
tmrTimeout.Enabled = False
Call EnableTransmitter(EnableDelay)
fncWaitForReply = Reply
End Function
```

Listing 12-1: Code for the RS-485 network's main window. (Sheet 5 of 16)

```
Private Sub cboIntervalValue_Click()
'Store the selected interval for data transfers.
DataTransferFormat.IntervalValue = Val(cboIntervalValue.Text)
'With shorter intervals, check elapsed time more often.
Select Case DataTransferFormat.IntervalUnits
    Case "seconds"
        tmrTransferInterval.Interval = 100
    Case "minutes", "hours"
        tmrTransferInterval.Interval = 1000
End Select
End Sub
```

```
Private Sub cmdStart_Click()
'Initiate data transfer.
Select Case DataTransferFormat.SingleOrContinuous
    Case "single"
        'Transfer data once.
        'Disable the Start button until polling is finished.
        cmdStart.Enabled = False
        Call PollSlave
        cmdStart.Enabled = True
    Case "continuous"
        'Do one transfer immediately, then let the timer take over.
        cmdStart.Enabled = False
        cmdStop.Enabled = True
        cmdStop.SetFocus
        PreviousTime = Now
        tmrTransferInterval.Enabled = True
        Call PollSlave
    Case Else
End Select
End Sub
```

```
Private Sub cmdStop_Click()
'Stop transferring data.
tmrTransferInterval.Enabled = False
cmdStop.Enabled = False
cmdStart.Enabled = True
Call DisableTransmitter
End Sub
```

Listing 12-1: Code for the RS-485 network's main window. (Sheet 6 of 16)

```
Private Sub DisableTransmitter()
'Set RTS true (high) to disable the RS485 transmitter
'by bringing its chip-enable low.
'Assumes that a second RS-232 receiver inverts RTS.
MSComm1.RTSEnable = True
End Sub
```

```
Private Sub EnableTransmitter(EnableDelay As Single)
'Set RTS false (low) to enable the RS485 transmitter.
'Assumes that a second RS-232 receiver has inverted RTS.
'Delay in milliseconds allows remote node
'to disable its transmitter.
Call Delay(EnableDelay)
MSComm1.RTSEnable = False
'Windows delay:
Call Delay(RTSDelay)
End Sub
```

```
Private Sub Form_Load()
Show
Call GetSettings
Call Startup
Load frmPortSettings
Load frmNodes
TransferInProgress = False
tmrTimeout.Interval = ReplyDelay
tmrTransferInterval.Enabled = False
tmrTimeout.Enabled = False
TimedOut = False
Call InitializeDisplayElements
SaveDataInFile = False
Call InitializeNodes
Call GetNewNodeSettings
'The master's transmitter is enabled,
'except when receiving replies.
Call EnableTransmitter(0)
End Sub
```

Listing 12-1: Code for the RS-485 network's main window. (Sheet 7 of 16)

```
Private Sub Form_Unload(Cancel As Integer)
Call ShutDown
Unload frmNodes
Unload frmDataFile
Unload frmPortSettings
Close #2
End
End Sub
```

```
Private Sub GetDataToSend(NodeNumber As Integer)
'Dummy data for testing: the current hour and minute.
Dim CurrentTime As String
CurrentTime = CStr(Format(Time, "nnss"))
Nodes.DataOut1(NodeNumber) = Val(Left(CurrentTime, 2))
Nodes.DataOut2(NodeNumber) = Val(Right(CurrentTime, 2))
End Sub
```

```
Public Sub GetNewNodeSettings()
'Store user changes made on the Nodes form.
Dim Count As Integer
    Nodes.Address(0) = CInt("&h" & frmNodes.cboAddress(0).Text)
For Count = 1 To 7
    Nodes.Cpu(Count) = frmNodes.cboCPU(Count).Text
    Nodes.Address(Count) = _
        CInt("&h" & frmNodes.cboAddress(Count).Text)
    Nodes.Active(Count) = frmNodes.chkNodeActive(Count).Value
Next Count
End Sub
```

```
Private Sub InitializeDisplayElements()
optSingleOrContinuous(0).Value = True
optIntervalUnits(0).Value = True
cboIntervalValue.ListIndex = 0
rtxStatus.Locked = True
rtxStatus.Text = ""
DataTransferFormat.IntervalValue = 1
cmdStop.Enabled = False
End Sub
```

Listing 12-1: Code for the RS-485 network's main window. (Sheet 8 of 16)

```
Private Sub InitializeNodes()
Dim Count As Integer
For Count = 0 To HighestNodeNumber
    Nodes.DataIn1(Count) = 0
    Nodes.DataIn2(Count) = 0
    Nodes.Status(Count) = ""
    Nodes.LastAccess(Count) = ""
    Nodes.Cpu(Count) = ""
Next Count
Call UpdateDisplay
End Sub
```

```
Private Sub mnuDataFile_Click(Index As Integer)
frmDataFile.Show
End Sub
```

```
Private Sub mnuNodes_Click(Index As Integer)
frmNodes.Show
End Sub
```

```
Private Sub mnuPortSettings_Click(Index As Integer)
frmPortSettings.Show
End Sub
```

```
Private Sub optIntervalUnits_Click(Index As Integer)
'Set the interval combo box to match the units selected.
Dim Maximum As Integer
Dim Count As Integer
Select Case Index
    Case 0
        Maximum = 59
        DataTransferFormat.IntervalUnits = "seconds"
    Case 1
        Maximum = 59
        DataTransferFormat.IntervalUnits = "minutes"
    Case 2
        Maximum = 24
        DataTransferFormat.IntervalUnits = "hours"
End Select
cboIntervalValue.Clear
For Count = 1 To Maximum
    cboIntervalValue.AddItem CStr(Count)
Next Count
cboIntervalValue.ListIndex = 0
End Sub
```

Listing 12-1: Code for the RS-485 network's main window. (Sheet 9 of 16)

```
Private Sub optPollUnits_Click(Index As Integer)
'Set the combo box items to match the units selected.
Dim Maximum As Integer
Dim Count as Integer
Select Case Index
    Case 0, 1
        'seconds, minutes
        Maximum = 59
    Case 2
        'hours
        Maximum = 24
End Select
End Sub
```

```
Private Sub optSingleOrContinuous_Click(Index As Integer)
Select Case Index
    Case 0
        DataTransferFormat.SingleOrContinuous = "single"
        'Disable interval selection:
        optIntervalUnits(0).Enabled = False
        optIntervalUnits(1).Enabled = False
        optIntervalUnits(2).Enabled = False
    Case 1
        DataTransferFormat.SingleOrContinuous = "continuous"
        'Enable interval selection:
        optIntervalUnits(0).Enabled = True
        optIntervalUnits(1).Enabled = True
        optIntervalUnits(2).Enabled = True
End Select
End Sub
```

Listing 12-1: Code for the RS-485 network's main window. (Sheet 10 of 16)

```
Private Sub PollSlave()
'Send the node address & wait for Acknowledge.
'If Ack received, send data, wait for reply.
'Store the results.
Dim AckReceived As Boolean
Dim AttemptNumber As Integer
Dim Buffer As Variant
Dim Count As Integer
Dim LastNode As Integer
Dim MessageToSend As Variant
Dim NumberOfTries As Integer
Dim ReplyReceived As Boolean
Dim TransmitFinished As Boolean
TransferInProgress = True
For Count = 1 To HighestNodeNumber
'Skip the node if it isn't selected (Active) on the Nodes form.
    If Nodes.Active(Count) = 1 Then
        'Clear the transmit and receive buffers
        MSComm1.OutBufferCount = 0
        If MSComm1.InBufferCount > 0 Then
            Buffer = MSComm1.Input
        EndIf
        'Create the message from the stored values.
        MessageToSend = fncCreateMessage(Count)
        'Store the time of the poll.
        Nodes.LastAccess(Count) = fncDisplayDateAndTime
        'Send the node address as a text character.
        Buffer = Chr(Nodes.Address(Count))
        'For Stamp and other slaves without input buffers,
        'poll more than once if needed.
        Select Case Nodes.Cpu(Count)
            Case "PC"
                NumberOfTries = 1
            Case "Stamp"
                NumberOfTries = 2
        End Select
        AttemptNumber = 0
```

Listing 12-1: Code for the RS-485 network's main window. (Sheet 11 of 16)

```
        Do
            MSComm1.Output = Buffer
            'Wait for the data to transmit
            Select Case fncConfirmTransmittedData(Buffer)
                Case -1
                    'If success, wait for Acknowledge.
                    AckReceived = fncWaitForAck(Count)
                Case 0
                    Nodes.Status(Count) = "Transmit error"
                Case 1
                    Nodes.Status(Count) = "Ack Timeout"
            End Select
            AttemptNumber = AttemptNumber + 1
        Loop Until AckReceived = True Or _
            AttemptNumber = NumberOfTries
        If AckReceived = True Then
            MSComm1.Output = MessageToSend
            'Delay to let the data transmit
            Select Case fncConfirmTransmittedData(MessageToSend)
                Case -1
                    'Data has transmitted.
                    'Wait for the slave's reply.
                    ReplyReceived = fncWaitForReply(Count)
                Case Else
                    Nodes.Status(Count) = "Transmit error"
            End Select
        End If
        Call UpdateDisplay
    End If
Next Count
If SaveDataInFile = True Then
    Call WriteResultsToFile
End If
TransferInProgress = False
End Sub
```

Listing 12-1: Code for the RS-485 network's main window. (Sheet 12 of 16)

```
Private Sub SaveResults _
    (NodeNumber As Integer, _
    Data1 As Byte, _
    Data2 As Byte, _
    ResultStatus As String)
    Nodes.DataIn1(NodeNumber) = Data1
    Nodes.DataIn2(NodeNumber) = Data2
    Nodes.Status(NodeNumber) = ResultStatus
End Sub
```

```
Private Sub WriteResultsToFile()
'Save received data and time in a file.
Dim Count As Integer
For Count = 1 To HighestNodeNumber
    'Skip if the node isn't selected (active) on the Nodes form.
    If Nodes.Active(Count) = 1 Then
        Write #2, _
            Count, _
            Nodes.LastAccess(Count), _
            Nodes.DataOut1(Count), _
            Nodes.DataOut2(Count), _
            Nodes.DataIn1(Count), _
            Nodes.DataIn2(Count), _
            Nodes.Status(Count)
    End If
Next Count
End Sub
```

Listing 12-1: Code for the RS-485 network's main window. (Sheet 13 of 16)

```
Private Sub tmrTransferInterval_Timer()
'See if it's time to do a transfer.
Dim CurrentTime As Date
Dim Units As String
CurrentTime = Now
Select Case DataTransferFormat.IntervalUnits
    Case "seconds"
        Units = "s"
    Case "minutes"
        Units = "n"
    Case "hours"
        Units = "h"
End Select
'If elapsed time since the last transfer is more than
'the selected interval, do a data transfer.
If DateDiff(Units, PreviousTime, CurrentTime) >= _
        DataTransferFormat.IntervalValue Then
    PreviousTime = CurrentTime
    'But don't start a new transfer if one is in progress.
    If TransferInProgress = False Then
        Call PollSlave
    End If
End If
End Sub
```

```
Private Sub tmrTimeout_Timer()
tmrTimeout.Enabled = False
TimedOut = True
End Sub
```

Listing 12-1: Code for the RS-485 network's main window. (Sheet 14 of 16)

```
Private Sub UpdateDisplay()
'Show the latest information for all nodes
Dim Column As Integer
Dim DataIn1Display As String
Dim DataIn2Display As String
Dim Count As Integer
'Set up 5 columns
With rtxStatus
        .SelTabCount = 5
        For Column = 0 To .SelTabCount - 1
            .SelTabs(Column) = 1000 * Column
        Next Column
End With
rtxStatus.Text = "Node #" & Chr(vbKeyTab) _
    & "Data out" & Chr(vbKeyTab) _
    & "Data in" & Chr(vbKeyTab) _
    & "Status" & Chr(vbKeyTab) _
    & "Last Access" & vbCrLf
For Count = 1 To HighestNodeNumber
    'Skip if the node isn't selected (active) on the Nodes form.
    If Nodes.Active(Count) = 1 Then
    Select Case Nodes.Status(Count)
            Case "OK"
                DataIn1Display = _
                    fncByteToAsciiHex(Nodes.DataIn1(Count))
                DataIn2Display = _
                    fncByteToAsciiHex(Nodes.DataIn2(Count))
            Case Else
                DataIn1Display = ""
                DataIn2Display = ""
        End Select
        rtxStatus.SelStart = Len(rtxStatus.Text)
        rtxStatus.SelText = _
             Hex$(Count) & Chr(vbKeyTab) _
            & fncByteToAsciiHex(Nodes.DataOut1(Count)) & "    " _
            & fncByteToAsciiHex(Nodes.DataOut2(Count)) _
            & Chr(vbKeyTab) _
            & DataIn1Display & "   " & DataIn2Display _
            & Chr(vbKeyTab) _
            & Nodes.Status(Count) & Chr(vbKeyTab) _
            & Nodes.LastAccess(Count) & vbCrLf
    End If
Next Count
End Sub
```

Listing 12-1: Code for the RS-485 network's main window. (Sheet 15 of 16)

```
Public Function fncInitializeComPort _
    (BitRate As Long, PortNumber As Integer) As Boolean
'BitRate and PortNumber are passed to this routine.
'All other properties are set explicitly in the code.
Dim ComSettings As String
If MSComm1.PortOpen = True Then
    MSComm1.PortOpen = False
End If
ComSettings = CStr(BitRate) & ",N,8,1"
MSComm1.CommPort = PortNumber
' bit rate, no parity, 8 data, and 1 stop bit.
MSComm1.Settings = ComSettings
'Set to 0 to read entire buffer on Input
MSComm1.InputLen = 0
MSComm1.InBufferSize = 256
'Input and output data are text.
MSComm1.InputMode = comInputModeText
'MSComm does no handshaking.
MSComm1.Handshaking = comNone
MSComm1.OutBufferSize = 256
MSComm1.EOFEnable = False
'No OnComm event on received data.
MSComm1.RThreshold = 0
'No OnComm transmit event.
MSComm1.SThreshold = 0
MSComm1.PortOpen = True
OneByteDelay = fncOneByteDelay(BitRate)
End Function
```

Listing 12-1: Code for the RS-485 network's main window. (Sheet 16 of 16)

Debugging Tips

Networks can be a minefield to troubleshoot, because the multiple nodes multiply the possibilities for trouble. A gradual and deliberate approach to putting together a network can save many hours of debugging later. This section includes suggestions that I've found useful for network developing and debugging.

Start with two nodes. Keep it simple at first. In a master/slave network, connect the master to one slave and get that working first. If possible, start with a full-duplex RS-232 or RS-485 interface. This way, you don't even have to worry about enabling and disabling the drivers at appropriate times.

```
Option Explicit
'Enables the user to specify the type & address of remote nodes.
```

```
Private Sub cmdOK_Click()
Call frmMain.GetNewNodeSettings
Hide
End Sub
```

```
Private Sub Form_Load()
Call InitializeNodeCpuComboBoxes
Call InitializeNodeAddressComboBoxes
Call InitializeNodeActiveCheckBoxes
Call GetSettings
Call frmMain.GetNewNodeSettings
End Sub
```

```
Private Sub Form_Unload(Cancel As Integer)
Call SaveSettings
End Sub
```

```
Private Sub GetSettings()
Dim Count As Integer
    cboAddress(Count).ListIndex = GetSetting _
        (ProjectName, "Startup", "NodeAddress" & CStr(0), 0)
For Count = 1 To 7
    cboCPU(Count).ListIndex = GetSetting _
        (ProjectName, "Startup", "NodeCPU" & CStr(Count), 0)
    cboAddress(Count).ListIndex = GetSetting _
        (ProjectName, "Startup", "NodeAddress" & CStr(Count), 0)
    chkNodeActive(Count).Value = GetSetting _
        (ProjectName, "Startup", "NodeActive" & CStr(Count), 1)
Next Count
End Sub
```

```
Private Sub InitializeNodeActiveCheckBoxes()
Dim Count As Integer
For Count = 1 To 7
    chkNodeActive(Count).Value = 1
Next Count
End Sub
```

Listing 12-2: Code for the Nodes window, which enables users to select and configure nodes in the network. (Sheet 1 of 2)

```
Private Sub InitializeNodeAddressComboBoxes()
Dim Count As Integer
Dim Address As Integer
'Address range is 67h to 6Eh
For Count = 0 To 7
    For Address = &H67 To &H6E
        cboAddress(Count).AddItem Hex$(Address)
    Next Address
Next Count
For Count = 0 To 7
    cboAddress(Count).ListIndex = Count
Next Count
End Sub

Private Sub InitializeNodeCpuComboBoxes()
Dim Count As Integer
For Count = 1 To 7
    cboCPU(Count).AddItem "PC"
    cboCPU(Count).AddItem "Stamp"
Next Count
End Sub

Private Sub SaveSettings()
Dim Count As Integer
SaveSetting ProjectName, "Startup", _
    "NodeAddress" & CStr(0), cboAddress(0).ListIndex
For Count = 1 To 7
    SaveSetting ProjectName, "Startup", _
        "NodeCPU" & CStr(Count), cboCPU(Count).ListIndex
    SaveSetting ProjectName, "Startup", _
        "NodeAddress" & CStr(Count), cboAddress(Count).ListIndex
    SaveSetting ProjectName, "Startup", _
        "NodeActive" & CStr(Count), chkNodeActive(Count).Value
Next Count
End Sub
```

Listing 12-2: Code for the Nodes window, which enables users to select and configure nodes in the network. (Sheet 2 of 2)

Keep the distance short. If possible, make it easy on yourself and place the nodes side-by-side, all in one room, until things are working.

Use a slow bit rate. This is especially useful if your debugging tools are limited. At 300 bps, you can see the LEDs flicker on a breakout box when a node transmits.

```
'Basic Stamp II RS-485 network node.
'The Stamp periodically waits for serial input.
'If it receives a byte that matches its node number,
'it sends an Acknowledge, waits for a message, and
'sends a message in reply.
'If the received byte doesn't match, or if the wait times out,
'the Stamp takes no action at the serial port
'and continues on with its other activities.
'All debug statements are for testing & may be removed.

'The RS-485 transmit and receive uses 3 port bits.
'One port bit is direction control.

'Each node must have a unique address!
'Allowed addresses are 68h through 6Eh.
NodeAddress con $6A

Constants:
'Serial-port settings: 2400 bps, non-inverted, 8-N-1
BaudMode con 396

'Serial transmit output
SerialOutput con 14
'Serial receive input
SerialInput con 13
'Direction-control output:
TRControl con 15

'Delay (milliseconds) before enabling transmitter.
'Allows previous node to disable its transmitter.
EnableTransmitterDelay con 500
'Time to wait for incoming data before giving up.
timeout con 2000

'Variables:

DataIn1 var byte
DataIn2 var byte
DataOut1 var byte
DataOut2 var byte
```

Listing 12-3: Code for a Basic Stamp II node. (Sheet 1 of 3)

```
'Configure I/O bits as input or output.
dir13=0
dir14=1
'Direction control:
dir15=1
'For debugging, bits 0-3 are outputs, 4-7 are inputs.
dira=%1111
dirb=%0000
'Bits 8-12 are unused.

'Initialize the output high.
high SerialOutput

'main loop:
  debug "RS-485 network",cr

Begin:
'Enable the receiver, disable the transmitter (default state):
low TRControl
gosub NodeActivities
'Wait until a byte is received or timeout.
'If a byte is received, store it in DataIn1.
'If timeout, give up.
serin serialinput,baudmode,timeout,NoData,[DataIn1]
  debug "received: ",hex2 DataIn1,cr
if DataIn1=NodeAddress then GetMessage
NoData:
goto begin
```

Listing 12-3: Code for a Basic Stamp II node. (Sheet 2 of 3)

```
GetMessage:
pause EnableTransmitterDelay
'Enable the driver, disable the receiver
high TRControl
'Send NodeAddress
serout SerialOutput,Baudmode,[NodeAddress]
  debug "sending: ",hex2 NodeAddress,cr
'Enable the receiver, disable the driver
low TRControl
'Read 4 ASCII Hex bytes & store as binary values.
Serin SerialInput,baudmode,timeout,NoMessage,[hex2 DataIn1,hex2
  DataIn2]
'Reply with the node address and 4 ASCII Hex bytes
'representing 2 binary values.
gosub ProcessReceivedData
'Wait to be sure the master's transmitter is disabled.
pause EnableTransmitterDelay
'Enable the driver, disable the receiver
high TRControl
Serout SerialOutput,baudmode,[NodeAddress,hex2 DataOut1,hex2
  DataOut2]
goto Begin

NodeActivities:
'Use for any activities the node is responsible
'for on its own.
return

NoMessage:
  debug "no data received",cr
goto Begin

ProcessReceivedData:
'Some test values and actions for debugging.
  debug "received: ",hex2 DataIn1, " ", hex2 DataIn2,cr
'Set output bits 0-3 to match bits 0-3 of DataIn2:
outa=DataIn2.lownib
'First byte to send is received byte + 1:
DataOut1=DataIn1+1
'Second byte to send contains the values of input bits 4-7:
DataOut2=inb
  debug "sending: ",hex2 NodeAddress, " ", hex2 DataOut1, " ",
  hex2 DataOut2, cr
return
```

Listing 12-3: Code for a Basic Stamp II node. (Sheet 3 of 3)

```
'Stamp II network example using open-baud mode.
'Master node
'The master sends a byte to each of up to 7 Stamps.
'In response, the receiving Stamp sends a byte to the master.
'Bits 5-7 identify the node the byte is addressed to.
'Bits 0-4 may contain data, commands, or other information.

'In this example, the receiving Stamp sets its port bit 0
'to match the received bit 4. Bits 0-3 are unused.
'When the master receives a reply, it sets its port bit
'corresponding to the node number to match bit 4 of the
'received byte. Bits 5-7 of the reply identify the master
'as the recipient (node 8). Bits 0-3 are undefined.

Node var nib
DataOut var byte(7)
DataIn var byte(7)
InputBits var byte
OutputBits var byte
NodeNumber var nib
temp var byte
'2400 bps, not inverted, open-baud mode
baudmode con 36081

'Pin used for serial I/O:
ComBit con 7

inputs:
dir0= 0
dir1= 0
dir2= 0
dir3= 0
dir4= 0
dir5= 0
dir6= 0
'This pin is input except during Serout
dir7 = 0
```

Listing 12-4: Code for an open-baudmode network's master node. (Sheet 1 of 3)

```
'outputs:
dir8= 1
dir9= 1
dir10= 1
dir11= 1
dir12= 1
dir13= 1
dir14= 1

'Bit 15 is unused.

begin:
GoSub DoPortIO
GoSub PollTheStamps
goto begin

PollTheStamps:
'Send and receive a byte from each Stamp.
For Node = 0 to 6
  'Send the appropriate DataOut byte.
  serout ComBit, baudmode,[DataOut(Node)]
  debug  "Node=",hex node, " Output=",hex Dataout(node),cr
  'Wait for reply; skip if no response.
  serin ComBit, baudmode, 500,NextNode,[DataIn(Node)]
  debug " Input=",hex DataIn(Node),cr
  NextNode:
  'Pause for Stamps to catch up.
  pause 500
Next
return

DoPortIO:
'Read and write to port bits.
'Read port bits 0-7.
InputBits=InL
'Store the bit values as bit 4
'in the appropriate bytes in the DataOut array.
'(Bit 7 is unused.)
outputbits=0
```

Listing 12-4: Code for an open-baudmode network's master node. (Sheet 2 of 3)

Serial Port Complete

```
For Node=0 to 6
  'Store bit 0 of InputBits as bit 4 of DataOut(Node)
  DataOut(Node)=(Node * $20) + (InputBits.Bit0 * $10)
  'Shift Inputs right to position the next bit as bit 0.
  InputBits=InputBits  >> 1
  'Write to port bits 8-14.
  'Store bit 4 of the received byte as bit 7 of PortOutputs.
  'Use Temp variable to get value of bit4 from array byte
     Temp=DataIn(Node)
     OutputBits.bit7 = Temp.bit4
  'Shift PortOutputs right to position a new bit as bit 7.
  OutputBits=OutputBits >> 1
'debug dec nodenumber, " rec: ",hex datain.bit4(nodenumber*8),
 "out: ",bin outputbits,cr
'debug hex dataout(nodenumber),cr
Next
'debug "output: ",hex outputbits,cr
'Set port bits 8-14 to match PortOutputs.
OutH=OutputBits
return
```

Listing 12-4: Code for an open-baudmode network's master node. (Sheet 3 of 3)

Use microcontrollers that allow a separate terminal interface for debugging. You can leave a Basic Stamp connected to a PC and add whatever debug statements you want to monitor what the Stamp is doing, while the network communications take place on their own pair of wires. Of course, this does require a spare PC, or at least a Windows PC with two ports. When the network is debugged, you can remove the debug statements and the PC connection.

You can do the same with any microcontroller that has two serial ports. To keep costs down in a commercial product, use 2-port chips for development and switch to 1-port chips for the final design. If a separate debugging interface isn't an option, at least add a few LEDs on port bits and code to toggle them on or off at appropriate times to indicate what the program is doing.

Monitor the network traffic. On a PC, the programming language's debugging features do much of the work for you. Set breakpoints and watch variables. In Visual Basic, debug.print statements are another way to get a quick look at values. You can do much of the same with a Basic Stamp, by hooking it to a PC and using debug statements.

As with RS-232, a digital oscilloscope or logic analyzer can help by showing exactly what's happening in the link. Many scopes have a math function that enables you to view a differential voltage as *Channel 1 – Channel 2*.

```
'Stamp II network example using open-baud mode.
'Slave node
'When the slave receives a byte, it sets its bit 0
'to match bit 4 of the received byte.
'Bits 5-7 identify the node. Bits 0-3 are unused.

'2400 bps, not inverted, open-baud mode
baudmode con 36081

'Pin used for serial I/O:
ComBit con 7

'Each slave node has a unique number, 0-6.
'The master is node 7.
Node con 0

DataOut var byte
DataIn var byte
Address var nib

inputs:
dir0= 0
'Bit 7 is input except during Serout
dir7= 0

'outputs:
dir1= 1

'Bits 2-6, 8-15 are unused.

'Set bits 5-7 to the master's address.
DataOut = $E0

begin:
gosub NodeActivities
'Watch for incoming data; quit if no activity.
'debug "watching"
serin ComBit, baudmode, 1000, begin,[DataIn]
'debug hex datain,cr
'If bits 5-7 match the node number, take action.
Address=DataIn >> 5
debug "Address: ",dec address,cr
if Address = Node then Respond
goto begin
```

Listing 12-5: Code for an open-baudmode network's slave node. (Sheet 1 of 2)

```
Respond:
'Set bit 1 to match bit 4 of DataIn
Out1=DataIn.bit4
'Read bit0 and set bit 4 of DataOut equal to it.
DataOut=$E0 + ($10 * in0)
debug hex dataout,cr
'Send the reply
serout ComBit, baudmode, [dataout]
goto begin

NodeActivities:
'Place other node activities here.
return
```

Listing 12-5: Code for an open-baudmode network's slave node. (Sheet 2 of 2)

Lacking these, you can do a lot with simple LEDs and switches. On a microcontroller node, connect LEDs to spare output bits and have the program toggle the bits as progress indicators. For example, turn on an LED when the node recognizes its address, and turn on another when it receives a message. Connect toggle or slide switches to spare input bits and have the program send the values of the bits in its messages.

Appendix A

Resources

This appendix lists resources that you may find useful in serial-port explorations. For additions and updates to this list, visit Lakeview Research on the World Wide Web at *http://www.lvr.com*, where I host a page devoted to the latest serial-port information and products.

TIA/EIA Standards

TIA/EIA is the source for the standard documents that describe the RS-232, RS-485, and related interfaces.

TIA/EIA-232-F: *Interface between Data Terminal Equipment and Data Circuit-Termination Equipment Employing Serial Binary Data Interchange.* (RS-232)

TIA/EIA-422-B: *Electrical Characteristics of Balanced Voltage Digital Interface Circuits.* (RS-422)

TIA/EIA-423-B: *Electrical Characteristics of Unbalanced Voltage Digital Interface Circuits.* (RS-423)

TIA/EIA-485: *Standard for Electrical Characteristics of Generators and Receivers for Use in Balanced Digital Multipoint Systems.* (RS-485)

EIA/TIA-530-A: *High Speed 25-Position Interface for Data Terminal Equipment and Data Circuit-Terminating Equipment, Including Alternative 26-Position Connector.*

EIA/TIA-561: *Simple 8-Position Non-Synchronous Interface between Data Terminal Equipment and Data Circuit-Terminating Equipment Employing Serial Binary Data Interchange.*

EIA/TIA-562: *Electrical Characteristics for an Unbalanced Digital Interface Circuits.*

EIA/TIA-574: *9-Position Non-Synchronous Interface between Data Terminal Equipment and Data Circuit-Terminating Equipment Employing Serial Binary Data Interchange.*

All TIA/EIA standards are available from:

Global Engineering Documents
15 Inverness Way East
Englewood, CO 80112
Phone: 303-397-7956
Fax: 303-397-2740
Email: global@ihs.com
WWW: http://global@ihs.com

Chips

The Internet is the quickest way to get detailed information about serial-interface chips. Many manufacturers also publish applications notes that show how to use the chips offered. These are some of the most useful sources for serial-port interface chips and information:

Company	Web address (http://)	Products
Dallas Semiconductor	www.dalsemi.com	Low power RS-232 interface chips.
Harris Semiconductor	www.harris.com	RS-232 interface chips.
Linear Technology	www.linear.com/	Many interface chips.
Maxim Semiconductor	www.maxim-ic.com	Dozens of interface chips, plus application notes.
National Semiconductor	www.national.com/	Many chips & excellent application notes.
Texas Instruments	www.ti.com	Many chips & application notes.

Product Vendors

There are many sources for electronic components and serial-port cards, switches, and related devices. The following is a selected list of vendors with good selections.

Company	Web address (http://)	Products
B & B Electronics Manufacturing Company	www.bb-elec.com	If it relates to serial communications, B & B probably has it.
Black Box Corporation	www.blackbox.com	Many products related to RS-232 and RS-485.
Blue Earth Research	www.blueearthresearch.com/	Microcontroller modules with RS-232 and RS-485 interfaces.
Cimetrics Technology	www.cimetrics.com/	9-bit network specialists
Digi-Key	www.digikey.com	Chips and other electronic components.
Jameco Electronics	www.jameco.com	Chips, components, and serial-port cards, switch boxes, and extenders.
JDR Microdevices	www.jdr.com	Chips, components, and serial-port cards, switch boxes, and extenders.
Micromint	www.micromint.com	Source for the 80C52-Basic chip and Domino microcontroller.
Parallax	www.parallaxinc.com	Source for Basic Stamps.
R.E. Smith	www.rs485.com	Extensive series of RS-485/RS-232 adapters.
Sealevel Corp.	www.sealevel.com	RS-232 and RS-485 expansion cards.
Scott Edwards Electronics	www.seetron.com	Basic Stamp add-ons and *PIC Source Book*

Other Useful Books

I hope you've found *Serial Port Complete* to be useful. But I know that one book can't cover everything. The following is a selected list of recommended books on related topics:

The Art of Electronics, Second Edition, by Paul Horowitz and Winfield Hill. 1989, Cambridge University Press, 1125 pages. An essential, complete introduction to electronic circuits of all types.

Communications Programming for Windows 95, by Charles A. Mirho and Andre Terrisse. 1996, Microsoft Press, 306 pages. Covers Windows API calls for serial-port access. Program code in C.

The Embedded PC's ISA Bus: Firmware, Gadgets, and Practical Tricks, by Ed Nisley. 1997, Peer-to-Peer Communications, 344. An outstanding, detailed resource on the internal workings of PCs, expecially as they relate to their use as embedded controllers.

High-Speed Digital Design: A Handbook of Black Magic, by Howard W. Johnson and Martin Graham. 1993, Prentice Hall, 447 pages. A technical but readable guide to a difficult topic. Covers cable and interface design.

The Personal Computer from the Inside Out, Third Edition by Murray Sargent III and Richard L Shoemaker. 1995, Addison-Wesley, 800 pages. A classic, detailed reference to the PC's hardware. Also includes a primer on assembly language, an introduction to digital logic, a chapter on computer control and monitoring, and even project construction tips.

Visual Basic Programmer's Guide to Serial Communications, by Richard Grier. 1997, Mabry Software, 302 pages. Much good information about accessing serial ports for all purposes.

Visual Basic 5.0 Programming Guide to the Win32 API, by Daniel Appleman. 1998, Ziff-Davis Press, 585 pages. An excellent reference for using the Windows API in 32-bit Visual-Basic programs. Contain many insights and tips beyond simply documenting the API.

Visual Basic Programmer's Guide to the Windows API, by Daniel Appleman. 1993, Ziff-Davis Press, 1020 pages. Same as the previous listing, but for Windows 3.1 programming.

And don't forget...

Parallel Port Complete, by Jan Axelson. 1996, Lakeview Research, 343 pages. The companion volume to this book has all you need to know about the PC's parallel port, including high-speed IEEE-1284 PS/2, EPP and ECP modes.
ISBN 0-9650819-1-5

The Microcontroller Idea Book, by Jan Axelson. 1994, Lakeview Research, 277 pages. An introduction to circuit design and programming with microcontrollers.
ISBN 0-9650819-0-7

Making Printed Circuit Boards, by Jan Axelson. 1993. TAB/McGraw Hill, 327 pages. Prototyping and PC-board making in small quantities.
ISBN 0-8306-3951-9

Appendix B

RS-232 Signals

The following page has the names and functions for each of RS-232's 25 pins, as defined by the standard document TIA/EIA-232-F. Only nine of the signals are in popular use on PCs.

A PC is normally a DTE; a modem or other peripheral is a DCE.

Pin Functions as defined by TIA/EIA-232-F

Pin #	Circuit Name	Popular Name	Source	Type	Description
1	Shield	-	-	-	
2*	BA	TD	DTE	data	transmitted data
3*	BB	RD	DCE	data	received data
4*	CA/CJ	RTS	DTE	control	request to send/ready to receive
5*	CB	CTS	DCE	control	clear to send
6*	CC	DSR	DCE	control	DCE (data set) ready
7*	AB	SG	-	common	signal common
8*	CF	CD	DCE	control	received line signal detector (carrier detect)
9	-			-	reserved for testing
10	-			-	reserved for testing
11	-			-	unassigned
12	SCF/CI		DCE	control	secondary received line signal detector/data signal rate selector
13	SCB		DCE	control	secondary clear to send
14	SBA		DTE	data	secondary transmitted data
15	DB		DCE	timing	transmitter signal element timing
16	SBB		DCE	data	secondary received data
17	DD		DCE	timing	receiver signal element timing
18	LL		DTE	control	local loopback
19	SCA		DTE	control	secondary request to send
20*	CD	DTR	DTE	control	DTE ready
21	RL/CG		DTE/DCE	control	remote loopback/ signal quality detector
22*	CE/CK	RI	DCE	control	ring indicator/received energy present
23	CH/CI		DTE/DCE	control	data signal rate selector
24	DA		DTE	timing	transmit signal element timing
25	TM		DCE	control	test mode

*Signals included in PC interface.

Appendix C

Number Systems

Many serial-port applications use number systems other than the familiar decimal system. Hexadecimal numbers offer an easy-to-read, concise way of expressing byte values. For applications that assign functions to individual bits, numbers expressed as binary values are convenient because they show each bit's value. This appendix is a review of number systems and related topics.

About Number Systems

A number system is a way to express quantitative information. Each of the number systems described below has a different base: 10, 2, or 16. The base determines how many characters are needed to express a given quantity.

Decimal Numbers

The decimal number system used in everyday (non-computer) life has ten digits (0-9). Each digit in a number represents a value raised to a power of 10.

This table shows the value of each digit in the decimal number 760:

Decimal digit	7	6	0
Digit multiplier	10^2	10^1	10^0
Digit value	70	60	0

Binary Numbers

In the binary number system, each 0 or 1 represents a value raised to a power of 2. The numbers use only 0 and 1 of the ten decimal digits.

Binary representations are useful when you need to see the value of each bit in a byte. For example, you might want to set, clear, toggle, or read a bit in one of the parallel port's registers. Visual Basic's logical operators offer a way to control and display individual bit values.

This table shows the value of each digit in the binary representation of the decimal number 760:

Binary bit	1	0	1	1	1	1	1	0	0	0
Bit multiplier	2^9	2^8	2^7	2^6	2^5	2^4	2^3	2^2	2^1	2^0
Bit value (decimal)	512	0	128	64	32	16	8	0	0	0

Hexadecimal Numbers

In the hexadecimal, or hex, number system, each character represents a value raised to a power of 16. There are 16 characters, with the letters A through F representing the decimal values 10 through 15.

Each character in a hex number represents 4 bits. This makes hex numbers a convenient, concise way to express 8- or 16-bit numbers. In Visual Basic, a leading &h indicates a hex value:

```
&h2F8
```

Other common ways of indicating hex values are with a trailing h:

```
2F8h
```

with a leading 0x:

```
0x2F8
```

or with a leading $:

```
$2F8
```

Visual Basic's Hex$ operator displays a value in hexadecimal:

```
debug.print Hex$(760)
2F8
```

This table shows the value of each character in 2F8h, which is the hexadecimal representation of the decimal number 760:

Hex character	2	F	8
Character multiplier (decimal)	16^2	16^1	16^0
Character value (decimal)	512	240	8

Another form of Hex numbers is ASCII Hex, which expresses values as ASCII codes representing Hex characters. Chapter 2 has more on this format.

Kilobytes and Megabytes

Two common and sometimes confusing terms for dealing with quantities in the computer world are kilobyte (k) and Megabyte (M).

In the metric system of measurement, kilo means 1000, but in the computer world, it commonly refers to a multiplier of 1024, which is 2^{10}, or 400h. An 8k RAM chip actually stores 8192 bytes, not 8000.

In a similar way, in the metric system, Mega means a million, but in the computer world, it commonly refers to 1,048,576 (2^{20}, or 1000h). One Megabyte equals 1024 kilobytes.

Multipliers

And finally, here's a list of the prefixes often used to express component values and other quantities in electronics and computers:

Prefix	Description	Multiplier
G	Giga-	1×10^{12}
M	Mega-	1,000,000
k	kilo-	1,000
m	milli-	1/1000
μ	micro-	1/1,000,000
n	nano-	$1/10^{-9}$
p	pico-	$1/10^{-12}$

Index

Symbols

A

Index

V

Val operator **48**
Visual Basic
    serial communication and **45–87**
    versions **45, 88**
voltage
    common mode **233–236**
    reflection **213–218**
    RS-232 **123**
    RS-485 **190–191**
voltage margin **124**
voltmeter, for troubleshooting **155**

W

wait
    See delay
Wait (Basic Stamp) **109**
win32api.txt **60, 82**
Windows
    registry, See registry
    See also, API functions, specific Windows
        version
Windows 3.x
    and Visual Basic **88**

Control Panel **28**
Windows 95
    Briefcase **183**
    Control Panel **28, 31**
    Direct Cable Connection **182**
    Hyperterminal **93**
    Regedit **31**
Windows NT
    and kernal-mode driver **85**
word, transmitted, defined **14**
writing data **47**

X

XModem **23**
Xon/Xoff handshaking **54**

Y

YModem **23**

Z

ZModem **23**